Moving Target

A Memoir of Pursuit

Address:
Bilingual Press
Hispanic Research Center
Arizona State University
P.O. Box 872702
Tempe, Arizona 85287-2702
(480) 965-3867

Moving Target

A Memoir of Pursuit

Ron Arias

Bilingual Press/Editorial Bilingüe
Tempe, Arizona

ISBN 1-931010-18-8

Library of Congress Cataloging-in-Publication Data

Arias, Ron, 1941–
Moving target : a memoir of pursuit / Ron Arias.
p. cm.
ISBN 1-931010-18-8 (alk. paper)
1. Arias, Ron, 1941—Childhood and youth. 2. Authors, American—20th century—Family relationships. 3. Korean War, 1950-1953—Prisoners and prisons, North Korean. 4. Prisoners of war—United States—Family relationships. 5. Prisoners of war—Korea, North—Family relationships. 6. Authors, American—20th century—Biography. 7. Fathers and sons—United States. 8. Arias, Ron, 1941—Family. I. Title.

PS3551.R427 Z47 2002
813'.54—dc21
[B] 2002026164

PRINTED IN THE UNITED STATES OF AMERICA

Cover and interior design by John Wincek, Aerocraft Charter Art Service

Acknowledgments

Partial funding provided by the Arizona Commission on the Arts through appropriations from the Arizona State Legislature and grants from the National Endowment for the Arts.

Contents

PART 1

1951-1970

PART 2

1985-2000

In memory of Emma Lou Arias

and Armando Arias

Your story as much as mine

Show me a hero and I will write you a tragedy.

—*F. Scott Fitzgerald*

We pretty much crossed Poland on foot, and the whole time I was with him he called himself Charley. I never knew him as Armando.

—Dr. Julius Parker,

FORMER AMERICAN PRISONER OF WAR, OFLAG 64

Information has been received by the Department of the Army which furnishes reason to believe that your retention in the Army Establishment is not clearly consistent with the interests of national security.

—U.S. ARMY BOARD OF INQUIRY

(regarding the elimination of First Lieutenant Armando Arias after three years as a prisoner of war in North Korea)

Armando & Emma, Circa 1946

My mother
Circa 1935
El Paso or
C. Juarez
Emma Estrada

PART 1
1951–1970

Feb., 1945
eastern Poland

Dr. Julius Parker, left, my father, at right. Between is the Jewish Polish engineer who befriended them during their escape from Nazi captivity.

Arias family, Oct. 29, 1949

Bobby, Mommy, Daddy, Ronnie & Jr. in front

Island

I try to busy myself. I read, I water the plants, I ride my bike, I go to work, I jog, I see movies with my wife. Whatever I do, he's there. He won't leave—he sits in my brain.

Most of the time I watch him. One moment he's quietly stretched out in his recliner, smoking his pipe. The next instant he's in a prisoner of war camp, hands tied behind his back, arms yanked up high enough so that only his toes are touching the snow on the ground. He's moaning and his arms must be just about stretched out of their sockets. I can only see him from behind, but I recognize his wide shoulders and the way his knees lock and arc backwards as if they're about to flex the wrong way. I remember whenever he stood, his legs always looked like that.

The moment holds longer than most. Then I move on, doing what I'm doing now—paddling a kayak out on the ocean, the bow of my little red boat blasting through whitecaps, throwing a light spray into my face. It's my morning's adventure, my exercise, a mile out from shore, alone under a cloudless sky.

I paddle in toward the shore, passing a gang of cormorants and gulls facing the breeze on a pile of rocks. Some days I go out to the reef or out two or three miles to where there's nothing but sea around me. If I have the time and the wind and waves aren't too strong, I'll go out even further. I'll stop and gaze at the distant, flat shoreline or at the gulls riding the swells up and down. In my boat, placidly bobbing and swaying, I'll lean back, stretch out my legs and scan the sky. Relaxed, I might even forget the man who lives in my mind.

Today I meander from point to point, shoal to rocks, aimless, dreamy. Ever since my coronaries clogged up some years ago, such escapes from work and worry are practically prescribed by my doctor. A change in diet, medication—I've learned what to do to stay alive. But it seems my father, the one in my brain, doesn't know this. Every now and then, I imagine him playfully clutching my heart and giving it a squeeze. He's strong and I don't think he's aware he could accidentally kill me.

Ahead, a tiny island, one of my favorites, beckons from about a mile away. Wind now at my back, I paddle easily toward the brick chimney and roofless stone walls. A century ago it was somebody's perfect sea home, an acre of beach and rock and a few windbent, spindly trees. There's a half-moon slice of beach on one side, and on the other an apron of flat rock pocked with mossy tidal pools.

I move the boat in a straight line, pushed by the wind and waves at my back. The double-bladed paddle rotates in and out of the water in short, smooth strokes, first one side, then the other. Trancelike, I pull on each side, my arms, shoulders, and back muscles hauling me and my little thirteen-foot marvel forward through the water.

By the time I reach the island, I'm ready for a rest. I coast onto the smooth, sandy bottom, swing my legs over the sides, and stand up, the boat now between my legs. I carry the paddle in one hand and the kayak in the other, moving them higher up on the beach.

I've got the island to myself. Boaters use the place for picnics and parties, but today my only companions are the Canada geese and swans nibbling grass in the tree shade near the ruins. I walk around the island looking for the odd piece of gnarled wood, length of rope, or something that might hook my attention, but I find nothing. Much of the flat rock on one side of the island glistens with whitish bird droppings, so I stay upwind of the smell. Empty beer cans and bottles have been heaped around a blackened, cut-down trashcan. I step through a doorless granite frame and into the main room of this three-room relic. Smooth, rounded stones rise up in different sizes and shapes. Crumbled chunks of mortar and brick litter the concrete floor amid sprouting trees trying to squeeze through the cracks.

Crossing the floor, I pass through another doorway and sit on a stone ledge or bench on the outside of the house. I face the sun, squinting from the silvery glitter of light reflected off the water. I've come here to relax, but I can't.

He and my mother appear as I remember them before the Korean War. I see clipped moments. I hear their laughter as he picks me up and holds me in one arm. Or we drive miles across Los Angeles, alongside the old trolley tracks to our favorite street stand called Sloppy Joe's. They buy me and my two brothers hot dogs in toasted buns slathered with diced onions, mustard, ketchup, and sweet pickle relish.

I look around at the crumbling stones, the broken bricks. A thousand years from now nothing of this house or even of the island itself will remain. Yet people did live here. Who were they? What did they do? Where did they go? What was their story?

I'll never know, just as I thought I would never know what really happened in the bedroom in Oceanside, California, where my mother died, unexpectedly and with enough clues to arouse suspicion that she died unnaturally. Suicide? Or did my father hurry her death? And was I complicit in this process? What were the forces that brought her to that moment when death seemed the only solution? When did it all begin? Was there an event, a single circumstance that pushed us all toward such a needless end? I see my mother. I remember her resting in the casket as we, her family, silently approach, pause, and retreat. Once beautiful and vibrant, she has grown old and small. Mommy: I now have a single answer to my questions. It's something you probably knew all along. But like today's little excursion on the water, to give you the complete answer will take time, will mean moving from place to place, point to rocky point, island to island.

I lean back, my head at one end of the stone bench, and doze off. It's a dreamless sleep, and when I awake, I hear only the breaking waves. I'm finally roused by the screeching of a lone seagull. I stand, stretch, and pick my way through the ruins and exit out the other side. I find my kayak and paddle, put on my life vest, and move toward the water. When I'm in up to my knees, I straddle the boat at its middle, then lower myself into the cockpit, stick my legs under the canvas deck, and head for home.

My mother
in N.M.
circa '37
or '38

Me with him
– in L.A.
probably in 1944
before he left
for Europe

Camp Pendleton

No one seemed to mind that I had a view of womanhood few boys my age ever get to see. It was January of 1951, and my tonsils and adenoids had just been removed at Camp Pendleton's naval hospital just outside Oceanside, California. Since I was a military dependent, I was entitled to free care at Pendleton. My mother had driven me down for the operation from our home in Los Angeles, and because of a bed shortage in the children's ward, they placed me in the maternity ward—thus, my first view of so many large ladies. And they didn't seem to mind my presence, probably because I was short for my age and looked a lot younger than nine.

After my operation, I could barely speak above a whisper. I was given only liquids and cold soft things to swallow. I stayed in bed, read my comic books, drank cold juices, and slurped up small bowls of vanilla ice cream and little cubes of Jell-O. I also watched the comings and goings of doctors, nurses, and my big-bellied neighbors. For reasons I didn't know then, the traffic moving awkwardly to and from the ward's only bathroom was steady, day and night. They had to go there *a lot*. Of course, now and then I would also have to leave my bed and join the parade shuffling toward relief.

There were a half-dozen toilet stalls on one side of the bathroom. On the other side were the washbasins and a long mirror on the wall. There were no doors to the stalls, and everybody wore skimpy hospital gowns open at the back. I usually waited my turn in line for an available stall, so I had no choice but to witness everything these women did.

When my mother came to visit me that first day, I told her that everyone was very nice to me. She just smiled and said she had brought me something to keep me out of mischief. From her purse she retrieved a number 40 spiral notebook with a blue cover and a coiled wire going through holes in the pages at the top. "Here," she said, handing it to me, "write down what you see. Write some stories." That was the first time I remember deliberately writing to create a kind of life with words on the page.

I amused myself by retelling *Little Toot*, *Mighty Mouse*, *The Three Bears*, and *Cinderella*. I also wrote something called "The Hospital," all about doctors and nurses "fixing" the patients. As for pregnancy and childbirth, not a word. I don't remember thinking much beyond all those big bellies and bare bottoms.

Today, flipping through that notebook I've kept all these years, I see that none of the restroom images ever made it onto those pages. Either I censored myself or I just didn't know how to describe what I saw. My mother always said writing your thoughts in notebooks "keeps idle hands and minds busy." What she didn't tell me was *how* I could write about something so new and wonderfully fascinating.

My spelling mistakes remain in that first little notebook she gave me—along with her corrections. *Toot* for *toat*. *Mighty* for *mighgy*. *Doctor* for *dgotgor*. Patiently she showed me the difference and I copied her words, mouthing the sounds of a long *oo*, a silent *ght*, and a throaty *octor*. For some reason she left uncorrected the title of my crude little collection, *Storieies*.

Mommy did not believe in the impossible. She predicted I would become a good speller, and I did. She told me I could do anything, be anything, if I set my mind to it. "Where there's a will, there's a way," she'd say. Whenever she wanted to punctuate some lesson-building moment for me and my two brothers, she would usually repeat one of her rules. They were gentle reminders about how we should live and behave, or how we should get over the hurdles in our lives. Her favorites were "Do unto others as you would have them do unto you," "Don't do in two steps what you can do in one," and "If it's worth doing, it's worth doing right."

I wasn't really aware of it then, but at about the time I was in the hospital, she was facing her own greatest hurdle. She was desperately trying to resurrect our father, Army Second Lieutenant Armando Arias. As a reservist in the infantry, he had been called up to fight in Korea, and in early November of 1950—five weeks after joining his unit as a platoon leader—Chinese troops overran his position. He was either captured or killed, and the army classified him as "missing in action." Later, we would learn that captured American troops were forced to march hundreds of miles north through a frozen countryside to the Chinese border. The few who survived the ordeal were imprisoned in camps in a place that came to be known as The Valley of Death.

Around Christmas, we heard on the radio that if missing troops were not listed as prisoners of war, then they were probably dead. But my mother would have none of that. To her our father was very much alive. In the first of many little notebooks she would keep for him, she writes (and I cite her words exactly as I found them—the same as I present all subsequent pieces of "evidence" in my quest to capture something approaching truth):

Jan. 1, Monday

My dearest,
I thought you might like it very much if I wrote you an account of our activities everyday.
Since I cannot mail you any letters, perhaps I will be able to send you this "diary" someday—but better still, you will read it yourself when you come home to us.

The boys go back to school tomorrow and that is a relief—they are better behaved than other boys, but I always like to lock myself up in our bedroom for an hour or so and think about us, cry a little, pray and caress your clothes. The boys' chatter disturbs me. . . .

She kept him alive with words, nightly entries with details of the day, and plenty of yearning and heartache. Familiar words also filled our blessings and prayers. We would recite them before every meal and during the evening radio broadcast of the rosary. Blessings and prayers would be followed by the phrase "guide, keep safe, and return our daddy to us." At night after dinner my mother, my older brother Bobby and I would kneel before the radio in the living room, each of us with a loop of black beads in our hands. My younger brother Armand—or Junior—had just turned two and was spared the ritual twenty minutes of rote responses we had to give to the singsongy, monotonous voice of the radio priest. Afterward, it was always to the *Virgen de Guadalupe* that we would ask to *guide, keep safe, and return our daddy to us.*

My mother also kept our father alive by speaking of him constantly. It became a reflex with her, referring to him as if he had just gone away for a few days and would be coming home that night. There was never any doubt that he would do this thing or that thing when he returned: *Daddy will take you camping. . . . Daddy will fix your bike. . . . Daddy will take us to the beach . . . When Daddy comes back, he'll take us to Mexico City . . . to the shrine of the blessed Virgin.* Like the prayer for returning him safely to us, the Mexico City trip became a promise we heard a lot. It was a vow she made to make a pilgrimage to the shrine of Our Lady to give thanks for bringing him home alive.

For three years such words kept our father alive in our minds. "When is Daddy coming?" I would ask. "I bet I know what he's doing. He's thinking of us. If you listen real good, you can hear him talking to us." I had no fixed image of where he was or what he was doing. Off in the war, I thought, captured or missing, living off the land, hiding. I imagined him crouched in a cave, in a forest, or in a river breathing under water through a straw. In my dreams he became a blend of Jesus Christ, Charles Atlas, and every one of my Saturday morning heroes at the movie theater—from Flash Gordon to Audie Murphy.

To my mother, though, he was much more than all those figures. Every night, alone with her thoughts and her notebook, her "Daddy" brought her a kind of salvation, a deliverance from an anxious, aching solitude.

March 2, Friday

My dearest beloved,
I really must be going crazy. I talked to your picture today, outloud for about 10 minutes! I needed your comfort, soothing words and caresses so much! The last few days have been bad mentally. How much worse they must be for you! I should keep that in mind always—but, oh, I do miss you so, my precious! Please visit me in my dreams, Daddy. That's the one reason I welcome the night.

My mother worked at a portrait photography studio somewhat misleadingly called the Hollywood Film Studios. There in a back room with other women, she color-tinted black-and-white photographs with blends of oil-based paints. Color photography had not yet taken hold, so she had plenty of work. She was fast and had a good eye, and ever since my father had been missing in action, Mr. Lemoste, the Filipino studio owner, would sometimes let her take a box of photographs to work on at home.

On a good day she could finish forty or fifty pictures. She would stay at it for hours at a time in a corner of our living room, sitting before a wooden easel with her brushes and puffs of cotton, swiping and daubing on paint that had been squeezed onto a palette out of little tubes. I'd watch her transform those gray faces into people with hues of pink, beige, and brown human skin. With just a few strokes and smudges, a few punctuating, pinpoint touches, she would transform drab, shadowy shapes into a rainbow of colors—red hair, green eyes, gold and silver necklaces, ruby-red earrings, blue suits, gauzy yellow curtains, mahogany brown chairs.

Each portrait required hundreds of tiny strokes and deft little movements of her hands. For the close-ups, practically every hair had to be painted separately. She seemed to caress everything, from eyebrows and lashes to the pinkish blush on cheeks or darkened hollows around eyes and in the creases of ears. She used Q-tips for the black dots of nostrils or for the white streak on a cherry red lower lip. And for the lacy lime green crosswork of a mantilla that framed a woman's face, she would use the tiniest of brushes or a toothpick.

Standing by her side, I heard and learned the names of new colors: magenta, ochre, auburn, turquoise, cordovan. With these and the rest of the dollops of color on her palette, she gave three-dimensional life to generations of Mr. Lemoste's customers—families, babies, children, newlyweds, white-haired old men, soldiers in uniform, and women in movie-star poses wearing off-the-shoulder dresses. She said that while they were on her easel, they were hers "to brighten up."

When my mother gave me that notebook in the maternity ward at Camp Pendleton, she told me to write what I saw, write some stories. For most of my life, that is what I've done. Now that I'm trying to recreate my parents as they were—she tinting pictures, say, or he lighting his pipe—I also see the heart of a much greater story, one she kept alive with words and a tenacious need for love.

Richelieu

A few months before my father went on active duty and then off to fight in Korea, my parents had cleaned out their savings to make a down payment on their dream house in El Sereno. Overnight we had become nobility. Compared to our little wooden home in the old neighborhood by the Los Angeles River, our new place looked like a villa, a long, white stuccoed beauty with a grand apron of grass spreading down a slope from the bougainvillea and oleander bushes to the street. It had four bedrooms, a big kitchen, a dining room, a step-down living room, a patio with grapevines hanging from a trellis, a huge garage and an orchard in back with peach, plum, walnut, and orange trees. Our street even had what sounded to me like a royal name: Richelieu. Avenue Richelieu, if you please.

To help clean our new palace, as well as cook and take care of Junior—who was still in diapers—my mother brought us Alice. Her real name was Alicia and she spoke almost no English, but that hardly mattered to me.

One afternoon Bobby and I had just come home from school when we heard the horn. Ever since my father had been missing in action, my mother would honk the horn to announce some new purchase she had made or some surprise she wanted to spring on us—like a new pair of roller skates for me, a leather jacket for Bobby, or a coloring book for Junior. Anything to "spruce up the day." Sometimes she would cheerfully declare, "Let's go to a movie!" and we'd pile into our old Chevy and head for the drive-in theater—with Fluffy, our first poodle-and-terrier mutt, eagerly poking his white head and black snout out a rear window.

Other times she would take us to Chinatown for dinner. Or, if she was really feeling down and needed to get away, she'd let us miss a day of school and we'd drive up to Mt. Wilson, Knott's Berry Farm, or the beach—usually Santa Monica or Long Beach. We never knew what she was cooking up for good times, but honking the horn always got our attention.

On the day she brought us Alice, she left the house with Junior, saying she was going to leave him with a friend while she "did some business" in Tijuana. So when she drove up to the house that afternoon, horn honking, we bolted out the front door, Fluffy leading the charge. We scrambled down the concrete stairs. When we reached the driveway, my mother and her passenger were getting out of the car. "Boys," Mommy announced cheerfully, "meet Alice. She's going to help me with the house."

My brother and I stood side by side, mute and motionless, looking like a dummy welcoming committee. Fluffy was barking and running around the car. But Bobby and I could only stare at the unexpected stranger in the pale yellow dress. Alice was slender and young—maybe high school age—with big, dark eyes and long, straight black hair. She held a small suitcase with one hand, and with the other she gripped the top of a brown paper lunch bag. Suddenly Bobby stepped forward and took the suitcase. Alice nodded and smiled. Then I reached out to unburden her other hand. "No, gracias," she said, clutching the bag but smiling. "Son mis zapatos." Then she followed my mother, Bobby, and Fluffy up the stairs. I lingered behind, softly pronouncing the word *zapatos* and wishing I could have carried the shoes that were in her bag.

I had learned to speak Spanish well when I was five and sent to live for a year with my grandmother in El Paso, Texas. Mama, as we all called my mother's mother, spoke very little English. And just about everyone else in Mama's world relied on Spanish—my relatives, my new playmates, the milkman, the ice man, the car mechanic, the grocery clerks at the corner store.

I'd been used to hearing bits of Spanish at home in Los Angeles, but my parents almost always spoke English, especially to us kids. And even though Bobby and I understood a lot of Spanish, we were never really expected to answer in anything but English. But with Mama in El Paso, all that was reversed and I quickly learned to answer in Spanish. Soon I was speaking Spanish most of the time. On my first day of school, I was even placed in the first-grade class for the Mexican kids who spoke little or no English.

A year later, in 1948, I returned to Los Angeles on the train. I remember the Sunset Limited pulling into Union Station and my mom standing on the platform, scanning the windows, then waving excitedly when she spotted me. My parents had sent me away to be with Mama while they were getting their new business started, a burger-and-fries malt shop. Unlike Bobby, who was old enough to take care of himself, I would just be in the way. So they had packed me off to Texas and a life that was more Mexican than American.

Because Mama had asked a conductor to look out for me during the trip, when we got to Los Angeles, this same man helped me down to the platform and into my mother's outstretched arms. She squeezed me and kissed me on the forehead, all the time chattering words I only heard as meaningless sounds. She handed the conductor some coins after he set down my suitcase, then said something to him, and they both stared down at me. More words, and the two waited for me to answer. In those days it didn't take much to make me cry. Other people were getting off the train, looking down at me with worried expressions. Confused and scared, I felt the tears coming on. Finally my mother bent down and my wiped my cheeks with her hands. "Ya, no llores," she said, "Mommy's here."

Somehow those few words telling me not to cry unlocked my mind. I understood and nodded. As we walked to the end of the platform and into the terminal building, a jumble of English words came rushing back to me. My mother chattered on, asking more questions. For the longest time I could only answer in Spanish.

So when Alice came to live with us a few years later, the two of us had no trouble communicating. Sometimes after school I would sit at the kitchen table and watch her chop vegetables, iron clothes, or wash dishes, my eyes fixed on her long, shiny hair swaying across her back. Her movements always seemed unhurried and gentle, and her voice was soft and calming. She would hum or sing Mexican songs, or recite nonsense rhymes, then laugh over how silly they were. Then I would say the rhyme and she would clap her hands.

Mostly Alice stayed in the house cleaning things or taking care of Junior. Once when my mother was gone and Alice was inside the house, Bobby and I were pulling weeds in the orchard. It was our chore for the day. After a while we started flinging dirt clods at each other. I must have hit him with a rock or a walnut, because suddenly he sank to his knees, his hands covering his face. Then he stood up and charged. I ran to the house, across the patio, and through the double doors into the living room, my brother right behind me. I screamed for Alice. When she appeared in the kitchen doorway, I hid behind her, then ran over to where Junior was seated at the kitchen table eating a banana.

In his rage, Bobby brushed by Alice, ignoring her pleas to stop. He chased me around the kitchen table. He was almost thirteen and tall, almost taller than Alice. Of course, he towered over me. I remember reaching the sink when I felt a hard thud in my back just below my left shoulder blade. Then I felt a vibration. Alice shrieked, "¡Dios mío!" and I heard Bobby say, "I thought it was a spoon." I felt a dull, aching sensation spreading over my back. It hurt but I must have been so stunned that I couldn't cry. I just stood there, leaning forward against the tile edge of the sink, still feeling the faint metallic vibration of whatever it was that Bobby had stuck in my back.

Alice began sobbing hysterically and Junior started crying. I kept thinking maybe I was some kind of hero—like my dad—for being hurt and wounded, even if it wasn't in a real war. Then I felt someone pull the object—it turned out to be a fork—out. It was probably Bobby because Alice was a puddle of tears and Dios míos. After a while, she called my mother and tried to explain what had happened. When my mother got home, Bobby was whacked with a coat hanger and punished with weeks of restriction. And Alice was scolded about her inability to speak English and about not knowing whom to call in emergencies.

Of course, I was not always the victim. Twice before Bobby drove me to such anger that I retaliated with my own nasty weapons. Once I struck back with a hatchet and landed a blow on his head that sliced into his scalp. Lots of blood, and for a moment the hatchet remained stuck on his head, then fell to the ground. Another time what I flung at him did stick. He had teased me into a rage, so I ran after him with a dart. Before he could escape, I threw it at his back as hard as I could. I caught him in the left ear, the metal point going clean through the flesh above the lobe. This time there was not much blood, but I felt relieved that I'd struck back, stunned him, hurt him, evened the score for the day. That was a few years before his four-pronged attack in the kitchen.

Mostly our violence was cooperative, sometimes explosive, like the rockets we built out of balsa wood, trying out different powdery propellants until one blew up in the right direction, launching our tubular craft forward and a few feet into the air, more grenade than thrusting propulsion. We were never injured by these experiments, although once I thought I might be set on fire when Bobby lit a match next to my rear end as I expelled a monster fart. With a whoosh, a small flame shot out, leaving a darkened burn spot on my otherwise white Jockey shorts.

May 3, Thursday

I had quite a scare today. Bobby struck a fork into Ronnie's back! They were fighting. And poor Alice, she can't really stop them. Oh, my Waddy, if only you were here. It's times like these I need you most. I took Ronnie to the Pasadena hospital and the nurse said he would be okay—the fork hit a rib.

If it's not one thing it's another, and some days I can barely cope. At the studio all day, as I'm painting, my thoughts are with you. So much that I just paint automatically. I wonder what you're doing, thinking, etc. The days are going by and no news—my prayers are always with you.

Santa Monica

I was proud of the four wounds on my back. They were bravery badges, little reddish dots that I could see in the mirror if I craned my neck around. I got lots of sympathy from my mother and Alice, and I impressed the kids at school when I told them what had happened and showed them the evidence.

What I didn't know then was that the war was crippling my parents with much more serious wounds. At the time we didn't even know if Daddy was alive. Not really. We prayed for him, dreamed of him, talked to him in our thoughts, and in her notebooks my mother wrote to him every night. But if he were alive, we knew from the news he'd be half frozen and starving.

Sometime during those first months of 1951 my mother stopped playing the piano, something she had enjoyed doing ever since the nuns taught her at Loreto Academy, the convent school in Las Cruces, New Mexico, that Mama had sent her to. Her black baby grand now sat neglected at one end of the living room, keys covered, top down, more decoration than musical instrument. Normally, my mother would just as soon sit down and play for pleasure than turn on the radio or put on a record. She'd play at the slightest provocation, usually romantic Mexican ballads and waltzes or American pop songs, even jitterbug. You could whistle a tune, make something up, and right away she'd play the melody with her right hand, then add the base chords with her left hand, fingers spread wide, pounding the keys, snapping the wrist, sometimes singing the words.

But that never happened anymore. Only Bobby and I would reluctantly open the piano to practice our lessons. We weren't very good, and for a few years we had limped along with a series of teachers who would instruct us in their homes. The lessons someday were to stop, too, but for now my mother chose to ignore the obvious: that we were hopeless musically.

A television set with a ten-inch screen was now the evening centerpiece. Bought in 1949 as an amusement, with the war it became a necessity. Every night we would watch the news. More battles, more men killed, more wounded, more missing, truce talks on and off, and occasional talk of an exchange of POWs. Meanwhile, my mother attended meetings of the wives of prisoners. She also corresponded with anybody who might have information about our father. And every now and then, some meeting or chance contact would help her fill out the picture she was imagining.

May 27, Sunday

In the morning I went to interview a Los Angeles boy that just arrived from Korea. He was in your Co. and fought in that battle of Nov. 2nd. He didn't know you, but he talked all about the fighting that day, and with every word he spoke, my heart bled for you.

Not long after writing this entry, she received a blurred photograph of a group of prisoners held by the Chinese along the Yalu River.

June 4, Monday

After getting thru the washing, I went down-town, as I wanted to get you your Father's Day gift. My, but you'll be busy opening gifts when you get back. Let's see—your wedding anniversary gift, Xmas gift, birthday gift and now Father's Day gifts. When will our reunion be? Received a letter from a Mrs. Miller in San Pedro. Her husband is also an M.I.A. She enclosed a newspaper photo of a POW in China—he looks exactly like you! Am going to send for an original print. Mrs. Miller says the newspaper is a workers newspaper in New York.

My mother sent a letter requesting a copy of the original photo, explaining who she was and that this likeness of her husband was the first real proof she had that he was alive. All she wanted was a better copy of the picture, just to make sure, and maybe more information about the identities and location of the men.

God has given me a gift! I have seen your picture in the paper! It is you—everyone agrees—so my mind is more at ease, knowing you are a P.W., instead of wandering around the hills, lost. Am sending the picture to War Dept. tomorrow. Will tell you how I came to see it, when I see you. Soon, dearest, soon now!

A few weeks later, two men from the F.B.I. came to the house to question my mother. They said the newspaper had published her letter alongside the same picture, and they wanted to know if she had had any further contact with the publication. She had not. Then one of the men patiently explained that her joyful letter was being used as propaganda by the communists. My mother apologized and said she didn't think about the consequences of sending such a letter. In her enthusiasm, she had even supplied the newspaper with a description of our father: his name, rank, serial number, unit, even his six-foot height and the fact that he originally came from Nogales, Arizona.

They lectured her about "consorting with the enemy" and doing anything that would give the impression that the communists were helping the wife of a missing U.S. army officer. After the F.B.I. men left, my mother had a bad case of stomach nerves for days. One night my Uncle Tuy even came over to calm her down. His name was Sal or Salvador Estrada, but all the adults called him Chalo and we called him "Tuy," which sounds like *Too-ee* and probably came from an early mispronunciation of *tío,* or uncle in Spanish. "You didn't do anything wrong," Tuy told her. "Anyone would have done the same thing in your place."

"Chalo," my mother said, "it was so embarrassing."

Tuy put his hand on her shoulder, then she began crying and he embraced her. He was Mommy's only brother, a few years younger, and he had fought in Italy and Germany during the last war. A gentle, deliberate man, just after the war while still in Germany he met a young freckle-faced redhead from Stuttgart who eventually became my Aunt Lore. They lived in our old neighborhood near the Los Angeles River, and he worked as a civilian accountant for the military. If my mother had any problems or questions about the army or the government's way of doing things, she'd ask my uncle. This time, Mommy just cried, and Tuy said, "Nothing's going to happen. You did nothing wrong."

"Ay, Chalo," I remember her saying, "why do we have wars? Why do men fight?"

After Tuy left, we all sat down in the living room and stared at the shiny photograph the newspaper had sent my mother. What it showed was four men in fatigue jackets and caps with the earflaps down. They're listening to what looks like a woman holding up a book and apparently talking about it. Her back's to the camera, her hair bunches out from under a cap with a bill, and she's wearing a quilted jacket and pants. My father, his arms down, is standing to one side next to two women with white armbands around the thick left sleeves of their jackets. The two women look Asian and the taller one has her lips slightly parted in a half grin. We could tell—at least my mother could—that the man standing next to these women was our father. "He's got sad eyes," she said, moving a finger over and over that part of the photograph, as if she could rub away his weary expression.

Wonderful news! The peace talks will start July 8th at Kaesong. But I also was given quite a shock from an unexpected source. The F.B.I. paid ME a visit!! Guess why? Because I wrote a letter to that Commie newspaper that published your picture, asking them to send me a print of it—and the newspaper published the letter without my consent. Chalo says not to worry about the F.B.I. They were just doing their job.

The next morning I was still in bed, rubbing the sleep out of the corners of my eyes, when Mommy came into my room, clapping her hands. "Chop-chop, up and at 'em!" she ordered. "Early bird gets the worm!" Bobby shuffled into the room in his pajamas, stretching his arms and yawning. "We're going to the beach," she said. "Vámonos—everybody get ready—chop-chop!"

Chop-chop meant double-time, get the lead out, move it. I think it was something she picked up from Wong's Market or some Charlie Chan movie. Of course, when we heard the word "beach," we woke up instantly.

Whenever my mother kept us out of school, it was as if she had just hatched a conspiracy against the school gods and we were her very willing accomplices. It was our secret, our little detour around the authorities. In a way, maybe she was playing hooky too. She would call Mr. Lemoste at the studio and say she was sick and that she would bring extra work home the next day. That was so he wouldn't get too far behind in photographs that needed tinting. Mr. Lemoste, a softie, would agree, and for a day she could be a kid again.

That morning we piled into the old Chevy and headed to Santa Monica. Alice, Junior, and I sat in the back with Fluffy, who sat up on the seat to stick his head out the open window. Bobby rode shotgun in the front, and between him and my mother was a basket of sandwiches, potato chips, and chocolate chip cookies. A watermelon was in the trunk; the soda pop we'd get later. As soon as my mother stopped the car in the beach parking lot, we scrambled out and unloaded the food, towels, and the big umbrella. Fluffy strained on the leash as Bobby and I led the way, plodding barefoot through the sand to a spot just above the slope going down to the water. We had our bathing suits on underneath our clothes, so as soon as we set up the umbrella, off came the clothes and we went whooping and laughing into the surf. My mother stripped to her one-piece bathing suit, but Alice just kept on the blouse and the knee-length shorts she sometimes wore at the house. "Es por el sol," she said when I asked her why she wasn't wearing a bathing suit—as if the sun were something bad and dark skin had to be covered up. I think that's the first time I was aware that skin color was for some reason an important matter. I looked at my mother—her shoulders, arms, and legs were pinkish white. Then I noticed Bobby's skin, which was fair all over, especially his chest and stomach. I examined my arms and legs, brown like Alice's. Only years later did I realize why my father called me Ink Spot when I was little.

We had been going to the beach since I could remember—usually Santa Monica or Long Beach. If we didn't drive there, we'd ride one of the Pacific Electric red cars, boarding at the stop on the hillside above Riverside Drive. The trip took about an hour, and on warm, sunny days, as we neared the ocean, the breeze would turn cooler, fresher. Pretty soon we could smell the seaweed and salt in the air, then see the glimmering water beyond the palm trees. One time, as soon as we were on the sand, Daddy dropped the umbrella and kicked off his loafers. "Last one in is a rotten egg!" he said, pulling off his polo shirt. Then he went racing ahead of us, kicking through the water, tumbling into the bigger waves. That day, maybe in the summer of 1948 or '49, he seemed just like one of us.

We missed him now, Bobby and I doing our best imitations of him goofing around in the water. Afterwards we built a fort with a moat around it, and Junior wandered over and plunked himself in the middle. Then, while Mommy read a book under the umbrella, we all went up to the amusement park on the pier. We bought cotton candy, and for free showed Alice how skinny or fat we were in the trick mirrors in front of the fun house.

In the afternoon, after we'd eaten our hot dogs, our mother took off her dark glasses, stood up, and suddenly bolted toward the frothy, shallow water, Fluffy right with her. Without a word, we sprinted down the slope after her. She ran in up to her knees, laughing and slapping water at us. Later, when we were eating the watermelon, she started pinching the little black seeds with her thumb and finger. Then she started chasing us, zapping us in the back with seeds. Alice, who had been collecting shells with Junior, set my little brother down in the umbrella shade and stared at my mother as if she were a stranger. I don't think Alice had ever seen Mommy's silly side.

We left in the late afternoon, driving back along Santa Monica Boulevard. No sooner had my mother turned the car onto Richelieu Avenue than she pulled over to the curb, put the engine in neutral, and said she didn't want to go home yet. "Let's go to a movie," she said brightly, and we all cheered. But quiet Alice complained that she wasn't feeling well enough to go with us, so we stopped at the house. Alice and Fluffy got out of the car. "Pobrecita," my mother said as we watched the slender figure with the beautiful long hair slowly move up the stairs. "I think we wore her out."

After leaving the house, we drove to an all-you-can-eat restaurant in Alhambra, ate too much, then from there we went to the Floral Drive-In Theater to see *The Thing From Another Planet.*

. . . an eerie picture. Junior got scared and got under the seat, Ronnie chewed on his knuckles, and I bit into a fingernail. Bobby was the only calm one in the group. But what a day we had! I was a naughty girl, Daddy, but it's just that I was so happy. Please, my precious, come to me in my dreams tonight.

La luna

During the summer of 1951 we became famous for a day. As my mother writes at the top of her notebook page for July 28, a Saturday, it was a "Red Letter Day."

I received two letters from you this morning! One dated Feb. 11, (your birthday?), the other March 12th. I kissed those precious letters—you were so very near—I could even touch you.

Chalo came over immediately—we called the Army, reporters came, took notes, pictures, etc. So much excitement . . .

The next day when the story appeared in the *Los Angeles Times*, the phone started ringing early in the morning and didn't stop until late that night. Strangers said they were happy for us, and many were people whose sons or husbands or brothers were also prisoners or presumed dead. The *Times* piece ran alongside that same picture we had of our father with four other prisoners and the three women, who were identified as Chinese nurses. It began by saying that the "two dramatic letters raised the hopes of all Southland mothers or wives whose husbands or sons have been reported missing in Korea." Then the story explained that "Lieutenant Arias, 32, had been reported missing in action November 2, 1950." Until then, I hadn't known his age, but I remember thinking he was the same age that Christ was when he died. Maybe I heard it from my mother during all our praying to Christ and the Virgin and the best saints for what we wanted. Or maybe the priest at Santa Teresa's mentioned Christ's age in his Sunday sermon. Wherever this came from, it never mattered to my mother. "Daddy," she said, "knows how to survive." His disappearance in combat, as the story explained,

> did not overly dismay Mrs. Arias. During World War II her fighting husband four times had been a prisoner of war of the German armies—and four times had escaped to make his way to the safety of friendly troops. He was awarded the Bronze Star for bravery.

The story also conveyed parts of his unmistakable, formal-sounding messages to us.

> From a prisoner of war camp somewhere in North Korea—passed by the "Chinese People's Committee for World Peace and Against American Aggression"—came the two printed notes.
>
> "I am in good health and still in one piece," said the first note, written Feb. 11, 1951, his birthday. "Remind my sons of their piano lessons and their good manners. Do not let them forget humility and respect for their elders. . . ."

Another letter dated March 12 declared:

"I have no way of knowing whether or not you have been notified of my captivity. But I continue to pray day and night that you may have been fully aware of that fact. . . ."

As in World War II, Lt. Arias served as a leader of an intelligence and reconnaissance platoon in Korea. His wife, Emma Lou, 31, said Arias was captured by the Germans at St. Lo during the Normandy invasion. He escaped to rejoin his outfit, only to be recaptured during another patrol action. This time also he escaped.

In December, 1944, he was captured a third time and sent to a prisoner of war camp in Poland. The following month he fled the camp to the advancing Russian forces and later returned to the American Army.

Upon receipt of the letters, the soldier's three sons, Robert, 12, Ronald, 8, and Armando Jr., 3, pounded the family piano with gusto.

Next to this story, with a caption that began with the words "Happy Music," is a picture of me seated on a stool playing the piano, with my mother and brothers behind me. My mother holds Junior in one arm and a letter in her other hand. Bobby holds the second letter. I remember that moment because the photographer kept telling Bobby to move closer to the piano and for us to keep saying "cheese." When we saw the picture in the paper, right away Bobby and I noticed that they got our ages wrong. Bobby was thirteen and I was nine, and, as I discovered years later, my mother's age was also wrong by a lot. We never mentioned the mistakes made in our ages, just as we almost never questioned our parents about anything we sensed might be off limits. There were certain things we just didn't bring up.

In fact, in my father's presence we weren't really supposed to "speak unless spoken to," as my mother would say. And we never questioned. We might complain and whine about having to go to bed early, or being told to mow the lawn a second time if the first mowing was a sloppy job. But we never questioned a fact like someone's age. We accepted what we were told the same way we accepted how we were taught to behave, like asking permission to leave the table after eating our meals. *May I be excused?* was as natural as breathing. And we always answered *Yes, sir,* and *No, sir,* to any order, any request. When I prepared myself for a belt strapping, bent over the bed, pants and underwear down around my knees, Daddy would invariably ask, "Do you know why you're being punished?" Trembling, I would answer, "Yes, sir!" even if I didn't know. Then he would calmly repeat my sin to me, followed by five or six or seven methodically applied whacks to my butt.

Right after the two letters came that summer, my mother decided to sell the house and make a few other big changes in our lives. For months now she had called our new place on Richelieu Avenue a white elephant, saying that the upkeep and payments were taking most of what the army sent her every month. So she put the house up for sale, and people started coming in to inspect every room and all around outside. Bobby and I had to make our beds so that you could bounce a dime off the top blanket, just as our father had taught us. Even Alice, who slept in the same room with Junior, couldn't tuck her sheet and blanket in as tightly as we could. "That's how they do it in the army," I told her, and she'd salute me with a grin and a "¡Sí, mi general!"

By the end of July the house was sold and my mother started looking for another one to buy. In the meantime, on the spur of the moment, she traded in our old Chevy for a new one, a "two-tone" green two-door sedan. It didn't have a clutch like most cars, but instead had something called "power glide," which made the shifting automatic. "Daddy's car," my mother said, "so let's keep it nice and shiny." And we did. Bobby and I kept it spotless. But when we were done waxing and buffing the dark green roof and the light green bottom part, we'd take turns sitting behind the steering wheel, smelling the newness and pretending to drive. Once, in the driveway, when I was playing driver by myself, Alice and Fluffy got in the back. I asked where she wanted to go, and she said, "A la luna, vamos a la luna."

"You sure?" I asked in English, my feet dangling over the floorboard.

"A la luna, mi general," Alice said, playing along and as usual calling me her general.

I made a throaty engine noise and jiggled the steering wheel. "OK, here goes. Next stop the moon!" Alice joined in with the engine noises, and Fluffy started barking. In the excitement, I must have released the hand brake or shifted the gear setting to neutral, because the car slowly started rolling backwards down the slight incline to the street. Alice shrieked and told me to stop the car, but I couldn't reach the brake pedal. We were now almost to the street. Then I heard a crunching, scraping sound and the car stopped halfway into the street. My little Red Flyer wagon that we were using to carry weeds had been mangled and was stuck under the rear bumper.

Poor Alice. It wasn't her fault, but she took the blame for allowing me to play in the car. "You should have known better!" my mother told her. "Thank God no one was hurt." I was scolded and punished with extra chores, but Alice would have to go. My mother said she could stay another week, then she would have to find work somewhere else.

When it was time for her to leave, my mother was waiting in the car. Bobby, Junior, and I followed Alice down the stairway steps to the driveway. Her shiny hair swayed like black silk and I could feel a thickness in my throat. I grabbed her suitcase and Bobby carried a stuffed pink-and-white giraffe she had won at a game booth on the Santa Monica pier. As soon as she opened the car door to climb in, Junior started crying. When she bent down to hug and kiss him, he cried even louder, and she drew back and looked at him with wide-open, surprised eyes, her lips forming an O. "Eso no," she said, moving her head slowly from side to side. Junior quieted down. Then she embraced Bobby and me together, kissed us on the cheeks, and asked us to be good. "Tú también," she told Fluffy.

By the time my mother had backed the car down the driveway, I was standing by my brothers wiping away my tears, feeling awful and thinking it was my fault she was going. Then the new Chevy started forward, my mother grim-faced behind the steering wheel. Alice, who was seated on the side nearest us, looked out the open window and raised her right hand over an eyebrow in a salute that lasted until they turned the corner.

That night in my sleep I kept hearing Alice say, "A la luna, vamos a la luna."

Farnsworth

Tuesday, Nov. 13

Little sleepy today. I received your check and went to deposit some money—also paid a few bills. Have talked of nothing but you all after-noon. There are times when you are so near to me, I can almost see you, touch you, and, yes, even smell your dear smell—so sweet to me. I'm so restless lately! I want to move and have a home ready for you to come back to. I can just picture us, with our three little brats, all of us together again.

Wednesday, Nov. 14

I took the car to be checked at the Chev. agency. While they were doing that, I went window shopping and ended up buying a pair of slacks.

I also read the most gruesome headlines yet, and was sick to my stomach. I read the Chinese have murdered 5700 P.O.W.'s (Americans). My prayers are stronger than ever for your safety. I know, just know, that you are alive and will come back to us. We need you so!

Before Christmas we had moved out of our palace on Richelieu and into our new home on Farnsworth Avenue, which was at the other end of El Sereno, near Alhambra. Like our new car, the house, my mother said, was bought for Daddy. She knew exactly what he would like, knew his tastes better than he himself did.

House styles on Farnsworth were all different, from wooden Cape Cods with verandas to pueblos with flat roofs and painted stucco. Squeezed onto narrow lots, the houses all had their own different species of trees. One would have a tall, bushy pine out front, and in the yard next door a big, leafy oak would have its thick branches spread out like so many smooth, cream-colored snakes, perfect for climbing. And dominating everything were the tall, shaggy palm trees that grew on each side of the street in the narrow strips between the curb and the sidewalk.

Our house, built just after World War II, had touches of the ranch look: wooden roof shingles and shutters, an old beam above the front porch, and patches of fake adobe showing through the tan stuccoed walls. Inside, everything was smaller than in our Richelieu house, and we only had a single bathroom. In the living room, my mother hung gauzy drapes over the venetian blinds, so that after we crammed in our same furniture, the suffused light and reduced space gave the room a dark, closed-in feel.

There was the sofa, my mother's rocker, a coffee table, the portable record player, the collection of LPs and 45s, the piano, and the bookshelves with her novels, a big Webster's, a row of

Reader's Digest books, and an *Encyclopedia Britannica* set she had just finished paying off in installments. Right after we moved everything in, the room became a kind of shrine to my father, a place where we could speak his name as if he were seated in the room's centerpiece, his dark brown Naugahyde recliner. It faced the fireplace and next to it we had placed a small table with his tobacco humidor and pipes.

I remember the different smoking pipes, each of them with whitish scrapes and bite marks on the removable stems. I kept the little wooden bowls shiny, and poked bristly cleaning wires through the stems. Sometimes I would put a pipe in my mouth, lean back in the recliner, legs out, and suck in the faint taste of burnt tobacco. Every few days I would also put water on the rubbery round plug under the humidor lid.

We called the area around the recliner "Daddy's spot." Like a sanctuary where the miraculous would occur, it must have had a special power because it was here toward the end of 1951 that my mother first heard my father's faint voice. She said she was sitting in the recliner after we had gone to sleep. It was quiet and she was thinking of him in the prison camp. Was he hungry all the time? Was he hurt? Did they torture him? Did he sleep on the ground? She imagined him lying down, thinking of her. Then she heard his voice. He told her she had to be strong and that she must wait until "September the twenty-third." Then his voice grew weak and stopped. That night in her "chatterlog," she wrote that maybe September twenty-third—ten months away—was the day he would come home.

Over the next three weeks she lost twenty-three pounds. She slept little, took on too much work from the studio, sometimes painting until two in the morning. Finally, the sciatic nerve in her right leg exploded in such pain that she was in bed for days. Sometimes she would crawl to the bathroom, whimpering, on hands and knees. Evelina, the sobadora from Boyle Heights, came and gave her massages, and Dr. Matson from our old Riverside Drive neighborhood sent over pain pills. He had treated her for this before and said it had something to do with her flat feet, her fallen arches.

Eventually, the sciatic attacks retreated, and the wait for letters continued. Work and the war went on.

Sunday, Dec. 16,
past midnight

Tired, tired, so tired! If I could only reach you—but these past few nites, even in my dreams you seemed far away. Last nite I dreamt you were almost home, but somehow you never seemed to get here.

My precious, this has been a cruel separation. May God never separate us ever again—even in death.

The next day, the Chinese government released a list of their prisoners of war. The newspapers and television reports put First Lieutenant Armando Arias near the top of the list, and again a reporter and photographer came over to take pictures and ask questions. That afternoon we bought a Christmas tree and decorated it with bulbs, tinsel, and cotton. Then Bobby and I put together our Lionel train set, plugged in the transformer, and ran the engine and four freight cars around and around the tree until Junior sat on the track and let the Southern Pacific pile up in his lap.

After the list of prisoners came out and the army officially confirmed our father as a POW, he managed to convey a brief Christmas greeting to us through an Associated Press photographer who was allowed to visit the officers' camp. My mother called the AP, and they verified the message.

Xmas, 4:15 a.m.

I'm just now going to bed. Tried to sleep a couple of hours before getting up and going to early Mass. Then came home to open presents—all except yours. Those we are keeping until you come home. We'll have a real Xmas then.

I had a few "girls" here for tamales. Wives and one mother of an M.I.A. man. They left at 3 a.m. Then I "played" Santa Claus and put out kids' gifts, washed dishes and came to bed. It is now 9:15 p.m. in Korea, my precious. You are probably just now going to bed. What kind of Xmas will you have?

Right after New Year's Day of 1952, the rains started. For weeks the water poured down on Los Angeles, flooding streets and causing landslides everywhere. Schools closed, neighborhoods were blocked off, the Arroyo Seco Freeway turned into a river, and about twenty people drowned. The newspapers said it was the worst flood since 1932.

Farnsworth Avenue was a mess. The street, sidewalks, and front yards were littered with palm fronds, tree limbs, and roof shingles torn off by the tremendous winds that came with the rain. We didn't leave the house much—at least Junior and I didn't. Bobby had his paper route, but he couldn't do it on his bike because of the flooding. For a while, even the milkman and mailman stopped coming.

I jumped at any chance to go out. I wasn't used to confinement if I didn't have to go to school. When we lived on Richelieu Avenue the grassy hills above the house were my playground, where the neighborhood kids would play war. We made wooden rifles and dug foxholes to duck out of the way of the dirt clods lobbed over from the enemy. El Sereno's hills were covered with dirt trails, some leading up to the concrete remains of an unfinished, abandoned resort hotel. If you got past your fear of snakes and spiders, you could hide out in the dark tunnels around the empty pool, then ambush the Nazis, the Red Chinese, or whoever the bad guys were that day. Of course, whenever we played war, I was always Daddy. On the outside I might look like the smallest soldier in the El Sereno hills, but inside I was the biggest. I was Daddy.

Fighting on Farnsworth was different. The only place suitable for war was the creek that ran behind the houses on our side of the street. There, among the tangle of overgrown bushes, vines, and tree limbs dipping over the creek, you could fight your battles in whatever jungle you could imagine. And the rules were simple. If you surprised some kid first and shot him with a shout—"Bam!"—he was dead. But if he got you first, you were the dead one. So it was all about being sneaky and quiet and knowing when to make a move to kill the other guy. Enough guys dead, and your side won.

Marcus, a seven-year-old who lived next door to us, never took well to losing. A skinny, freckle-faced kid, he would flail around in circles, shrieking, "Pow! Pow! Pow!" whenever we'd nab him hiding somewhere ready to pounce on us. It didn't matter whose side he was on, Marcus would always die. So when we'd choose up sides among the six or seven of us, Marcus was always the last to be picked.

When those weeks of rain came, the creek almost overflowed with muddy brown water mixed with trees, bottles, cans, even dead animals. One gray, nasty morning, wearing my rain poncho, I was taking the trash out to the incinerator behind our garage when I heard a slapping sound. Then I heard the slender voice of Marcus shouting above the noise of the storm, "Pow! Pow! Pow!" I peeked through a crack in the wooden fence separating our yard from the creek. There he was, all by himself, soaking wet in his shorts, swinging a gunnysack over his head. There was something in the sack, and as he brought it down on a flat chunk of concrete that jutted out near the top of the creek bank, I heard the final slap. Then he turned the sack upside down over the water and out plopped what looked like the limp body of a white rabbit or cat. Afterward, he dipped the sack into the water, rinsing away dark stains.

"Marcus is a sick boy," my mother said later after I told her what I saw. "A bad boy, but he's sick." She had spoken to his mother, and what we didn't know was that the whole family had problems. The father was a policeman who used to keep a gun under the driver's seat of his car. When Marcus was four, he found the gun and started playing with it in the back seat. His mother was in the front with his baby brother, and just as his father was backing the car out of the driveway, Marcus pointed the gun ahead and pulled the trigger. The bullet went through his brother's heart and then into his mother, killing the baby and wounding her.

After I saw Marcus with the cat that day, I never saw him again. Maybe he went to live with a relative the way I lived with Mama in Texas. Whatever the reason, he was gone and no more cats went missing in the neighborhood. Shooting the gun was probably an accident, but catching and killing kittens and cats? I knew it wasn't like Mama chopping the heads off the chickens she raised. I used to watch her do this on the tree stump with a hatchet, and somehow it always seemed right and normal because later on we ate whatever she killed—except once when Bobby couldn't bring himself to eat his favorite rooster, Major. That was Mama's perverse version of shock humor.

When the rains finally stopped and the streets were cleared of everything that had blown down, Bobby could deliver papers on his bike again and we could return to school. Eventually, as the jungle grew back on the sides of the creek, the kids on the block started playing war again. I played a few times, but it wasn't the same as before. I didn't think about it then, but maybe we should have taken Marcus prisoner instead of shooting him. Maybe that way he wouldn't have done what he did.

Fri., Feb. 8

Went to buy groceries, but first we went to Alhambra to buy Ronnie shoes. Nothing very much that's news, my dearest. Same routine at work.

Yesterday I received a letter from the War Dept. "informing" me that your status is "captured"—mind you, after more than a year of trying to have them declare you "alive." I certainly didn't want you to keep on being listed as M.I.A.

ogales Soldier Missing In Korea

A Happier Moment Recalled

ews that First Lieutenant Armando Arias of Nogales was missing in on in Korea recalled a happier moment in 1946 when the four sons Ir. and Mrs. Julio Arias, Sr., were the key figures in a family reunion. ured above (left to right) are: Eugene, Gold Hill, Oregon; Florencio, les, both whom served in the U. S. Navy; Armando, his parents, and Jr., U. S. Army, now with the U. S. Consular Service in Cebu.

Family Of Lt. Armando Arias Receives News For Second Time In Five Years-In Another War

The mother of a Nogales soldier tearfully learned this week that her son is again missing in action—for the second time, in a different war, in five short years.

Missing in action in North Korea is First Lieutenant Armando Arias, 27-year-old son of Mr. and Mrs. Julio Arias, Sr., 417 Elm Street.

The Department of Defense telegram was withheld from Mrs. Arias by members of the family until earlier this week.

"I thought it was time to tell her," the father commented.

Lt. Arias has been missing since November 2nd after he led a unit of the First Cavalry against first elements of Chinese Communist troops in the Changjin Reservoir district near the Manchurian border.

During World War II, Lieutenant Arias was listed as missing in action in Germany. Many months later he was released by advancing Allied units from a Prisoner of War camp.

Lt. Arias' wife and baby arrived here this week to visit from their home in Los Angeles.

Lt. Arias attended Nogales public schools and was well-known. He was inducted into the Army the first time in 1940. In March, 1942, he was a machine gun instructor at Fort Bliss, Texas. He graduated from the Fort Benning Officer's Candidate School in 1943 as a second lieutenant.

He was assigned to the ETO. He was released from the POW camp on February 22, 1945, and arrived in Nogales on April 27 of that year.

After his discharge he was employed at the Los Angeles Ambassador Hotel. He was recalled into uniform last August.

In the same Prisoner of War camp in Germany with Arias were: Frank A. Bennett and Jack Tidwell, both Nogales.

Wife Of Missing Soldier Visiting Nogales In-Laws

Mrs. Armando Arias and baby, of Los Angeles, are visiting with Mr. and Mrs. Julio Arias, 417½ Elm Street.

Mrs. Arias and Mr. and Mrs. Arias have not heard from First Lieutenant Armando Arias, who has been reported missing in action in North Korea since November 2.

Nogales, Arizona, news story, 1950.

L. A. Captive of Reds Fled Nazis 4 Times

"Thank God!"

Mrs. Emma Lou Arias gasped that exclamation and then sank to her knees in silent prayer last night on learning that her husband, 1st Lt. Armando Arias, had officially been reported as a prisoner of war.

A few minutes later, the house at 3172 Farnsworth avenue took on the appearance of a victory celebration as Mrs. Arias gave the joyful news to their three children and began to call friends and relatives.

"In his last letter, written last September 16 from a prisoner of war camp in North Korea, he told me not to give up faith or hope, and I and the children prayed for him every day," said Mrs. Arias through tears.

"Now, I hope he'll be coming home soon."

Attached to the First Cavalry Division, Arias was reported missing in action on November 2, 1950. He had left Camp Stoneman three months earlier.

Being captured was no new experience for Arias. The Nazis captured him four times during World War II, and he escaped each time.

1ST LT. ARMANDO ARIAS

He was awarded the Bronze Star for bravery.

The Arias children are Robert, 12; Ronald, 8, and Armando Jr., 3.

Los Angeles news story, 1951.

HAPPY MUSIC—Ronald Arias, 8, pounds piano happily after getting unexpected notes from father in China Red prison camp urging sons to keep at lessons. Watching are his mother, Mrs. Emma Lou Arias, holding brother Armando Jr., 3, and brother Robert, 12, waiting turn. Times photo

Notes From Father in Red POW Camp Cheer Family

Los Angeles Army Officer Feared Dead After Being Reported Missing in Action

Two brief notes, passed by Chinese captors of an American Army officer, brought relief yesterday to a worried Los Angeles family.

Lt. Armando Arias, 31, of 2211 Richelieu Ave., was reported missing in action Nov. 2, 1950, when Chinese Communist hordes swept down from Manchuria to overwhelm his unit of the 1st Cavalry Division.

Being captured was not a new experience for the soldier.

Escaped Three Times

Three times he was captured by the Nazis in World War II. Three times he escaped to rejoin American forces.

But the pattern of warfare in Korea, the character of his captors, and other factors, made his disappearance in battle even more trying for his worried wife and their three sons.

From a prisoner of war camp somewhere in North Korea—passed by the "Chinese People's Committee for World Peace and Against American Aggression"—came the two printed notes.

"I am in good health and still in one piece," said the first note, written Feb. 11, 1951, his birthday. "Remind my sons of their piano lessons and their good manners. Do not let them forget humility . . ."

It was unquestionably written by the soldier, his wife said.

A letter dated March 12 declared:

"I have no way of knowing whether or not you have been notified of my captivity. But I continue to pray day and night that you may have been fully aware of that fact . . .

"Please, my dearest, try not to worry too much. Just trust to God and have faith that I should find myself once again in my family's embrace.

"Do not let my sons forget humility, manners and respect for their elders. Also let them continue their piano lessons."

Lt. Arias won the Bronze Star for meritorious achievement in World War II. And, as in that war, he served as leader of an intelligence and reconnaissance platoon in Korea.

Sent to Polish Camp

His wife, Emma Lou, 31, said Arias was captured by the Germans at St. Lo during the Normandy invasion. He escaped to rejoin his outfit, only to be recaptured during another patrol action. This time also he escaped.

In December, 1944, he was captured a third time and sent to a prisoner of war camp in Poland. The following month he fled the camp to the advancing Russian forces and later returned to the American Army.

Arias was sent overseas to Korea in August, 1950, and promoted to first lieutenant Oct. 21, 1950.

Upon receipt of the letters, the soldier's three sons, Robert, 12; Ronald, 8, and Armando Jr., 3, pounded the family piano with gusto.

They are keeping up their piano lessons.

One of the first news stories on us and my dad's captivity.

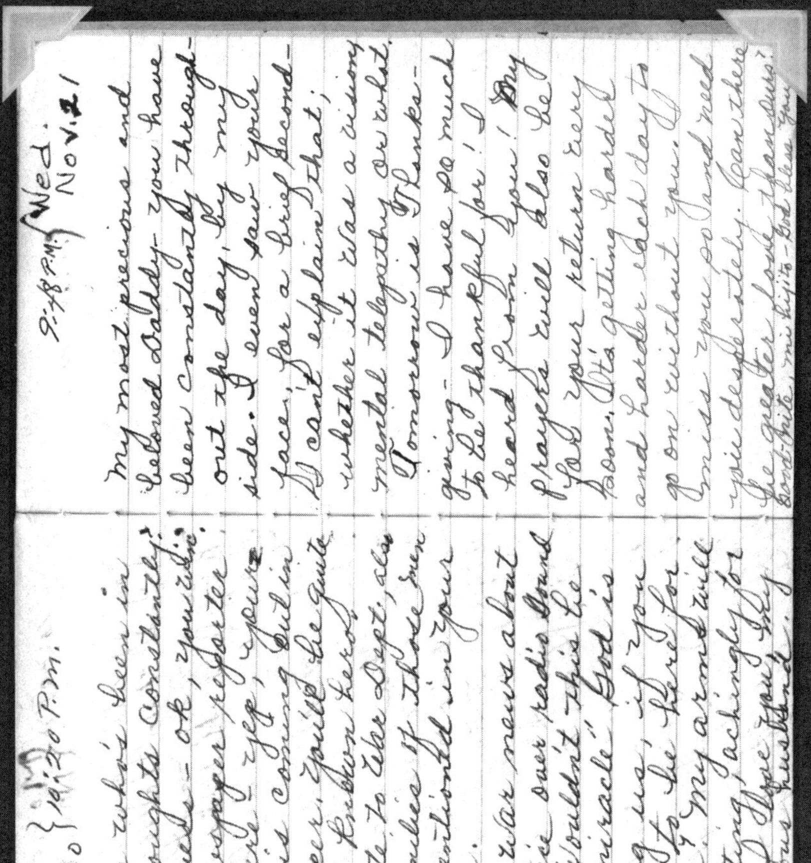

Tues. } 10:20 P.M.
Nov. 20

Guess who's been in my thoughts constantly? One guess – ok, you win: A newspaper reporter was here – yep, your story is coming out in the paper. You'll be quite a well known hero.

I wrote to War Dept., also the families of those men you mentioned in your letters.

Also, war news about Armistice over radio sound good. Wouldn't this be our "miracle" God is granting us, if you were to be here for Xmas? My arms will be waiting, achingly for you. I love you, my precious husband.

9:48 P.M. { Wed.
Nov. 21

My most precious and beloved Daddy – you have been constantly through-out the day, by my side. I even saw your face, for a brief second – I can't explain that; whether it was a vision, mental telepathy or what.

Tomorrow is Thanks-giving – I have so much to be thankful for! I heard from you! My prayers will also be for your return very soon. It's getting harder and harder each day to go on without you. I miss you so and need you desperately. Can there be greater love than ours? Good-nite, mi hijito – God bless you

My mother's journal. #3, 1951

Limbo

Tues., Feb. 26

What joy! While I was at work at the studio, Bobby called me from home to tell me I had five letters from you!

I started crying, rushed home, locked myself in our room and read and re-read your beautiful, dear letters. . . .

I don't have these letters. I only have these little pocket-sized notebooks she wrote in every night. They are well made, stitch-bound, the black, blue, red, and green covers stiff, their outside surfaces slightly rough with tiny corrugations rippling all in one direction like cured leather. I choose the green notebook with the words *Memo Book* stylishly emblazoned in gold-colored lettering on the worn cover. Of the nine notebooks, it has the thinnest, most flexible cover. I open the front cover and see where my mother wrote *1953*, underlined twice. I flip open to a few pages, scanning for anything interesting, any clues about him, about her, about their real lives together, not just her monotonous details of the day, her nightly yearnings and saccharine professions of love.

In February she writes,

Went to pay some bills—also painted some pics for Mr. Lemoste and delivered them today. Nothing much else. Wrote you a nice long letter today. We all went to church. Ash Wednesday. Lent starts. Let me dream of you tonight!

And the next day:

Had another upper tooth pulled out—that makes 3, with 6 more to go—ugh! If I keep on at this rate, you'll be coming home to a toothless old hag. . . .

Week after week of dreams and tedium and longing. On March 11 she fills the usual single-page entry with trees:

From where I'm writing here in our bedroom, I look out and I can see a lonely lime in our lime tree—the only one so far this spring. We also have an orange tree and a plum tree—the plum tree bears fruit each season—and there's also an avocado tree, but no avocados.

I flip more pages. When I first found these notebooks, I used to look for any glimpse of myself through her eyes. A few times I found a page entirely devoted to the two of us, like the entry for August 9, 1952:

Ronnie's first dancing lesson—and you wait, Daddy, what a surprise he'll be to you—he actually loves it and seems to have a nice sense of rhythm. After that, we came home, had a bite to eat and then we all four went to the plunge and Ronnie is teaching me to swim!

I savored this page not because it produced a sweet memory, which it didn't—my mind is blank on both the swimming and dancing—but because it brought me closer to my mother as I'd like to remember her. Playful, carefree, not a touch of what she was to become.

I finger a page in the 1953 notebook. I see she had a another Daddy dream, a vision of the two of them together,

like the time you drove us from El Paso to L.A. Do you remember, Daddy?

I expect to read more, but that's it, end of page. I ask my uncle Tuy about that trip taken so long ago. Was it before the war? Tell me about her, about growing up in the thirties in El Paso, in a city she said she never liked. How did she and my father meet? Was he a soldier then? What was he like?

Tuy, now bent from age and illness, says he will write me a letter with his memories of that time. "Ronnie, I'll put it all down for you," he says, "all I can remember about my poor sister and why she left our hometown." That would have been five or six years before I was born. I thank him for anything he can share with me, someday when he gets a chance.

Sat., Mar. 28

What wonderful news! The Reds have offered to exchange all POWs! God forgive me, but this is the first time I've hoped you're sick. Kids so excited, talking about plans for your return. They're reporting that the exchange will take place "within a few days."

That day I ran outside to tell Fran and Rye, neighbors we'd become friends with, that my daddy was coming home. Then I scrambled back to listen to the news on the radio, which was in the living room near the table with his humidor and pipes. We all sat on a piece of the big recliner, Bobby and I on the armrests, Junior hanging onto the raised footrest, and Mommy in the middle. The radio news announcer wasn't saying much else, except that General Clark would probably start the truce talks in "forty-eight hours." They didn't, but when they did, the talks bogged down, although now and then a breakthrough would be reported. We'd get excited for a few days, then things would go gloomy again. "No long faces," my mother would say. "Daddy doesn't want caras largas."

About this time my Aunt Helen came to live with us, staying in a backyard rental cottage. Helen was my mother's younger half-sister and we called her Auntie. Ever since she gave birth to my cousin Sandy, she had been a huge burden on everyone. At least my mother devoted many pages to Auntie's "problem," her stays at the state "loony bin" in Camarillo, her shock treatments, her visits with us, her "escapes" from the house, and her incessant talking.

I met Helen at the Alhambra station and after staying here a few hours, I took her to Chalo's. She gave us quite a time—her illness seems worse if anything—on top of a terrible persecution complex. I wish God would help her get well soon, for her baby's sake.

And the next day:

Helen was committed to the hospital (psycho ward) again. This time here in L.A. Her husband and the doctor had to do it, for her own protection.

As much as my mother felt burdened by Auntie, I never did. Mostly I remember a beautiful, cheerful young woman who used to treat me like a favorite little brother when I lived with Mama in El Paso. Auntie would take me to Ysleta High School to watch basketball games, buy me ice cream cones, and protect me from Mama's punishments whenever I did something wrong. I once wet my pants walking home along Highway 80. Auntie found me crying, sized up what was wrong from the stain on my pants, and had me remove them along with my underwear. In minutes she had them washed and drying on a fence out by where we kept the chickens, where Mama wouldn't notice them. I put on another pair of underwear and short pants, then Auntie combed my hair, kissed me on the forehead, and gave me a big hug.

Auntie's mental problems began when she was about nineteen and all set to marry Rubén, a handsome, happy-go-lucky marine stationed at Camp Pendleton. The night before the wedding, Rubén was apparently driving too fast around a curve and went off a bridge. They say he died instantly. At the funeral, Auntie kept her head covered in black lace, crying the whole time.

On April 2, my mother had another dream, similar to the inexplicable premonition dream she had a year before about September 23.

I dreamt you were in some sort of hospital laying down on a table with a Chinese doctor standing by you—and the trouble seemed to be that you were having great difficulty in passing water and were in great pain. Suddenly you gave out a piercing scream and were able to relieve yourself.

Finally, toward the end of April, both sides agreed to exchange prisoners. The American and other UN prisoners began to be released in groups of twenty, thirty, and forty men. Then suddenly, the POW exchange stopped. Daddy wasn't among the men who were freed. More waiting. Then in mid-May we began getting letters and calls from some of the freed prisoners or their wives passing on news that Daddy was OK. This led to more visits by reporters, and soon we were reading headlines about "L.A.'s Most Captured Soldier" again.

Then, on June 7, my mother describes another dream so different from her others. It's a rare two-page peek at her fear of rejection:

You were home and so different toward me. So cruel! I was actually pleading with you to be with me, alone, just for a few minutes and you refused me. I finally pulled you by the arm into a room and you wouldn't have a thing to do with me physically. You were with a woman and some man and another strange couple. You were actually enjoying humiliating me in front of them. I wonder what all that means?

More than two months later, on July 19, her birthday, my mother writes that *our time in limbo will soon be over.* For this day, on the final page of notebook number six, she writes that an armistice is about to be signed and she believes she finally has a reason to celebrate. Then she adds,

Now that your homecoming will soon be a reality, this will be the last page I'll write on my "Way by Way" account I started when you became an MIA casualty.

Whatever anxieties she may have had about his homecoming must have been swept away by the attention the newspapers gave us, followed by a television appearance on an NBC daytime program called *Glamour Girl*, which was similar to another popular show, *Queen for a Day*. She had to tell the audience why she wanted to win a makeover as well as lots of prizes and a vacation for two. After explaining to host Harry Babbitt that she and her three sons had been waiting for more than two and a half years for Daddy to come home from a Chinese prison camp, the audience overwhelmingly chose her to be “glamourized.”

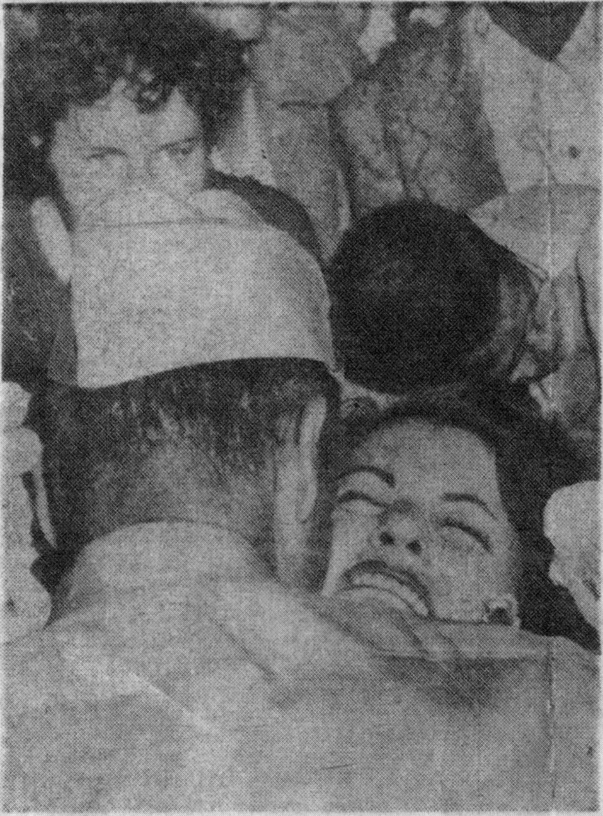

—AP WIREPHOTO

L.A. WAR PRISONER BACK HOME

Mrs. Armando Arias of Los Angeles weeps with joy as she embraces her husband, Lt. Armando Arias, who was first of 290 returning POWs ashore as transport Gen. Howze docked at San Francisco yesterday. They and their three sons will return to their home at 3172 Farnsworth Ave. tonight by United Air Lines.

My mom greets my dad after their three years of separation.

POW Returnees

$3000 Prize For L. A. Man

By Associated Press

SAN FRANCISCD, Sept. 23.—The transport Gen. R. L. Howze brought home the last 290 repatriated prisoners of war from Korea today. Again there were tears of joy in the eyes of the crowd that pressed onto the dock at Fort Mason.

This was the group that included the "biological warfare" fliers—men who had been tortured into false witness on the story of dropping of "germ bombs."

The first man off the ship was First Lieut. Armando Arias of Los Angeles. His wife told him the news that she had won $3000 in prizes and a two-week vacation on a radio "giveaway" program.

The big transport carried 1985 military passengers. In addition to the 290 POWs, there were 1695 rotation troops returning from combat duty in Korea, including 565 men of the First Ma-... Division.

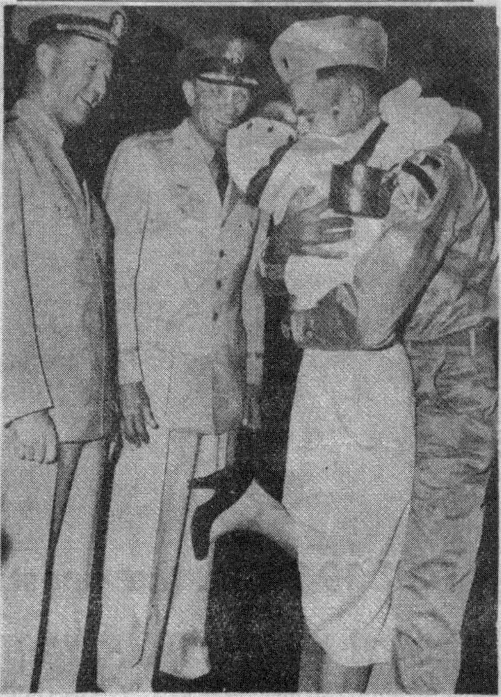

—Associated Press Wirephoto

THAT WELCOME HOME HUG

Gripped in tight embrace are Lieut. Armando Arias of Los Angeles and his wife a moment after he disembarked from troopship at San Francisco. When Mrs. Arias got her breath again, she informed her repatriated prisoner-husband that she had just won $3000 and a two-week vacation on a radio show. The interested spectators at left are a navy rear admiral and army major general.

Los Angeles Times Story, September 23, 1953.

Nation's ace POW now back with L. A. family

By DON DWIGGINS
Daily News Staff Writer

SAN FRANCISCO, Sept. 24.—America's "ace prisoner of war," Lt. Armando Arias of Los Angeles, came home to his native soil yesterday in an emotion-choked arrival of the last Korean POW troopship.

San Francisco's port of embarkation went all out for the slim, handsome cavalry officer, the first man among 1994 aboard the USNS General R. L. Howze to step ashore.

BUT MORE than that, the pretty red-haired wife and three sons of seven-times-captured Lieutenant Arias were there screaming a welcome above the din of harbor tugboat whistles, roaring jet planes and the blaring Ft. Mason band.

For shy Mrs. Emma Lou Arias, the spectacular arrival was an overwhelming experience that climaxed long years of waiting, wondering and hoping while her husband fought to escape and come home, then fought just to stay alive until Operation Big Switch.

"Armando!" screamed the wife, dressed in white so her husband could see her. There on the troopship, as it pulled alongside the crowded dock, she saw the gaunt, thin face of her six-foot husband, for the first time since July 1950.

FOR ARIAS, the arrival was the end of a terrible nightmare behind the barbed wire of a Communist prison compound.

It had followed the years he spent as an infantryman and Intelligence officer in World War II, when he was captured four times, only to escape, on advance patrol during Intelligence missions. In Korea he was captured three more times—twice after daring escapes.

Arias told the grimly familiar tale of forced marches in biting cold, of prisoners crammed 14 to 18 in a single room, living on dried corn and millet, and once in a while some rice.

The officer was a rugged 200-pounder in good health when he was captured but the harsh diet took its toll and he dropped to less than 150 pounds. The rock-hard corn also broke out several fillings in his teeth and they became badly infected, he said.

"During the last month or so," he said, "the Communists treated us better, apparently in an effort to live up to the Geneva Conference rules of war where they hadn't before."

The Howze homecoming, one day after Gen. William Dean's return to the United States, brought back in all 290 POWs, 29 from Southern California.

Among these was First Lt. John S. Quinn, 1051 N. Marengo Ave., Pasadena, whom the Communists had at one time loudly claimed had signed a "confession" that he had engaged in germ warfare missions.

With Quinn was his observer, Lt. Kenneth L. Enoch, of Youngstown, O., likewise used in the Red propaganda smear.

WHILE QUINN, Enoch and others in the germ warfare fiction have been officially cleared of complicity in the scheme, they were hustled ashore discreetly to spare them repeating the denials.

The Arias family, which lives at 3172 Farnsworth Ave., will stay over in San Francisco until Lieutenant Arias straightens out his orders for hospitalization.

And when they come home, "I hope it will be forever," said the Army wife, mother of three sons, Robert, 14; Ronald, 9, and Armando Jr., 4.

Due to arrive tonight on United Air Lines, the family is planning a surprise "Christmas-in-September" party for Armando, around a pretty tree sent over by the City Parks and Recreation Department.

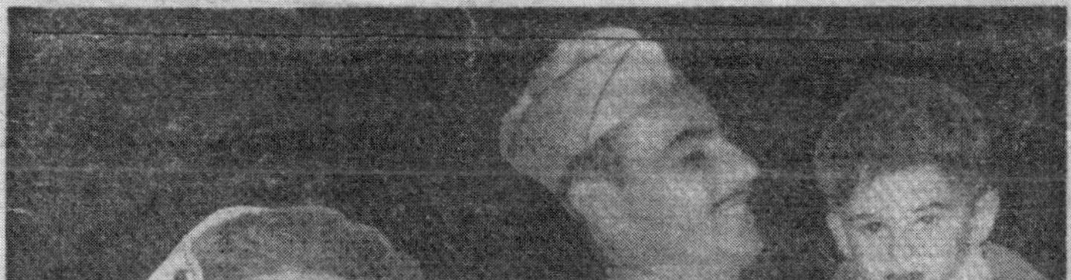

—U.P. telephoto.

AMERICA'S ACE PRISONER OF WAR REJOINS FAMILY AFTER 3 YEARS IN KOREA
Lt. Armando Arias was met in San Francisco by wife, Armando Jr., 4, and two other sons

Los Angeles Daily News story, September, 1953.

My mom & dad Sept. of 1953 only days after returning to U.S. from North Korean POW camp. They were awarded a vacation in La Jolla, Calif. by the Glamour Girl TV program that also sent us to San Francisco for our father's arrival.

San Francisco

Bobby and I made paper airplanes with the hotel stationery, then proceeded to launch our creations one by one out the windows of our suite in the Mark Hopkins. Most of the planes, with their creased and swept-back wings, spiraled or drifted down to the cobblestone parking area in front of the lobby entrance. But I remember that one caught an updraft of wind and drifted off, gliding over the city, a white speck disappearing in the direction of the Golden Gate Bridge.

I imagined it flying over the sea, zooming out to the ship that was bringing Daddy home. He was on deck and about to catch my little paper plane when I heard a knock on the door and someone said, "Breakfast!" Bobby opened the door and a man wearing a black suit and white gloves pushed a cart with two trays of covered food into the room. Like a magician presenting an illusion on stage, he made a flourish with one hand over the cart, then spun around and left the room. Speechless, Bobby and I stared a moment at the silvery, gleaming apparition, then we began removing the heavy metal covers from the plates and bowls. Scrambled eggs, bacon, sausage, pancakes, fruit salad, toast and warm muffins, little cups of jellies, glasses of milk and orange juice, and a single red rose on each tray. I picked up a fork, then a spoon. Real silver—thick, heavy, spotless.

By the time we finished eating, I could hear my mother's excited voice from outside the room. "Boys! Chop-chop! Up and at 'em!"

"Yes, ma'am," we answered together.

"Daddy's day, so look your best."

"Yes, ma'am!"

She and Junior were in the suite next to ours, though as soon as Daddy joined us, Junior would stay with Bobby and me. It was all part of a plan that began the moment she won the television contest.

> **MATE OF POW NEVER LOST FAITH IN SEPT. 23**
>
> Mrs. Armando Arias, her heart full of love and faith, flew to San Francisco yesterday to meet the transport USS Gen. Howze—and her long-missing husband, Lt. Armando Arias.
>
> Lieutenant Arias, one of the last prisoners of war to be released by the Communists in Korea, is due in San Francisco on Wednesday—a day of fateful meaning to Mrs. Arias.
>
> For Wednesday is Sept. 23, and for three years, during most of which Mrs. Arias didn't even know if her husband was alive or dead, she has had a conviction he would return to her on Sept. 23.
>
> Although she knew her appearance would mean nothing to her husband as compared to his thoughts of just being with her once again, Mrs. Arias felt that she should do something to make herself as alluring as possible.
>
> Toward this end, she competed with three other women on the NBC television program "Glamour Girl" and was chosen by the studio audience to be "glamourized."
>
> In a new wardrobe, with happy tears in her eyes, Mrs. Arias and her three sons boarded a United Airlines plane for San Francisco, where they will be put up at the Mark Hopkins Hotel by the show's producers to await the arrival of the ship.

I keep this news clip with the other stories, all of them sealed in a plastic bag. The fragile newsprint has yellowed from age, but the image of my mother smiling at the camera as the show's host pins a corsage to her suit jacket remains as vivid as if she were standing next to me now. Shiny hoop earrings dangle over her shoulders, the lipstick bright red, her dark wavy hair pulled back from her widow's peak. And I imagine the sweet scent of Chanel No. 5, her favorite.

I've often thought that her winning the contest was something others arranged to promote what they did. The show's producers must have sensed they had a winner when they read the news stories and saw the pretty mother with the three sons waiting for their soldier hero. It must have been easy to make it happen. All I remember of the show was watching in the audience behind the camera, newly combed, a starched white shirt clutching my neck.

I remember very little about the homecoming event itself. We left the hotel and were driven to a covered dock at the Embarcadero. As the long gray hull of the ship eased closer, the shrieks from my mother must have been continuous. But was I there? Were there thousands of other families cheering and shouting? I don't hear them. And were we brought to the front of the crowd, ahead of everyone, where the generals and admirals were? Was the military band playing? Tugboats blasting their whistles? And were there jet planes overhead? I don't know, but I have the *Daily News* story.

Nation's ace POW now back with L.A. family

SAN FRANCISCO, Sept. 24.— America's "ace prisoner of war," Lt. Armando Arias of Los Angeles, came home to his native soil yesterday in an emotion-choked arrival of the last Korean POW troopship.

San Francisco's port of embarkation went all out for the slim, handsome cavalry officer, the first man among 1994 aboard the USNS General R. L. Howze to step ashore.

But more than that, the pretty red-haired wife and three sons of seven-times-captured Lieutenant Arias were there screaming a welcome above the din of harbor tugboat whistles, roaring jet planes and the blaring Ft. Mason band. . . .

What I do remember is when he bent down and embraced me. He was wearing his khaki tan uniform, and the shirt felt stiff from the starch. Suddenly I was smelling cologne or deodorant, and I was kissing his cheek, clinging, crying, laughing, buried in his smell, his voice, the touch of his moustache. Bobby says he talked to all of us, but my memory hears nothing of his words, only his chuckling when he held me tightly against his chest. It seemed for forever and all I could do was breathe the good smell and not want it to go away.

The newspaper picture shows my father holding Junior with his left arm. My mother leads the way. In another picture taken at the Embarcadero he's embracing her while a rear admiral and a major general, both with big smiles, look on. The caption mentions she has just won $3,000 and a two-week vacation.

The only other image I have of that time is a glossy photograph of my parents seated and posed together on the middle part of a diving board at the La Jollan Hotel. "Our second honeymoon," my mother said of their first days together. Mama came and took care of Junior and watched over us until the honeymoon was over and they came home.

In the three years since Daddy had left us, we had grown. Bobby was shaving now, Junior was in kindergarten, and I had begun seventh grade. We had changed, but we had also rehearsed our routines so many times that we practically tripped over each other trying to impress him. At the first dinner together at home, Bobby got to recite the blessing. But I finished eating first and asked to be excused. I ran off to prepare The Scene, followed by Bobby and Junior.

Later, when Daddy first sat in the recliner, I lit his pipe for him, Bobby gave him the newspaper, and Junior brought him his slippers. A little coffee? Cognac? Some television? Maybe watch *The Hit Parade*? We even sang "How Much Is That Doggie in the Window?" That first night and for many nights afterward we all competed for his approval. Before going to bed, we lined up for the gesture of respect and obedience. "Mano," we said, and with a solemn expression he would offer up his hand for the quick kiss on the knuckles. It all seemed so regal, so holy, like kissing the priest's ring at St. Teresa's.

My mother seemed happy, full of plans for the house, Daddy usually listening, smiling. When he spoke, it was softly and with big, measured words. He never shouted, never raised his voice, and never showed anger. Mommy told us our father had things "bottled up inside" from the prison camp. As she did with me, she gave him a notebook to write stories about his experience. He did begin writing something he called "The Lighter Side," but he only filled a few pages. It was all about a skeletal camp dog that competed with the starving prisoners for scraps of food.

"He would wolf down everything in one swallow," Daddy said, reading his description to us. "He was like the camp thief. He would eat anything and everything."

On a rare day when the prisoners were fed potatoes, someone tossed the dog a big boiled steaming one. The mongrel snapped the potato out of the air and gulped it down in one effortless swallow. "You should have seen him!" Daddy said, chuckling at the memory. "He ran off howling and hopping, jumping in the air. We never saw him again."

About that time I started noticing how Daddy would sometimes look at people, moving his eyes from side to side without turning his head. His posture stayed stiff and erect, and you wouldn't know he was looking all around if you didn't see the eyes moving all about. He might have done this before going to Korea—I don't know—but at the time I thought it was some survival trick he'd learned in prison camp. I tried looking around without moving my head, but I could never do it for very long. I couldn't see things clearly and my eyeballs would hurt.

One thing he did teach me after Korea was how to breathe while running. We started out at a slow jog on the sidewalk in front of the house. He explained how to count intakes of breath—two sucks in, two blows out. As we speeded up, the two-in, two-out routine continued, only faster. "Don't lose the rhythm," he said and he would breathe in loudly through his nostrils, then blow it out hard in two whooshes through his mouth. We ran to the corner and started back. I tried to keep up, trying to imitate his breathing and his stiff, mechanical stride. But just as he was moving ahead, he slowed, stopped, and faced me. I was gasping.

"Good," he said approvingly. "If you get the rhythm and you run at the right speed, you can run for hours."

"Did you run in Korea?" I asked, still gulping air. "Did they let you run?"

For a moment he didn't answer, then he slowly dropped his chin to his chest. It looked as if he were saying yes or just thinking about my question. Suddenly his eyes rose and he fixed me with a hard stare. "Just take care of number one," he said.

"Yes, sir."

We walked back to the house, not saying much, if anything. He had a long stride and I was trying to keep up, thinking of what he'd just told me, wondering if I could survive on the run, if I could someday run for hours.

Figueroa

During assembly in the school auditorium, the principal said he was proud to present a hometown hero, a man who had survived nearly three years in North Korea as a prisoner of war. The principal also mentioned Daddy's various medals, his shrapnel wound, and his escapes from the Germans in World War II. As a seventh-grader at El Sereno Junior High, I was pointed out as the hero's son and I had to raise my hand from where I sat near the side exit.

Then the principal pronounced Daddy's name. Since a lot of kids were from Mexican families, when they heard the name Armando Arias, they cheered and applauded. Daddy walked out onto the auditorium stage, in front of the California and American flags, looking like a general in his brim cap and dress tans all spiffy with medals, chest ribbons, braid, and shiny brass buttons. The kids went crazy, stomping their feet and chanting, "Hee-RO! Hee-RO! Hee-RO!"

When they calmed down enough to listen to him, it was suddenly so quiet I could hear my heart thumping. Daddy didn't talk for long, didn't say anything about being a prisoner, just that he was proud to be an American soldier and happy to be home again with his family. He told the students to study hard and stay in school, that they were the future of America. I don't remember the words, but he went on about the price of protecting freedom and that a lot of men gave their lives in Korea. Then he said thank you for listening and waved to the crowd. The place exploded with applause, shouts, and whistles, settling into the hero chant again. As the band started playing a loud military march, the principal, who maybe had been a soldier too, saluted Daddy as he left the stage.

My brother Bobby recalls the moment:

Seeing him in uniform like that, with his ribbons and all, made me so proud. The other kids didn't have anything like that to relate to. He was a very attractive individual, very handsome, and always on the positive side—like his vocabulary. He was always striving for perfection, always pushing us to quantify and qualify. I remember how our punishment sometimes was to listen to classical music and then read the album back and be able to recite it to him. And we'd talk about it. To this day, when I hear Sheherazade, *boom!—it just clicks and I hear a* Thousand and One Nights. *I think he got that from his prison experience. Someone taught him about classical music.*

For weeks at school I was the soldier's son, the handsome hero's kid. Some of the boys would ask me what my father said about the war and the fighting, and I had to make up things because he almost never talked about what happened. I just said he was in some big battles and a lot of guys died and finally the Chinese captured him. I had to imagine it all because at home we never asked him what happened. The subject was off-limits. When he did say something about the war and the prison camp, it was usually about another POW, like the Catholic chaplain who was sort of a saint in the officers' camp and died there.

Daddy would mention a few other names and details, like stealing a skinny chicken once or breaking his teeth on hard, half-cooked corn. But he seldom told stories, and was never much of a talker, anyway. After he returned from Korea, he seemed even quieter, more remote than he was before Korea. That was during the years after World War II when we were living in our old house on Coolidge, just off Riverside Drive. In those days, during the late 1940s, he'd lecture to us as if we were recruits, showing us how to do something, explaining right from wrong. That's when he would talk the most, when we heard him best.

One summer, before Korea, when I was seven or eight, he bought us two pairs of maroon leather boxing gloves. Bobby and

I made a big deal out of setting up a ring in the backyard, with corner poles and ropes all around. Daddy put the gloves on me, then patiently, with that deep voice and dead-sure, confident manner of his, showed me how to crouch, how to protect myself, how to bob and move my feet. Then he went through the arsenal of allowed weapons I could use—right hook, left jab, uppercut, feint, roundhouse, on and on.

Other kids on the block came around, and he lectured them too. Before long, we were organizing an afternoon of boxing matches. Some of the parents came, bringing folding chairs and setting them up ringside. Mommy made punch and set out cookies by the back porch. When everything was ready, Daddy announced the first bout, which would feature me and my best friend, Sammy Smaldino, who must have outweighed me by twenty pounds.

Sammy's dad sold fish from a truck, and sometimes, if he was home, Sammy helped wash out the truck, getting the smell of fish heads and fish slime all over himself. Even when he washed himself with soap, he couldn't get rid of that smell. Earlier that day he had helped his dad with the truck, then had raced over to my house. Most of the gladiators were barefoot and shirtless and wore short pants. They were still punching the air over by the clotheslines, practicing their moves against imaginary foes.

When Sammy arrived, I was in my corner, jogging in place, slick with sweat from my lesson in the afternoon heat. Louie Smaldino, who would later fight Bobby, laced up his kid brother's gloves, then pushed him toward the roped-off grassy patch. I don't know why we were paired up to fight, but maybe Daddy, who was the ref, figured my newly absorbed boxing knowledge would compensate for the mismatch in size. Whatever the reason, Sammy and I were the first to fight.

We touched gloves in the middle of the ring, then Sammy loomed over me, grinning. The reek of stale fish hit me first, immediately followed by a crunching wallop to my face that dropped me on my back. The crowd was counting. "Four! Five!" I struggled to my feet, stood, and wham! Fish boy bashed me again. I went down, this time for ten. Peering over the blades of grass, I could see Sammy hopping around like a frog, punching his pillowed hands to the sky, yelling, "I beat him! I beat him!"

Daddy propped me up and unlaced the gloves. No lecture, no slow, deliberate explanation of my weaknesses or what I could have done to avoid the pasting I got. Instead, after the other fights, after everyone had left, he took me to Curry's for ice cream. I don't remember if Bobby came with us. All I remember is Daddy and me sitting in silence on the counter stools at Curry's, licking our sugar cones of vanilla ice cream.

After he returned from Korea he seemed to grow silent more often than before, as if he were craving a kind of isolation in which he could think by himself. He'd sit in the darkened living room with the blinds and heavy shades over the windows. There in his recliner, he'd smoke his pipe, the sweet scent of tobacco smoke spreading through the house. He'd also listen to the classical records he had bought since returning—Tchaikovsky, Beethoven, names I'd never heard before. "Daddy's resting," my mother would say protectively, shooing us away from those grand, brooding sounds so heavy with emotion.

He also ate more slowly since coming back, and this probably had something to do with the starvation conditions in the POW camp. I remember one afternoon the heavenly smells of my mother's cooking were coming from the kitchen, teasing us, so that when she finally set the food on the table, my brothers and I must have looked like the ravenous prison-camp dog Daddy told us about. We sat down, said lightning-fast prayers of thanks, then began plundering the platters of Spanish rice, refried beans, and chicken with mole poblano sauce. "Slowly, slowly," Daddy said. "It's more nutritious if you take your time."

I looked at Mommy and she gave me a wink. The steam billowed up under our noses but we couldn't touch our meals. We had to watch the demonstration. With slow, measured movements, Daddy scooped up a forkful of beans and raised them to his lips. Then he delicately placed the beans in his mouth, after which he spent a minute or two to chew and swallow them. At one point, he closed his eyes, smiling and making a soft purring sound.

Finally, we got the nod to eat. We plunged into the feast, trying hard to slow down our plate-to-mouth movements and our chewing. The whole time I had the feeling he was watching me especially, sneaking peeks with his sideways glances, hardly turning his head, always moving his jaws at half speed. For a while, all of us—even Mommy, who could be a chatterbox—kept silent, concentrating on this new way to eat. We sat with our backs straight, lifting food to our mouths like robots, then chewing and chewing like a family of cows.

Not long after Daddy spoke at my school, the Veterans of Foreign Wars invited him to speak at the Patriotic Hall on Figueroa. This time he wrote a speech and asked Tuy if he could type it out for him. I didn't hear the speech, nor did I know what happened until many years later when I asked my uncle about it. Unbothered by my questions and small tape recorder, Tuy seemed anxious to unload this memory that had lived uneasily in his mind for more than three decades, a stream of vivid images he'd never been asked to release.

He had been in the papers and all. He was quite excited about it. He had a bunch of stuff written down, and I read it. But it didn't make any sense to me. It rambled on and on, and I thought the audience wouldn't be interested. I asked him if I could line-out some things, and when I did, he wrote more things in the margins. I told him his audience would be veterans and they probably want to know how he was captured, what was prison life like with the Chinese. And they want to hear all this in a down-to-earth manner.

So I went with him and your mother. We sat in the audience. A lot of veterans and their families showed up. Armando went up on stage when they called his name, and everybody applauded. That was fine. Then he started to speak. He asked the audience if they would mind if he took the mike and walked back and forth. "That's the best way I can describe myself," he said.

That started the thing. The more he talked, the more he rambled. He had memorized part of the speech and he had notes, but he started rambling on and on. Nothing that anybody would really be interested in. The words he was trying to use—big words, sometimes the words were not appropriate at all. And that was embarrassing. He was throwing out all these big words, and I thought, My God, what's he doing? Instead of saying the food they got was such and such, he'd say there were grains. He kept repeating the word grains, but he wouldn't say what grains. And he talked like that for so long, maybe about eight or nine minutes. I thought, "He's really making a fool of himself." Your mother and I, we were so embarrassed. He was walking back and forth on the stage. In his uniform, very serious but rambling on and on.

I looked around and I saw people whispering, and I was thinking, "This is terrible." But what could we do? He went on like that for about fifteen or twenty minutes, not making any sense. I don't think he was aware of anybody. He couldn't stop. It was gibberish, words just pouring out. Finally, when he finished, they didn't applaud or anything. In his mind I'm sure he was trying to do something, to tell them I don't know what, trying to build it up with all those words that didn't make sense.

Emma and I were so happy it was over. And the veterans, they were very stiff. Nobody applauded. They thanked him, but nobody really said anything. They just wanted him to leave.

I never knew this had happened. No one had ever told me, and in those days I don't think I would have believed it if I had heard the story. It was so different from the speech I heard at school. In my eyes Daddy was too commanding, too perfect as a soldier and a father, for that to have happened.

Now, however, almost a half-century later and knowing what I do about his life, I can easily believe he flipped and lost control. He had only just returned to us and the memory of abject hunger and deprivation must have been so strong that at one point during his description of POW food, he was suddenly back in the camp eating lice picked from his scalp, craving anything to feed his starving body. He was not aware that he was speaking before a roomful of men and women who simply wanted to hear an articulate, vivid presentation of life as a prisoner of war. Instead, he showered them with words and more words, words that might convince his audience he was knowledgeable. Patriots all, they wanted to honor him, like him, applaud him.

But how could they applaud rambling nonsense? In those moments of awkward relief when he was led off the stage, maybe someone, perhaps a veteran who had also faced combat and imprisonment, should have stood up and paid honor to the truth: *What you saw and heard from Lt. Arias was as close to the truth as you can get without actually being sick and cold and starved to the point of incoherence. Grains, he wanted grains, just a few more grains. Life was in those grains.*

My mother,
mid 1930s,
El Paso Texas

Coming home
from vocational
school

My uncle Sal,
my grandmother,
and my mother.

Mid 1920's
El Paso, Texas

Mexico City

In the black-and-white snapshot, my mother is the only one smiling. We're all standing stiffly in front of one of the flower-decorated canal boats of Xochimilco—the *X,* I learned, pronounced like an *S.* We've just completed a long, dusty drive from Los Angeles to Mexico City, and a boat ride through the canals is one of our first outings. The sun's in our faces, and Bobby, Junior, and I are caught squinting at the camera. My father, though he's out of uniform and dressed casually in slacks and a short-sleeved shirt, gazes too seriously at the lens. Next to him Mama has a stern, almost disdainful, expression. She's come with us to Mexico because, like Mommy, she had to make the pilgrimage to the shrine of the Virgin of Guadalupe.

I believe my mother must be smiling because she has already given her thanks to the Virgencita. She has already shuffled on her knees, moving a towel under her over the stone walkway and up the steps of the old chapel on the hillside. There, in front of an image of the woman she believed appeared to the Indian peasant Juan Diego nearly five centuries ago, my mother released some of her years of hurt and longing. In my snapshot, which has darkened and faded around the edges, my mother smiles, most likely because she has her man and we're all together again.

Spontaneity wasn't Daddy's style, but on that trip to Mexico City, just after he had returned from Korea, there were moments when the curtain of quiet reserve rose and another man emerged. It didn't happen often, but now and then he broke free and we had a peek at what I'd like to think of as the real Daddy. Once I remember him in the car singing along with the Mexican radio music, his voice rising in a long, broken falsetto. Windows down, dry desert wind on our faces, we waited—Junior, Bobby, and I scrunched together on the rear seat with Mama—giggling as he tilted his head back, oozing love lines to my mother, who was snuggled up to him, head on his shoulder.

At other times on the trip, he would take us exploring, like the hot afternoon when he steered the Buick off the asphalt highway onto many miles of a bumpy dirt road to the town of Teocaltiche. I remember the name because years later I turned onto that same road, this time with my own wife and kids. Maybe Daddy saw a sign or heard something at our last gas stop, but that's how he found a full-blown fiesta underway, complete with cockfights, mariachi bands, fireworks, and a charreada, the Mexican rodeo.

Another time he spotted a half-dozen horses in a corral. Off we veered to the rancho. At the corral, Daddy talked to the vaquero, and right away both of them were busy cinching up saddles and adjusting bits and bridles on four horses. After mounting them, my brothers and I bounced after our leader, leaving Mommy and Mama on a blanket in the shade of a tree.

Sometime during the afternoon ride through the scrub, Daddy let us catch up, then gave us a demonstration of how to post by moving up and down in the saddle in a certain rhythm in order to make the butt-thumping trot easier. When he finished the lesson, he slapped the end of the reins on his horse's flanks, grunted "Hyeah!" and galloped away, shouting as if he were the Lone Ranger disappearing through the brush.

The trip to Mexico City seemed to free him from military stiffness. For those two weeks, he was like the man Tuy describes "in the good old days" before Korea.

> *We took a trip to Big Bear, and he and your mother were ice-skating. They were so funny. He would fall, sliding and laughing and making funny noises. Really letting go. None of this reserve, just*

natural. And I imagined that was his real self, and the other was just a put-on for everybody that he would never discard. He always wanted to have that like a protection. . . . Or they'd go dancing. They were good dancers. We used to go to this thing called Command Performance, in Hollywood, and you had to go in uniform. They had movie stars and all. Not exactly premieres, but it was an Army program transmitted to troops in Europe. Bob Hope, Lucille Ball, Joan Crawford, Cesar Romero. Very entertaining. Only military invited. He'd swing your mom around, acting so funny. Like watching The Three Stooges . . . But after Korea we never saw that side of him again. It could have been his mind. He went through something that changed him. Little by little you could see he wasn't the same. They weren't the same.

One peek into this change occurred when we crossed over from Juárez to El Paso. The U.S. border patrol agent, after asking us what nationality we were, eyed Daddy's mustache and tanned face, then asked for some identification—a passport would do.

In a gruff, loud voice, Daddy instantly said, "Why?"

The agent smiled and casually said, "For all I know, you could be a wetback."

"Sir?"

"A wetback, you know, a mojado. Swims across?"

I don't remember all of this incident, but Bobby recalls that "Daddy went ballistic." He shouted in the man's face as if he were dressing down a recruit. In a rush of words, he informed the agent that he was a U.S. Army officer and had just spent three years in a prisoner of war camp in North Korea. He had survived for three years, all in the line of duty for his country, for people like the agent now before him.

Daddy then plucked the passport from his shirt pocket and held it up in front of the pale-faced man with the stunned expression. Bobby says he thought Daddy was going to throttle the guy if he cracked wise again.

"All right," the agent said, probably relieved but annoyed that his little redneck joke had fizzled on some crazy man's pride. "Go on through."

Mama also shouldered the baggage of her Mexican origins. As we drove north back through the state of Chihuahua to El Paso, she scoffed at just about everything—the toilets that didn't work, the holes in the streets, the cockroaches in the hotel rooms, the candies in the open markets, flies. She railed against all that was rascuachi—that is, junky, mended, half-done, seat-of-the-pants, frayed, faded, shabby, dirty, and definitely poor. "Ay, qué feo"—how ugly! she would say after spotting a barefoot, raggedy boy peeing against an adobe wall. She didn't have to say the word, but I knew the image was quintessentially rascuachi (properly spelled *rascuache*). To this day, I like pronouncing those three syllables of scorn: *rra . . . SCUA . . . chi*, imitating my grandmother's tone of lofty, arrogant pity. If she was at all compassionate, she hid it well, calling all such Mexicans she felt were beneath her "gentuza"—low-class, ill-mannered riffraff.

At the time, as a kid riding through Mexico in the backseat with Mama and my brothers, I sensed my grandmother was passing off her judgments as Bible truth—with my mother, who shared some of Mama's uppity pretensions, sometimes chiming in. But much of their attitude toward Mexico and Mexicans grew out of Mama's sorrowful origins in Chihuahua. She was the daughter of Faustino Terrazas, a cattle baron in Valle del Rosario, a remote mountain-valley town in the Sierra Tarahumara, where he reigned as the local patrón, the lord and master of one son, four daughters, a long roster of house servants and ranch hands, dozens of horses, and a large herd of cattle.

The 1910 revolution and Pancho Villa, who arrived in person at the Terrazas ranch, forced the family to escape to El Paso, which is where my mother eventually was born. The fighting, the loss of land, the race north to Texas—this was family lore. What I didn't know—until I discovered and read a pocket-size notebook my grandmother had written in 1942—was that her early life was continually plagued by personal disappointment. This would account for her sour view of so many things Mexican.

The notebook was probably my mother's idea. In it, Mama summarizes her life in simple, straightforward Spanish, careful to give names and dates and to mention milestone incidents and events. Beneath the name *JULIA T. ESTRADA*, in pinched, ungraceful, ink-penned words, sometimes misspelled or corrected, Mama begins (and I translate):

> *I was born in El Valle del Rosario, Chihuahua. According to papers that exist, I was born on June 19 of 1893. My life seems to me one of pure heartaches, because since the time I could reason or learn about life, I saw my mother suffering with all her children. We were five and others had died. My mother suffered because my father liked to drink and would almost lose his mind, and we were horrified to see him like that. My poor mother had heart problems and when I was seven she died, leaving us five orphans, Jesús Miguel, María del Refugio, Eufemia, Concepción and me, in the care of my grandmother and my eldest sister, María, the one we call Cuca.*
>
> *Later that year in 1901 my father married for the second time. . . . We never had freedom to do anything, and by 1910 when life became so insufferable, I accepted the offer of marriage from the first young man who asked me. But my father was very strict and wouldn't let me marry because the family needed me. My boyfriend and I loved each other very much but he became desperate and took up arms in the Mexican Revolution of 1910 and was killed in battle. I was so sad and in mourning for a year.*

Mama's father, Faustino Terrazas, and her brother slipped away to El Paso before Villa could catch and execute them. But the four daughters and their new stepmother had to stay behind. Villa—Mama always called him a bandit—put the Terrazas servants and ranch hands in charge of the imposing adobe mansion and the hacienda's huge spread of land, then confiscated all the family property and livestock. By 1915, after years of humiliation—she's not specific in her account—by their new masters, the women finally managed to escape to Ciudad Juárez. There they crossed the border and joined the men. When the family money ran out, Mama and her sisters went to work cleaning houses of the wealthier Americans in El Paso. Then one night her brother, Jesús Miguel, was assassinated because he was allied to an old-guard general, Pasqual Orozco, who was about to launch a counterattack against Villa.

> *So our sufferings continued, until at last I thought I should marry, which was arranged for May 17, 1916, even though my father did not accept the marriage. But I was very much in love with the man who would be my husband, Salvador Estrada, and we went through with it with all the decency possible. My family was disgusted with me, but I did it anyway. . . . I was blindly in love, but my sufferings were to go on.*

Poor Mama. Now married to a man who entrusted her with the care of three illegitimate young children he had had with another woman, she soon discovered that, like her father, her new husband, an enterprising dairy farmer with lucrative interests in other less reputable businesses (several Juárez brothels, for example) also "liked to drink, but fortunately he was a good man with me." Then, in July of 1917, Mama's first child, my mother, was born, followed a year and four months later by the birth of my Uncle Tuy, or Chalo, named Salvador after his father.

Burdened with the raising of five children, Mama—who also sheltered the mother of the three inherited kids—was then hit with another blow. Her husband, while on a trip to Los Angeles, suffered a diabetic attack in Deming, New Mexico. Soon afterward in El Paso, he died of peritonitis.

A widow with five children, a dairy farm to run, and an ailing father to look after, my grandmother somehow soldiered on. Then the family's grizzled, gout-ridden patriarch, Faustino, died. Eight years later, she writes, *the silliness occurred to me to marry again.* Fortunately, before that could happen, the three children and their mother, whom Mama had inherited years before, left the household. As for the urge to marry, it soon returned. But by all accounts, husband number two was a philandering opportunist who saw brief matrimony as a chance to get at my grandmother's savings, business profits, and jewels. Before exiting, he not only managed to help himself to her assets, but he also, as she decorously puts it, *left me in an interesting state.* Months later, on January 1, 1931, Mama gave birth to Elena Socorro, my Auntie Helen.

Nearly twenty-three years later, as our Buick sped north across the Chihuahuan desert toward the U.S. border, I knew nothing of my grandmother's grief, nor of her grudges against Mexican men. I only knew the stern, gray-haired presence who made us sandwiches and chicken tacos from her backseat food stash and scorned all things backward and rascuachi in Mexico.

Decades later, when Mama was almost eighty, I stopped by to visit her in Los Angeles. I had just bought a guitar and told her I was taking lessons. "Let me see it," she said. She was sitting in the kitchen of her little one-bedroom house between the freeway and the river. I lowered the volume on the radio, which was emitting music from the Spanish-language station. Then I retrieved the guitar from its black case.

Before taking it, she smiled, clapped her wrinkled hands, and rubbed them together as if she were about to open a present. She cradled the instrument in her lap, smoothly running a bony hand up and down the nylon strings. Then she propped it up and began to strum a few chords. In a thin cooing voice she began to sing the lines of an old corrido, probably some ballad from a hundred years ago. In that moment, I saw beyond her bluff. I glimpsed the girl she had been in Mexico riding her horse, roping calves, maybe singing love songs in the moonlight.

Camp Polk

In early 1954, courtesy of the U.S. Army, we moved from Los Angeles to a cramped, mildew-smelling house-trailer that was parked among spindly pine trees just outside Camp Polk, Louisiana. My mother called the whole place "cracker hell," and the drab, slate-gray trailer a "cracker box." Away from Mama and Tuy, from her friends, from her work, from her doctors, and from all the other anchors and diversions of L.A. life, she now had to fill her days tending to us, her sons, and to the social duties of a junior-grade officer's wife. For his part, Daddy was usually off on war-game maneuvers, at the battalion office, or out on the drill field marching his troops.

Despite the dismal trailer-camp setting, my mother tried to make our box as homey as possible. In the front, in the tiny "living room" next to the kitchen, she covered the sofa chair with lacy white doilies and a tasseled green-red-and-white rebozo, or Mexican shawl. She also hung beige curtains over the window blinds and decorated the walls with framed mirrors, a posed portrait of our family that she had tinted, and a St. Jude calendar. The most refined touch was a white porcelain figure of a woman in a long, ruffled flamenco dress, all of it topped by a head comb and delicate mantilla. This little lady, which my mother had made from a mold in a ceramics class the year before, watched us all from her linoleum-covered perch in one corner of our cramped combination dining-study-and-living room.

Bobby and I went to the white kids' school, grades seven through twelve, in Leesville, which turned out fine for him but, as I soon discovered, was painfully awkward for me. The first inkling of my coming school crisis happened after we left Los Angeles and headed to Louisiana. What we didn't put in storage after selling the Farnsworth house, we strapped to the top of the Buick. With Fluffy's windblown snout pointed out of the front window on the passenger side, and a mess of boxes, suitcases, and duffel bags piled on top, we looked like eastbound hillbillies going the wrong way.

We had stopped at a gas station somewhere in Texas and the attendant, an old guy in overalls, looked at us—especially me—with a frown. I had to pee pretty badly, so I got out and gingerly stepped toward the restroom. Fluffy was already zipping around sniffing and squirting anything vertical.

"It's locked!" the man shouted. I turned around, came back, and looked up at the hardened freckled face, which after a moment eased into a slight smile. "I don't know if I should give it to you," the attendant said, not teasing. Then he glanced at my mother, who was glowering at him from the front seat, and pulled the key out of his pocket. "Here," he said, "don't make a mess."

Everyone in the family but me was fair-skinned, and my mother was the fairest. She even dyed her black hair a reddish brown, something she began doing before I was born. I grew up with the acrid smell of hair dye wafting through the house whenever she was "touching up the roots." I never knew why, unless it was to look less Mexican and more acceptably white American. I think she was trying for the sultry, long, wavy-haired look of Rita Hayworth or Ava Gardner, two of my father's favorites. Whenever questions of origin or bloodlines came up, Mommy would insist we were "French, Spanish, and Portuguese," always in that order. The family's main unspoken rule in these matters was of course never to question anything our parents said. No adult in the family ever discussed our origins with us. We were to believe, as my mother once suggested, that the "purity of our stock" came from Europe, though tracing it back through centuries of emigrations to the New World would be impossible. It was the first time I'd heard of purity and stock to describe people, as opposed to dogs or cattle.

So we accepted the French-Spanish-Portuguese line even when we traveled to Mexico, never mind that Mama told me in later years that the Terrazas men had often taken Tarahumara Indian women as wives and mistresses. "That's the way it was," she once told me. "We're all mixed."

I walked off to the restroom, the grizzled attendant eyeing me suspiciously. As the darkest in the family, my skin color was some shade between light brown and what my medical records in later years listed as "olive." Nothing like Bobby, who was almost as creamy pink as Mommy, nor like Junior or Daddy, who were a few shades lighter than me. The story I grew up with was that when I was an infant, my mother one cold night set me in an open warming oven. "I forgot you," she'd say. "You were toasted!" Whenever the story was told, there were grins all around. I would even laugh at the image of me toasting until done just right.

So as I walked away with the restroom key, knees together, I wasn't really aware of what was going on. Then I reached the door, and there, neatly painted in red, were the words

NO NEGROES
NO MEXICANS
NO DOGS

At first I was so afraid of wetting my pants that I didn't comprehend the warning. Only later, on the way back to the car, did I wonder why the old buzzard might not like Mexicans. And why he was giving me the hard looks? In any case, in those days I thought I was Spanish, French, and Portuguese.

Weeks later, when I started school in Leesville, which is just down the road from Camp Polk—now Fort Polk—I remember being placed in the rear of my seventh-grade class and not making any friends that first week. I was entering after the beginning of the spring semester—unhappily behind in everything. I struggled with the subjects, especially algebra. To make things worse, from my first day of class, the teacher, a young hawk-nosed guy with a blond crew cut, ignored me. Between stints at the chalkboard, he would walk up and down the aisles as we wrote essays or worked on math problems. Now and then he would stop to help my classmates, but not me.

After a few quizzes, which I fumbled, the teacher probably decided I was a lost cause. The Ds and Fs piled up, and I withdrew into a haze of indifference and loneliness. At recess I usually crossed the dirt playground and stood by the scarred trunk of a big, shady oak tree. With the toe of my shoe I'd trace lines in the dust, making patterns and designs. Sometimes Bobby would come by with a few of his new classmates, but mostly I kept to myself.

At home I moped around the trailer, sometimes wandering off through the pine trees to look for crawdads in a nearby stream. When Mommy saw my grades, she knew something was wrong at school. I had always been an above-average student. In fifth grade I had even won a science contest with a silkworm project. But now the sadness in my eyes must have looked like lead weights to her. One day after school she tried to pry out of me an explanation for my hangdog manner. But I couldn't understand what was happening myself. So she interrogated Bobby, who confirmed my isolation during recess. It all must have made sudden sense to her because she immediately telephoned the school and asked for an appointment with the principal.

I didn't go with her, but knowing how my mother could erupt when she felt wronged, she must have burned his ears. The next day the teacher greeted me with a clap on the back and later stopped at my desk and patiently explained a particular algebra equation. At recess, a few classmates stayed with me and even let me shoot marbles with them.

After about a week, the friendly treatment in and out of class tapered off into a rote acknowledgement of my presence. "You can do anything you set your sights on," Mommy would say. "You're as good as you think you are. Don't let anyone tell you different." I don't know if I really believed her, but her words at least gave me a nugget of self-confidence.

I had never been so ostracized or ignored as I was then. On the bus going to and from school, we would pass groups of "coloreds" going off to their school, and one morning I asked the kid next to me about segregation. He gave me a scrunched-up, quizzical look, then blurted, "They have their place and we have ours. Ain't never been no different." I nodded, thinking this may have been the point my mother made so emphatically to the principal: that we were better than poor blacks and cracker whites, and that no one should ever confuse us with immigrant rascuachi riffraff from across the border.

The other crisis I had in Louisiana was resolved with crisp, military precision by my father. It happened early one morning when the trailer began to rock from side to side. Bobby and I were still in our bunk beds and it seemed as if an earthquake had followed us from Los Angeles. Fluffy, in the rear by our parents' bed, barked. I asked Bobby, who was in the bottom bunk, "Is that you?" He said he thought it was me moving around.

I swung my legs around and dropped down to the floor with a thunk. Then Bobby and I, both in our pajamas, followed by little Junior, who was rubbing sleep from his eyes, left the trailer by the side door at the front. We saw nothing outside except a little morning ground fog and the boxy gray silhouettes of neighboring trailers among the pine trees. Our home was the only one about to rock itself off the cement blocks underneath.

Slowly we edged around to the other side. There we saw a cow contentedly rubbing her back against the trailer. "Shoo!" Bobby cried, throwing a rock at the massive black-and-white rump. Our visitor finished one last jiggle, then ambled away. Bobby went back into the trailer while Junior and I stayed outside, making sure the cow did not return. After a moment, we moved away from the trailer and began to pee on a patch of red dirt. That's when I felt a little bump on the skin of my scrotum. I lowered the top part of my pajama bottom and bent down to look. The round, shiny black shape glistened in the early morning light. Hard and nubby to the touch, it was about the size of a pea and seemed to be rooted in my skin. I had seen a tick on Fluffy's ear once, but this one was bigger and blacker, and though I was afraid and disgusted at the sight, I was calm enough to know Daddy would know what to do.

Back inside the trailer, when he saw the tick, he ordered me onto the kitchen table, struck a wooden match, and put the flame just above the insect's bloated body. Everyone gathered around to peer at my pitifully bald privates, waiting for the little hitchhiker to withdraw. As soon as it pulled itself out, Daddy pinched it between his fingers, popping the bubble of blood. Then he swabbed some alcohol on the spot where the tick had dug in. My audience applauded.

"Thank you, Daddy," my mother reminded.

Embarrassed, I yanked up my pajama bottom and said nothing.

Daddy mussed my hair with one hand and nodded. I felt as if I had passed some kind of soldierly test without a whimper.

"Well?" Mommy insisted.

"Thanks," I finally said and waddled off to get dressed.

Fort Riley

We spent the hot summer of 1954 in Kansas after our father was transferred to Fort Riley. The army housing office gave us a ground-floor unit of a converted barracks building. Our new home had partitioned spaces for bedrooms, a kitchen, a living room, and all kinds of storage space. Although the "apartment" lacked a proper bathroom, it did have a complete military latrine. This spacious wonder included a shower area with about ten nozzles, a lot of porcelain washstands, a huge mirror, a row of toilet stalls, and a dozen or so floor-length off-white urinals.

Junior and I roamed around these accommodations for a few weeks, pretending we were recruits, standing for bed inspection, carving initials on the wooden ceiling posts, doing KP with the dishes, taking a scrub brush to a urinal or two.

Eventually, Daddy found us more traditional quarters off base in Junction City. It was a weather-beaten two-story wood-frame structure with small rooms and floors covered by buckled linoleum. After the wide-open spaces of barracks living, the place was tiny by comparison.

Bobby, Junior, and I squeezed into an upstairs atticlike bedroom with a low ceiling sloped steeply to the sides. With only a layer of wood slats and tar-paper shingles between us and the daytime sun, the bedroom would sizzle during the midday and afternoon hours. So most of the time we stayed downstairs, playing out back, watching TV, or doing some of the chores that Mommy had listed in columns under our names on a sheet of paper taped to the refrigerator: take out trash, burn trash, bathe Fluffy, water lawn, clean windows, wash car, wash dishes, dry dishes, sweep upstairs, dust furniture. Her rote question, "Did you do your chores?" was as predictable as the buzzing drone of the cicadas that cut through the still heat every afternoon. She hated housework, but she loved to cook—and that's how she divided home duties. Eventually we even learned to iron our own shirts, sew on buttons, and patch our torn trousers.

To earn "pin money," as she would say, I got a job delivering newspapers. Early every morning a fat, nicotine-smelling man and his even fatter wife would stop by in their station wagon to pick me up. I'd climb in back with three other boys and we would fold newspapers on the short drive to Fort Riley. When we got to our routes, we'd hop out, our gray canvas bags bulging with papers front and back. My route wound through a half-dozen barracks, and as I would walk through the two floors of each building, the bag hanging from my shoulders, my head popped through a hole in the middle, I would shout, "News! News! Get your newspaper!"

At this time of the morning, the men were mostly getting dressed, showering, shaving, or heading out to the mess hall for breakfast. It was my first close look at another kind of soldier, at men so different from my father. They were young, loud, and sometimes possessed of an explosive physical energy I'd never before seen. The towel fights, the wrestling, the cursing, the name-calling—all of it seemed born of raw impulse.

One time I even saw a kind of contest of sexual release. It happened in the last barracks on my route. The morning rush was over, the place nearly empty. I walked between the rows of neatly made beds and army-green footlockers toward a small group of men gathered around something happening at the far end of the barracks. They were yelling as if they were at a track meet. I thought of cockroaches being raced on the floor. Then, as I got nearer, I could see two guys seated on a footlocker, pants down, leaning back with their eyes shut, each man pumping himself as fast as a hand can move. I was fascinated yet scared by all the shouting, the grimacing, and the red-faced fury of the two guys in the middle.

Finally, when the winner erupted in what looked like tiny, liquid spaghetti, the other men cheered. They had made bets, and now they brought out a lot of coins and dollar bills. "Newspapers!" I shouted, and they turned to look at me, all except the loser, who was still pumping away. "Sure, kid," the winner said with a big grin. "We'll buy your papers." I had about a dozen left, and the soldiers bought them all, giving me tips and some good-natured thumps on my back. As I was walking away from the barracks, I figured the other guy must have finished, because my customers started cheering and whistling again.

Most of the money I earned I saved. I even had a bank account that my mother opened for me. "A penny saved is a penny earned," she'd say, adding "So's a dollar." With the savings from my paper route and my allowance money that I got for doing chores, I soon had enough to buy a metallic-green, three-speed Puch made in Austria. It was my first bike with gears and thin tires. I cleaned it just about every day, waxing and buffing the fenders, oiling the chrome-coated axles, polishing every spoke. I'd ride around town, zipping down the main street, exploring neighborhoods, cruising, cooling my face. Or I'd take Junior on little excursions, placing him on the crossbar between the seat and handlebars.

Junior was the first kid I ever loved. Even though seven years separated us, he was so cute, so smart, and so good-natured that I liked doing things with him. And I don't remember fighting with him, at least not with the same blazing anger that took hold of me when I fought with Bobby when we lived in Los Angeles. In those days I would tag after my older brother and his friends, and if I annoyed him he could tease me into a froth in seconds. All it would take was a little jeering or some trick to lose me, or just a shove, and I would go nuts.

But as teenagers in Kansas, we no longer fought. With different interests and impulses, we now went our separate ways. I was thirteen, busy selling papers and pedaling my new bike around

Junction City, while Bobby, at sixteen, was usually off on dates with a girlfriend, sometimes borrowing the Buick at night after Daddy came home.

I don't think we ever really teased Junior. He was too brainy, too observant for that, frowning you into seriousness if necessary. When he was still in diapers, because of the way he said "baby," I started calling him Beebe. And Daddy's affectionate name for the kid with the big head and soft brown curls was "Pumpkin Head," which came out sounding like *pung-kin HAID*. Or that could sometimes change to "Punkeeto." Because Junior was the youngest and smallest, Daddy could still pick him up, hold him in one arm and pinch his cheeks. He could dote on his Punkeeto in a way he could no longer chum up to us teenagers—one gangly and already shaving, and the other shedding baby fat and too large to cuddle. Junior had none of these complications. Daddy could be as playful with his affections as he pleased with Junior, which made what he did to him one night that much more unexpected and terrifying.

It happened a few days after Bobby came home later than he said he would. The next morning Daddy had gone berserk, slapping and punching my brother around upstairs with blows that we could hear downstairs. Bobby, his new deep voice cracking, begged him to stop. But the beating went on. Finally, it ended, and all we could hear were Bobby's whimpering cries and Daddy's footsteps coming across the floor and starting down the stairs where Junior and I were with Mommy. My brother remembers:

> *Mommy could really be aggressive, yelling profanities whenever she was mad, but you never heard a nasty word from him. He always spoke firm and direct. He had complete authority, and he never raised his voice or screamed. He never man-handled me, just beat the holy heck out of me at times. My butt usually. But Mommy would throw everything at us and then ten minutes later it was over and she was the affectionate one. I never felt affection from him. When we were living in Kansas, I went out with some friends and when I came back I didn't want to wake anybody up. So I slept in the kitchen with the dog. And then I got up early and I went to work—at a malt shop or something. He wouldn't believe*

me that I spent the night at home. He just wouldn't believe me. He never did when I told him something. And he would believe anything you would tell him. But not me. Maybe it was because I was so cocky. I must have resented it when he returned from Korea.

In Junior's case, no house rules were broken, no chore left undone, no white lie to cover up a mistake. Instead, Junior's fear of sudden loud noises and of insects, especially the flying kind, produced Daddy's creative remedy for a weakness in character. It was early evening on July Fourth, hot and stifling. Bobby and I were outside on the front lawn lighting firecrackers while Junior kept his distance from our explosions. Daddy must have noticed Junior's wincing, frightened expression, because he suddenly ordered him over to the porch. "Come on," he said sternly. "Move it, double time!"

Junior, then six years of age, warily moved toward my father, who was standing on the front porch under the hanging light. The glow had attracted a swarm of noisy, fat cicadas, big locustlike insects that made a high-pitched droning sound. And there were all kinds of other winged creatures, from June bugs, moths, and dragonflies to tiny gnats and no-see-ums—all of which terrified Junior, though Daddy seemed to be oblivious of their presence.

Junior slowly mounted the half-dozen creaky wooden stairs and when he reached the spot directly under the light, Daddy sternly ordered, "Stand at attention!"

"Yes, sir," Junior said meekly, automatically, and straightened up. Junior, unlike Bobby and me, seldom if ever was spanked. Ever since Daddy had returned from Korea—like *"some stranger in our house,"* Junior remembers—his method of punishment, of imparting lessons to his youngest son, was to have him stand at attention. Sometimes he'd have to stand for hours and for some reason usually in the center of a doorway. Over the years, Bobby and I had done our share of attention-standing, but Junior seemed to get more of this than we ever did—and not just in doorways. Tonight the site would be the porch. Junior recalls:

"Here," he said. "This will make you a man." And then he made me hold up my arms and hands so that the insects could crawl over

my skin. "Touch them, pet them, make friends with them," he said, and he made me do it.

The bugs zoomed around in the light's glow, enveloping my little brother for what seemed like hours. Mostly his hands hung down and his slender body trembled. He'd shake his head or twist away from the light's center. He'd shift his weight from one leg to another, squirming, lifting one foot, then the other. I couldn't see Beebe's face, since he was facing the street, but he probably had his eyes shut and maybe he was crying.

From inside I watched him through the windowpane, powerless to help the trembling, fragile figure under attack. Mommy pleaded for the punishment to stop, but my father must have had a fixed length of time in mind because the ordeal stretched long into the night. Before Junior was allowed back in the house, my mother turned off the light, then rushed out and brushed away the bugs from his face and clothes. Inside the house, she combed a few of the smaller critters from his hair.

Armand—no longer Beebe or Junior—today downplays the incident, shaking his head. I let him read what I've written of that night. He corrects me on a few points, then says,

I don't know what it was, but all I remember is after he came back from Korea there was this stranger telling me what to do. The first thing he did when we got home from San Francisco was cut my hair. Mommy let it grow long, in curls, and the first thing he did was cut my hair. Like we were now his men. I resented him changing our lives, taking over, in a way also taking Mommy over, taking her away from us. I know he was only doing what he thought was best. I can't blame him for that. But there was this dark side, like when he'd make me stand at attention, like in Kansas with all those bugs.

Maybe I have thinner skin, but the image of my little brother standing in a cloud of insects beneath the porch light has always plagued me. Something was not right. It was as if some violent beast had surfaced in our midst for just a moment, then slipped away without further fuss.

Before going to Korea, our father would punish us in a straightforward military manner. A brief lecture, a butt-strapping with his hand or a belt, counting the whacks, pausing between each one as if to let the hurt sink in before the next stinging slap. It was a methodical, ordered ritual, and we knew exactly what was coming. He always remained calm, his voice deep and measured, his movements deliberate. No histrionics, no yelling, no punching or slapping, nothing that seemed cruel. We could squeal in fear or protest our innocence, but once ordered to bend over, we submitted to the inevitable.

Now Bobby and I weren't sure what to expect. We were older, bigger, maybe more like his recruits. As for Junior, other than the insect episode, he was mostly spared the kind of strappings we got at his age.

Our Kansas summer also brought another change in our lives. Mommy, perhaps suffering from too much dampness in Louisiana, suddenly grew weak and began to cough flecks of blood. Diagnosed with tuberculosis, she was immediately quarantined and sent to Fitzsimmons Army Hospital in Denver. We never really said good-bye to our mother, but Daddy explained that he was being transferred to Colorado Springs so we could be closer to her. "As soon as she's better," he promised, "you can see her."

We all wanted her back, especially Junior. In those last days of packing up for Colorado, we began talking about her TB "spot" as if it were this tiny, awful bug hiding in her lungs and making her sick. "My spot," she explained, "showed up loud and clear in the Xrays." The idea, we were told, was that she could not smoke cigarettes anymore and she needed lots of rest and good food so that her spot would die. It hated sunshine, hated milk, hated bed rest, and those were her weapons.

One day I told Junior, "I'm taking Mommy milk and donuts. You can take her the sunshine." Junior looked puzzled, then laughed. Later, when we were in bed at night, he asked about the donuts, but I couldn't answer. For the longest time I tried to imagine how something that tasted so good could hurt Mommy's spot. Before we slipped off to our dreams, I'm sure we both imagined her making the sign of the cross with her thumb on our foreheads. As usual, she whispered, "Sleep and God bless. Duerme y que Dios te bendiga."

Fort Carson

We unpacked and settled into an old wooden rental Daddy had found at the foot of the mountains on the west side of Colorado Springs. Mama came from Los Angeles to watch over us boys while he was away at Fort Carson during the day. But unlike Mommy, Mama wouldn't allow us to do anything in the kitchen. "Manos de bragueta," she would scold, shooing us away as if our hands were constantly fiddling with our fly zippers. She didn't trust males, especially boys, to do anything domestic. In the kitchen they were clumsy and dirty.

However, outside Mama's domain, we did as we pleased, just as our mother had trained us. Armed with years of lessons as spic-and-span soldiers, we persisted in doing our chores—sweeping, dusting, cleaning windows, washing and ironing our clothes. The beds were made, the lawn watered, the dog fed, and every night even Daddy's big black-leather combat boots were shined to a mirrorlike luster. We so impressed Mama that after a few weeks she saw she wasn't really needed and returned to Los Angeles—but not before making one last trip to visit her ailing daughter in Denver.

In the fall of 1954, tubercular patients at the Army's Fitzsimmons Hospital inhabited a first-floor ward where everyone—patients as well as doctors, nurses and even janitors—wore white masks. Children weren't allowed in, but I remember one time peering through a visiting room window at a small, shuffling figure in slippers and a hospital gown. She came close and for a moment she pulled the cloth down from her nose and mouth, blew me a kiss, then covered up again. In that moment, I glimpsed a thinner face than when I last saw her, but she still used lipstick and wore little gold hoop earrings. She raised a thumb to the windowpane and with two strokes made a tiny cross on the glass. Then Daddy, also wearing a mask and standing next to her, took her hand, and the two returned to her bed, one of many I could see lined up on the right side of the ward.

Though we never coughed blood or got Mommy's "spot," as the regular Xrays showed, we had our own ordeals during those two and a half years in the Springs. I don't remember talking about it, but I believe we all missed her terribly. We were her brave little men and she was "tickled-pink" proud of us for "fending for yourselves."

But underneath the little show, there were cracks of neglect. Our mother was absent for many months, so every time Junior or one of us would hurt himself, there was no soft comfort to turn to. Certainly, we would never seek sympathy from Daddy. He was our father and the law, not a referee and never a buffer between us and the hard facts of life. Bobby would fight a severe acne problem alone, for example, or by myself I would carry my obsession with being tall to, as it were, ridiculous heights. If Mommy had been around, she might have lavished us each with one of her you're-my-hero-you're-the-best talks.

Mommy called me a late bloomer, and I desperately wanted to grow. But upward progress was so slow that I would sometimes help nature along. I'd gain maybe half an inch by stuffing wads of tissue paper in the heel part of my shoes. Using a gooey pomade, I'd also comb my crew-cut hair straight up, adding another few centimeters. And I never stood or walked with a hunch. Always soldier straight. Eventually, I joined the Harrison High junior varsity basketball team. As the squad's "manager"—really just the towel-and-water boy—maybe I thought hanging around tall guys would start my spurt.

One year I would even become the smallest member of the school's considerably beefy football team. Lost in my padded suit,

I'd regularly throw myself in front of tanklike running backs in practice or in games we were already winning by lopsided scores. Nothing seemed to work. Manhood—tall, deep-voiced, and hairy—would not open its door. When they lined us up for class pictures, I still had to stand in the front row with the shorter girls. And it wasn't until I was fourteen when the dark fuzz in the usual places started to sprout.

I don't know if I would have talked to Mommy about my worries over being short. I might have, since she was on the short side herself and might try bolstering my self-confidence, something I could have used when I had my first and only fight with a stranger. It happened at a playground and in front of a lot of other kids. I don't recall what provoked him, but this skinny boy about my size started shoving me, asking me to hit him. "You chicken?" he challenged. "Here chickie-chickie." I pushed back, and that's when he let fly with his fists. After he smashed my nose and I fell to the gravel near the swings, he started kicking me, then abruptly stopped. I was scared, trembling. When I got up, the kid was gone, so I limped away, holding my head up to keep the blood from dribbling on my shirt. I could have used the refuge Mommy would have provided had she been at home.

About this time Daddy would begin his own big fight—though it was a legal, not a physical bout. As Mommy would tell us, our father had a few crosses to bear. If we caught on to anything, it was usually by overhearing a conversation or noticing a change in the nightly routine of chores, play, dinner, homework, and TV time. I first heard of it at our second Colorado Springs house, which we bought in a new tract of identical square homes.

I used to sneak into the living room at around midnight to watch movies with the volume on the television turned way down. Face close to the black-white-and-gray images, once or twice a week I'd lose myself in stories that always seemed to have happy endings. One time early in the summer of 1955, as I tiptoed out of the bedroom into the hallway, I could hear Mommy's voice coming from the kitchen. Cured and back home with us now, she sounded as if she were reading a list of names. Every so often Daddy would tell her to stop. He'd read an address and telephone number, then she'd continue. Before I retreated to my bed, I heard her say one last name, then ask, "What about him? Will he defend you?"

I waited, and after a long pause, I could barely hear the words, "I don't know—I'll ask McClain."

I shut my bedroom door, quietly stepped by Junior's bed, and lay down on mine. Before I fell asleep I thought a while about what I'd heard. *Defend you,* she said. From what? Who was after him? What about all those names and addresses? And they all had ranks—first lieutenant, major, captain, colonel, chief warrant officer. Who were these people? And who was McClain?

In the months ahead, I would hear his and many other names. For long stretches there were no more late-night movies for me because my parents usually stayed at the kitchen table with papers and folders, lists and letters spread out in front of them. It was all about Daddy's "hearing," I was told, and one time I overheard him call it an "elimination hearing." The only thing I got straight at the time was that someone in the army, someone he had been in the prison camp with, thought he was a traitor and a "collaborator" with the communists. The year before we used to watch the McCarthy hearings on TV, and when Daddy one day left us to go to Washington, D.C., I thought he might have been ordered to testify before the senator's "witch-hunting" committee, as my mother called it.

When Daddy returned, they went back to their lists and letters. Whatever was happening, they would never explain it in any detail, at least not to me. The army was trying to eliminate him from military service, and we knew we should stay out of the way. You just didn't ask about something so serious, so out of bounds. Looking back now on our reluctance to ask questions about "forbidden subjects," I see we were living alongside a shadow world of unpleasantness, things Mommy was either shielding us from or hiding in order to create an ideal, happy picture of herself and the family. But there were some things she couldn't completely conceal, like her time in a tubercular ward or Daddy's elimination hearing.

Actually, I wasn't paying much attention to what was mostly a blur of background activity. That summer I was busy lugging golf bags around the course at the Broadmoor Hotel and Country

Club, sometimes hauling two heavy sets of clubs for thirty-six holes. After work I was also pursuing a dark-eyed, pretty girl named Marnie, who was as wild about Elvis and Bill Haley and the Comets as I was. I had just bought an old Cushman motor scooter, painted it primer gray, and kept cruising her neighborhood, hoping she'd see Mr. Cool in the white bucks and black turtleneck sweater. Out of the house, I seemed to be racing off every day to a new adventure. Who had time to think about The Hearing? Whatever the army was about to throw at him, Daddy could beat it. I wasn't worried.

A few times Father Prohens, a Spanish priest at the church we attended, would visit and stay for my mother's paella or one of her Mexican meals. Father Jaime Prohens, a round-faced, bespectacled man with a jolly demeanor, would say grace in Spanish, then bless us all. He usually stayed to finish his wine and smoke a cigar with my father. But once, after we were excused, Father Prohens stayed on to recite a rosary with my parents. Beads in hand, the three knelt and prayed before a black wooden cross with a white ceramic Christ figure in crucifixion pose. At the end, I overheard something about God protecting Daddy at the hearing.

The next day my father wore his black patent-leather shoes and his dressiest uniform. The brass buttons, medals, and his silver lieutenant's bars gleamed, and the trouser creases were as thin and straight as a stiletto. He kissed Mommy good-bye and left the house with a briefcase bulging with papers.

About two weeks later, the hearing was over. What happened was never clearly explained, but it appeared that for the time being he could remain in the army. I never knew if he was cleared of the charges or what the specific outcome was. At any rate, the matter was over—the case was apparently closed, and our life went on. Bobby continued driving his own Chevy convertible, canvas top usually down and a girlfriend at his side; Junior stayed happily in grammar school, and I went on still trying to be tall and cool in my white bucks and black turtleneck.

A year later we moved to Fort Sill, Oklahoma, but not before we heard that Daddy was up for promotion to captain, which probably meant that the army trusted him again. Mommy started saying "Captain Arias," testing the words, trying them out, gleeful but serious underneath. When we said grace at dinner, she would even ask the Virgin Mother to give the army a nudge, so that he could wear the two silver bars she had already bought, but the promotion was delayed awhile longer.

In the early summer of 1956, we had all promoted him in our minds. Then I made a wrong turn on my scooter, and my blind enthusiasm for Captain Daddy soon disappeared. It happened during the time I was working two jobs—carrying golf bags around the Broadmoor during the day and running a softball concession stand two nights a week a few miles from the house. Since I was fourteen and still under the age for a driver's license, I would ride my scooter there, always taking back roads and alleyways to avoid run-ins with the police. One afternoon a cop in a patrol car, probably suspecting I was too young to be driving, switched on his lights and siren and came after me. I raced around blocks and through alleys and empty lots, but I couldn't lose him. Then, just when I thought I was free, I turned into an alley and there was the patrol car coming in my direction.

When the cop finally caught me, he told me to leave the motor scooter and he would drive me home so we could hash out my crime with my parents. At the house, the officer explained to my father what had happened and that I would be fined and the scooter temporarily impounded. Daddy apologized for allowing me to drive it and promised I would sell it to pay for my fine, which was $55. The cop, maybe still smarting from another previous chase I had won, lectured me about breaking the law, then warned me not to disgrace my family again. Afterward, the two men shook hands, and the cop left.

I'm sure Daddy considered the old-fashioned strapping. I hadn't been punished like that for two or three years. Whatever he thought, he must have sensed that taking money from me was like taking away my freedom, and that that would hurt me more. I had a debt that went beyond the police fine, and over so many months I would have to pay it off. To him.

We sat facing each other at the kitchen table. Fluffy was the only witness, curled on a carpet by the door. After delivering one of his typical, even-toned discourses on doing right and doing wrong, he asked me, "Do you understand?"

"Yes, sir," I said, never daring to protest or even remind him that it was he who allowed me to buy the scooter in the first place.

"You may go now," he said.

Dismissed, I stepped over Fluffy and went outside to shoot baskets in the driveway until it was too dark to see. I sulked for days, though months later—after moving to our third house in Colorado Springs—I realized that perhaps his real message to me was: *If you're going to do wrong, make sure you don't get caught.* He would have said it with bigger words. Maybe he did and they just blew by me in a whoosh of elevated sounds with very little meaning—so different from the young soldiers I was hearing at the Fort Carson bowling alley where I set pins.

There, because they still had no automated pin setting, I would court death or severe injury each time the ball struck the pins. The wooden missiles would explode into the padded pit, missing me by inches, my feet and legs yanked up out of the way after finishing the previous pin-setting. You had to be fast or you'd get clipped. All the boys had bruises, a few had broken bones, and one kid was knocked unconscious and taken to the base hospital.

The sweaty bowlers in snot green T-shirts would drink a lot of beer, and better than a strike would be to take out a pinsetter. So for a few hours every night these glistening, muscular figures would face us, hurling those heavy black balls at us with as much maniacal glee as they could muster. "Yeah!" you'd hear after one of the kids went down. "I got that little shit! Little fucker ain't never coming back!"

Toward the end of our stay in Colorado Springs, I was finishing my freshman year, reading more and writing for the school newspaper. Increasingly, I was discovering music in language—from the sodden expletives of the bowling alley yahoos to the rhymed lines of Robert Frost. It was then that I began to hear how unnaturally my father expressed himself, casually mixing lofty tone and military formality with comic-book cheerfulness. Up until then I wasn't really noticing how other fathers spoke, how *anyone* spoke. I didn't think much about style.

I keep a postcard given to me by Max Medema, a onetime friend of my dad's from Arizona. On the back of the postcard, sent in the spring of 1956, my father's neatly printed words are evenly spaced, the first letter of most words capitalized. The crisp-looking, buoyant lines are typical of how my father tried to speak. Only the signature, A. Arias, with its loose and swirly A's, is written with cursive letters.

Hi Maximiliano!

Been Traveling All Over The CounTry BuT Never Seem Able To Pass Thru L.A. In Our Travels ~ So NexT To Seeing You, I ThoughT The Medium Of Correspondence Would Be MosT EffecTive Means Of CommunicaTing WiTh You. Wasn'T ThaT An Original ThoughT? I Seem To Recall Your STaTemenT Of Some years VinTage: "I'll Answer Or Have Answered All LeTTers Recvd from you". Here's Hoping you STill Adhere To ThaT View—& WiThin This Year!

Family Here In Good HealTh, WiTh Bobby GraduaTing Sr High Sch NexT MonTh & Hence InTo Army for Six MonTh Tng Program. Emma Lou STill ATTending Ceramic Courses AT Carson & Yours Truely ATTending Business Law Courses AT Colorado UniversiTy Evenings.

Family Sends Regards To You & Yours & Please ExTend BesT Wishes To BeTTy & Baby for All Of Us.

A. Arias

Fort Sill

In Oklahoma I became a thief. My new friend Larry and I would hang out at the base gym, watch the soldiers play basketball for awhile, then leave the building, double back, and slip into the men's locker room. One of us would check the unlocked compartments, fishing into pockets and shoes, while the other would stand lookout by the door. We usually managed to find a handful of coins, a few dollar bills, and sometimes a wallet with a five- or ten-dollar bill. On a good day we'd split about fifteen dollars apiece, enough to splurge at the Dairy Queen and see a few movies in downtown Lawton.

Larry was a skinny, pale-faced guy with a cocky walk and a taste for pink silky shirts and shiny white loafers. Even though he was a year older and a head taller than I was, we were in the same grade because he had ditched classes so often that he had to repeat his freshman year. The son of a mess sergeant who'd been stationed at Fort Sill for three years, Larry knew his way around the base and the city.

Long before rap, he was speaking in rhyming pop-song lines. It was talk but always with a rhyme and a beat. Our gym heists were the "thrill on Strawberry Hill," which sometimes became the "kill on the hill." Once he appeared at my open bedroom window, whispering, "Come-on-a-my-house, the house of come-on," and with the Rosemary Clooney line tapping after us, off we'd go to the gym for our "candy."

Besides mentoring me in locker-room thefts, my thrill guide for the summer of '56 showed me the occasional rewards of never passing up a coin-operated machine without dipping a finger in the coin return slot. He also took me to Indian bars where we could buy beer and smoke cigarettes without anyone making a fuss over our age. And at night, between the red brick homes of dependents' housing, he taught me the stealth needed to peek into lit bathrooms and bedrooms. Unfortunately, I never saw any of Larry's promised delights, having to content myself with his blunt descriptions of the girls and women he swore he had seen naked.

I tagged after my lowlife wizard whenever I could and by some miracle we were never caught stealing or peeking into windows, nor was I ever questioned about my absences at home. I probably wasn't even missed. My father was busy attending artillery and guided missile classes and my mother was occupied as the unofficial hostess to a visiting group of Spanish and Latin American officers who were students with my dad. So as long as I showed up for dinner, there were no lectures, curfews, groundings, strappings, middle-finger thumpings to the forehead, or commands to stand at attention. Nothing but free rein to outrun trouble.

We had come to Fort Sill so my father could study in a program attended by American as well as foreign officers. From the start of classes my father began inviting the Spanish-speaking students over to the house to study together. Suddenly, my mother found a summertime mission: mothering a half-dozen Spanish and Latin American "orphans," as she called them. Two or three times a week she would prepare the dining room table by the air conditioner, setting out a pot of coffee and plates of her cookies, potato salad, and sandwiches. She'd move back and forth from the men to the kitchen, filling their cups and glasses, emptying ashtrays, bustling about like a gracious domestic angel who must have reminded our guests of a sister, aunt, wife, or girlfriend back home. On those study nights, the long linoleum-covered dining room would fill with cigarette and cigar smoke as the laughter mixed into discussions punctuated by coefficients and decimal points.

These men from Spain, Puerto Rico, Uruguay, and Colombia showered Mommy with all the courtesies and compliments of visitors at a queen's court. Far from their own homes and yoked to weeks of dry lectures and algorithms calculating trajectories, they addressed her respectfully as Doña Emma. I knew my mother could be beautiful—certainly she had been so before Korea and her illness—but now she was radiant. The eager, giggly laugh, the dark red lipstick, the lustrous swirl of her permed reddish brown hair, the sparkle in her eyes—all were back. She probably felt as if she were sixteen again at her cousin's party in Chihuahua, la gringa from El Paso, circled and courted for dances by handsome young men who wrote her poems as easily as they gave her flowers.

As for my dad, he not only seemed to bask in Mommy's new glow, but he also appeared to settle comfortably into the role of senior soldier, the modest but savvy veteran of two wars. Our visitors, who could relax and loosen up after hours of class time in uniform, might have seen him as the ideal son of Spain, a latter-day knight without the lance and clunky armor. At least that's what I saw.

I also thought Daddy was super smart in math. In those pre-calculator days, my father's slide rule calculations were just so many digits and squiggles to me. But to him they seemed to provide clear, clean answers to every question about speed and distance. He always seemed so confident, so *right*. For the first time I began thinking we were opposites. I imagined his world as one of equations, of everything reduced to rules, to black-and-white, yes-no answers, of human life conducted coldly, efficiently, as a matter of time, speed, mass, and distance.

By contrast, my mother's world of guidelines and maxims was one of practical *advice* to get through the business of living. A penny or a dollar saved might be as good as one earned, depending on whether or not you spent it on a mood-lifter like ice cream and chocolate fudge. Mommy's handy hints for her boys were forgiving; they weren't do-or-die rules; her prayers to the Virgin and St. Jude sought common-sense solutions, not just comfort and solace.

That summer, borrowing from my mother's collection, I read *Anthony Adverse, Quo Vadis?, The Black Robe, Moby Dick,* and other sagas in which every day was a problem-solving adventure—emotional, ragged, dramatic. It was my mom's world and mine—although like Larry's easy, ever-ready rhymes, there was something attractively sturdy in my father's clear-eyed military approach to life, more mathematical than emotional.

My brother Bobby chose the military path, joining the army reserves after high school graduation and going away to boot camp, then to military police training. Maybe he and my parents felt he needed the discipline the army could give him after years of paying more attention to girls, cars, and good times than his homework. As for Junior, in Fort Sill he was usually off playing with his new friends, too young to ponder the basic personality differences between his parents.

At the end of summer, when the guided missile course concluded, my parents threw a good-bye party for the study group. The night before the big day, I stayed up late in bed reading *The Sun Also Rises*. Eventually, as I eased into sleep, I found myself running with the crowd down a cobblestone street, just ahead of the bulls, confident I would not be trampled or gored.

The next morning I woke up to my mother's painfully cheerful voice: "Chop-chop! Out of bed—let's go!"

I peeked at her silhouette against the fuzzy daylight filtering into my room, rubbed my eyes, opened them, trying to focus, then saw her round, smiling face above me. "Today's the day," she said brightly. "Up and at 'em!"

After she left the room I raised my head, putting the pillow up against the headboard, then leaned back into a comfortable position. Now that Bobby had left, I had a room to myself. We had left most of our things in storage in Colorado Springs, so our Fort Sill house, courtesy of the army, had only the basics—beds, chairs, tables, stove, refrigerator. To these my father added a makeshift barbecue spit-and-grill erected over a hole in the reddish orange dirt behind the house. The crude-looking framework of metal rods and wires was vintage rascuachi, his own hastily built invention for roasting the baby pig I was starting to smell.

Daddy and a Puerto Rican officer had brought home the whole animal, slaughtered, pink and scraped of hair. Now, with a skewer through the mouth and out the rear, it was just starting to sizzle for the afternoon party. Mommy meanwhile had turned into a kitchen dervish, tending pots of beans and rice, chopping onions, squeezing lemons, and baking three kinds of pie and a pineapple-upside-down cake. My parents hadn't given a party with such preparations in years, since before Korea.

We were also celebrating Daddy's overdue promotion to captain. After his return from Korea, Mommy had grumbled a lot about the army's passing him over year after year. She said most of the other POWs in the officers' camp had already been promoted. I never heard Daddy complain about the delay, but she would harp on it. She was convinced the hearing to oust him dishonorably from the service had caused the delay. "They cleared you, didn't they?" she'd ask him. "How much more do you have to do before they give you that cotton-pickin' promotion?" In Colorado she had started calling the elimination hearing a "trial," saying the army was "ungrateful" for all that Daddy had given his country. When he finally made captain, for her it was too late in coming and still an insult. Only on the day of that party did I see her happily embrace the army and her role as an officer's wife.

The afternoon was hot, pork smelling, and smoky. We gathered on chairs and benches arranged around the cement slab outside the back door. The skewered, fat-dripping lechón fed us all, slice by succulent slice. Daddy did the honors, serving my mother, our guests, and us kids. Mommy added servings of beans and rice, scooped out of big metal trays my father borrowed from the mess hall. The Uruguayan made a toast to Doña Emma, then they all sang "Cielito Lindo" and a few other songs in her honor. After the singing, the young Puerto Rican officer taught me how to "shoot" beer-bottle caps by snapping them between my middle finger and thumb. I got to where I could flip the caps across the yard, popping Junior in the back at about thirty feet away.

Later, when my mother asked my father why he wasn't drinking beer or rum and Coke like the others, he raised his glass of grape juice and said that for three years as a prisoner in Korea, even at his thirstiest, “I dreamed of grape juice, ice-cold, just like this.”

After I heard this, I looked in the refrigerator, then searched the kitchen for the obvious. He’d taken the last of the grape juice.

Schwäbisch Hall

To me it seemed the slide in my parents' marriage began in early 1957 when we were stationed in Germany. My father now commanded an artillery company and was away on maneuvers much of the time, leaving my mother alone in a gray, charmless apartment on the base outside Schwäbisch Hall. Junior was in school during the day, and during the week I was four hours away in Nuremberg, where I boarded and attended an American high school for military dependents.

My mother learned just enough German to speak to our cleaning lady, Lisel, and to shop in town. She never liked Germany and never really got to know any Germans as friends. Sweet-natured Lisel, a middle-aged matron, was the exception, but she only came to clean once a week. Whatever my mother's fears, real or imagined, the nearness of the last big war must have affected her feelings toward Germans. After all, only twelve years had passed since Daddy had been imprisoned by the Nazis. If they had killed Jews and gypsies, how safe would a Mexican in Germany have been during the war, even one who professed to be "Spanish, French, and Portuguese?"

I think she felt trapped and rootless in Germany. Even though she carried out the duties of a company commander's wife—hosting get-togethers of other wives, attending regimental parties and parade ground reviews—loneliness seemed to take over. She had no close friends, Daddy was often gone on war games, and her sons had little or nothing to do with her day-to-day life. No longer a diarist, she wrote letters, mostly morose ramblings to Mama and Tuy, informing them of her sciatica attacks, her recourse to a local masseuse, and her intention to visit the shrines of Lourdes and Fatima. She intended to pray for a cure and a mending of her marriage. I have none of those letters, although years later my grandmother told me that it hurt her to read that her daughter had problems. "They didn't love each other like they used to," she said.

Occasionally there were outings, tours of old churches and ruined castles, trips to the Schwäbisch Hall marktplatz to buy bread, schnitzel, or Italian gelati. Once my parents even visited me in Nuremberg, where I took them by the war crimes trial building, then to Soldiers Field, which is where the Nazis held their largest rallies during the war. It was also where I ran sprints and hurdles at school track meets. Using the running tricks Daddy had taught me in Los Angeles, I learned to run fast if not for long.

Another time they traveled south on the Stuttgart-Munich autobahn to the Bavarian town of Dachau. I was away at school and didn't go along but I wish I had. I can only imagine why one or both of them wanted to see the Third Reich's first human death factory. When they returned, they were quietly somber about their impressions. "Horrible" was my mother's dominant description.

My father never spoke to us, his sons, about his wartime missions against the Germans or if he had seen Dachau or other extermination camps during the war. Given his reticent nature, I doubt that we could have pried specifics out of him. Besides, there were the usual areas off limits to discussion, which included just about everything in the past. So we never asked. Of their visit to Camp Dachau, all I have now is an illustrated, authorless booklet entitled *Never Again*, and a snapshot they took of the Krematorium entrance with our '57 Buick parked just inside the open gate. I also have a single memory from when we were driving south to Italy for a three-week vacation that summer. Daddy was at the wheel, Mommy beside him in front, and the three of us in back—Bobby having finished his army training and now visiting us. As we passed the autobahn exit for Dachau, she said something about evil never really dying. After a moment's silence, he added, "like weeds with deep roots." That was it. As we zipped past Dachau, I imagined certain roots growing all the way to hell.

Italy opened the skies for us. Whatever gloom we'd felt at home slipped away as we motored south in our new maroon Buick through Munich, Garmisch-Partenkirchen, and up into the Austrian Alps toward Innsbruck. It was our first vacation together since the pilgrimage to Mexico City three years before. But this time we would camp, although, as we were to discover, Daddy might have said *bivouac* or *overnight deployment*. He had borrowed army-issue sleeping bags, a portable stove, fold-up cots and a monster heavy-duty olive green tent, all of which reeked of kerosene. Most of this gear he piled onto a metal rack tied hillbilly-style to the roof of the car. Food, clothes, and everything else we crammed into the trunk.

We stopped the first night at a campground just outside Innsbruck. There, among all the colorful lightweight tents of other campers, my father's heavy canvas monstrosity slowly rose, gray-green and foreboding, looking like a sad, sullen Gulliver tied down by the Lilliputians. Embarrassed, I grumbled to my mother about our temporary home's ugliness. It was late afternoon and we were sitting on a picnic bench near the campground restrooms. "That's Daddy for you," she said, shaking her head.

Pointing to the dark, sagging shape looming in the distance, I asked her, "But why'd he have to bring *that*?"

"Humor him," she said. "Once you're inside, you won't even notice."

My mother was right. I stopped fretting about how different we looked from the other campers and actually began to like pitching our tent every night. Wherever we stopped, we tackled the chore like Eagle Scouts. Center poles up, stakes pounded in, lines pulled and tightened fast, tarp spread on the ground, cots opened, sleeping bags rolled out. Efficient and tidy, our movements were made with crisp military precision. By the time we got to Italy and our final destination, the Lago di Garda resort for military families, the drill had become automatic—like saying *mano* and kissing the extended parental hand, something I did until I was nineteen or twenty.

Whatever martial spirit we had absorbed driving down evaporated as soon as we walked onto the spacious, well-tended campground and lakeside resort. Craggy, snow-tipped mountains loomed across the water, soft sunlight broke through leafy trees, butterflies flickered among the flowers, moving on in the warm afternoon breeze. In the following days life at Lago di Garda came as close to a perfect existence as I had ever known. All day and into the night we played at everything from Ping-Pong, hula hoops, badminton and tennis to cards, chess, and checkers. Even Daddy relaxed, for a time shedding stiffness for silliness—he liked doing back flips off a platform tethered in deeper water out in the lake.

He also taught Junior and me how to swing a tennis racquet, toss the ball, serve, volley, and play at the net. From then on, tennis would become the family sport, at least for Daddy, Junior, and me—since Bobby wasn't all that interested in running around trying to whack fuzzy little balls over a net. I don't know where our father learned to play, but it must have been after he returned from Korea. The only other athletic activities I saw him do were swimming and playing basketball at a gym with other army reservists during the period between the wars. When tennis entered our lives, it was as if he had found an emotional meeting ground for a kind of affection with us. Ever the patient, earnest instructor, he would coax us with easy shots, urging us to bend the knees, run faster, keep an eye on the ball. But once we learned the basics, he played with gusto, never holding back. So when we occasionally won points with good shots, they were so obvious that he never had to praise us.

After games he would shake our hands or pat us with a casual arm on the shoulder. Dripping with perspiration, we'd pick up loose balls together, towel off together, leave the court together, head for the water fountain together. In the years ahead, playing tennis under the midday sun or under the night lights, on asphalt or clay, in the morning fog or in blowing dust—whatever the conditions, tennis would become a bonding ritual but with no doubt about who was in charge.

Daddy not only won the key points, but also his mental hardness, his *purpose* in playing the game, was unshakable. You could not rattle him. Frustration seemed to bounce off him as soon as he uttered an *Ay Dios, Oh my!* or *Darn it!* In later years, even when Junior and I had surpassed him in form and shot-making ability, somehow he could still beat us with an uncanny talent for unnerving us. Now and then we might win a string of games, a set, or an entire match. But there could be no celebration because we knew in our bones who was still the toughest player.

Little did we suspect in 1957 that the Lago di Garda courts would be our friendly, civilized initiation to competition, to physical discipline, and to a sort of knowing comradeship with our father. As novice gladiators in white T-shirts and shorts, we were as eager to please him as he was to pull us into the arena, our mother offering cheers for both sides. Usually she would walk an aging Fluffy along the lakeshore, browse in shops in the nearby town, or read one of her novels while stretched out on a lawn chair in the shade up by the big white clubhouse. Once our tennis games became a regular, twice-daily event, she would do her reading closer to the courts. From there she would look up now and then, clap her hands and let out little yips and squeals, Fluffy managing a few excited barks himself. It didn't matter if the point was over or not, Mommy rooted for whatever was going on, never taking sides, apparently cheering only the effort or perhaps just the sight of us having fun.

My younger brother now remembers our Lago di Garda stay as the "last happiest time" we would have as a family. Away from Germany, away from the army routine, embracing Italian sun and food and constant, spontaneous activity—for that moment in our lives I believe we were fulfilled and content, together in good spirits as we would never be again.

1951 Arias Family – Farnsworth Ave. home, Los Angeles

Christmas 1956, Colorado Springs, Colorado

Pamplona

In June of 1959 I left my parents in southern Germany, determined to backpack my way through France and Spain. Daddy had been transferred from Schwäbisch Hall to another post outside Schwäbisch Gmund, and I had just finished my senior year at the American dependents high school in Stuttgart. I was yearning to get out on the road and see more of the world, to find adventure naturally, away from all the rules and required work of the classroom.

I also wanted to escape the increasingly gloomy atmosphere I felt at home. Mommy had taken to wearing a kerchief and dark glasses most of the day, even indoors. She was smoking more and forever listening to her Mexican "crying" records on the big Gründig console we had bought the year before. Beset by chronic headaches and immobilizing sciatica attacks, she managed to endure Daddy's usual departures to war game maneuvers by withdrawing into a kind of survival shell alternately hardened or softened by prescription drugs.

As for Junior, I remember he had a tough time fitting in at the local German school to which my parents insisted on sending him—despite his having to contend with a different language and culture, not to mention the inevitable slights from his new classmates. My ten-year-old brother, weighed down by this experience, could only add to the morose mood at home.

So I fled, surprisingly encouraged by my father and leaving my mother near tears by the sight of my leaving and the monster load on my back. "Mi'jito, do you have to take so much?"

"I have to," I boasted. "Got a long way to go. I need the sleeping bag and the tent."

"You can't take the bus or train?"

Then Daddy: "He's got to see things on his own. Don't worry, he'll be fine."

At that moment, Daddy and I connected. He was me. Somewhere, at some time when he was young, he had done this same thing. He had gone off on his own to discover life down the road after the next town, beyond the next hill. I could see the excitement in his eyes. "Have fun," he said. "Enjoy, enjoy!"

And I did. All through France and into Spain, hitchhiking, walking, sleeping in campgrounds, in barns, and once in a ditch by the side of a highway. By the time I reached Pamplona, I was living on a few dollars a day. Fortunately, the Sisters of Mercy shelter put me up for free as a charity case. The only strict regulation was the curfew they kept. If you weren't back in the shelter by nine P.M., too bad—the front doors would be locked until morning.

I didn't mind the regulation. I was grateful to have clean white sheets and a blanket on my simple, wood-frame cot, one of dozens lined up against the long walls of the cavernous basement. On one side of me was an old man who looked like a character Don Quixote might have met on the country roads of La Mancha. Bald and bearded, he was a rheumy-eyed derelict with missing teeth and garlicky body odor. He kept asking me for money, and I kept saying I didn't have any. Actually, I still had two fifty-dollar traveler's checks, which I kept with my passport in a strip of cloth wrapped around my waist. Eventually my smelly neighbor stopped talking, lay down, covered himself, and went to sleep. This left me free to talk to the thin, fine-featured man on the other side of my bed. He had just finished removing his trousers and shirt and was neatly folding them over the crossbar at the head of the cot.

Francisco Zabaleta had come to Pamplona for the festival of San Fermín almost every year since he was sixteen, and he was now "crawling toward fifty," as he put it. A bullfight aficionado since childhood, he had first run with the bulls in 1926 and had seen at least one corrida on each visit to the city. "I'm a poor bookkeeper, a life of numbers," he said. "The bulls revive me."

I told him I had read the autobiography of the great matador Juan Belmonte and that I liked how as a boy in a moonlit field he challenged fighting bulls with only a stick and a ragged piece of cape. Poetry of the campo, Francisco said, and we talked about tomorrow's run through the streets. In all his years he had never fallen down or been hurt. He wasn't as fast as he used to be, but he knew every doorway of the route, "every place where I can escape a disgrace."

Francisco had just arrived by bus from Madrid and he intended to do the run in the early morning, attend the afternoon corrida, then return in the evening to Madrid. Pamplona was his one risky extravagance of the year, away from his childless wife and all the predictable comforts of a modest man marking time toward a pension. He said he couldn't afford to stay more than one night and one day.

Our talk trailed off and Francisco fell asleep before I did. The long, dimly lit room slowly filled with a chorus of wheezy breaths, snoring, and occasional grumbles about not being able to smoke or drink. "God gave us wine for a reason!" someone muttered. But the good Sisters, in exchange for a small contribution to their mission, had exacted a promise from all guests to abstain from alcohol and tobacco. Still, the grumbling continued, goaded by drunken voices from the street singing the praises of San Fermín.

Pamplona.
Staying at the refugio de las Hermanas de Misericordia.
Stuffed in next to a bum on one side and the Madrid guy
Francisco on the other. Reminds me of Daddy. Deep voice,
long nose. But more talkative. He's really up for the bul—

The word trails off on the page. I must have been drifting toward sleep. My mother had given me the small leather-covered address book just before I left on my summer odyssey. She had entered a few addresses of relatives and told me not to forget to send postcards to them. The blank pages at the back were for impressions of my trip. No one saved the cards that I sent from Paris, Poitiers, Toledo, and Barcelona, but I still have the address book.

That night in the Pamplona shelter was the first time I had ever written about someone who reminded me of my father—at least physically so. Mostly it was the nose that did it, Francisco's prominent "Spanish nose," as my mother would have said. The only ones in my family with that nose were my dad's four brothers, sister, and father, Julio Arias, born in Spain near the city of León. I have only one image of my grandfather. He was visiting us in Los Angeles. I wasn't quite seven and I remember that he got out of the car with my parents, walked across the front lawn of our Coolidge Avenue house and extended a hand to touch my head. I looked up and froze as this longish, knucklelike appendage descended toward my face. At the last possible moment it stopped and retreated. Apparently my grandfather only wanted a closer look at me.

I intended to tell Francisco about my own Spanish connection and that as a young man my grandfather had immigrated to Mexico before settling in Nogales, Arizona. But my friendly bed neighbor was asleep. For a man almost three times my age, he had an easy kind of openness that was relaxing, not as cautious, as guarded as Daddy might have been sharing his life with a kid in a poorhouse shelter most likely filled with petty thieves and hustlers. Although I was already seventeen, it was only then, in Spain, that I began feeling a need to connect with an older person, someone to follow, even if only for a few steps. I had learned to take orders from Daddy, focus on instructions, properly smack a tennis ball. But I rarely ever traded spontaneous thoughts with him. We would sometimes laugh together, but there was no whimsy, no hint of stories, memories, nothing from the past.

Waking up in the shelter that first morning, I immediately turned to face my neighbor Francisco, but he was gone, up hours earlier to do the run. Unfortunately, the geezer who reeked of garlic was still around, shuffling back from the big restroom at one end of the long room. "Ah," he said, blowing his nose in toilet paper. "Good morning." He loomed over the bed.

"Yes," I said, shrinking back and rubbing my eyes.

"Ernesto's here. You can see him right up the street. He's in the plaza."

"Who?"

"Ernesto, the writer. Ernesto Hemingway."

"Oh," I said, finally comprehending.

He smiled and waited, maybe for a tip. I turned over on my side, closed my eyes for a while, and eventually the odor and its owner left in search of more promising prey.

Later, after I washed up and left my pack at the shelter's office, I went looking for Hemingway, excited and hoping the news was true, yet thinking the old wino had fed me a line he'd used for years on naive gringos and other foreigners, most of whom were here to recreate their own version of *The Sun Also Rises*. I had read the novel, had seen the movie with Ava Gardner and Tyrone Power, and in my American literature class we had discussed *The Old Man and the Sea*. Beyond that, all I knew was that he was someone you read along with all the greats from Shakespeare on.

At the plaza where he was supposed to be, I bought a program of the afternoon's fight, then made my way through the crowd of tourists and locals—many of the men wearing red neckerchiefs and berets—toward the shady side of the square. It was only midmorning, but it looked as if the party had started hours ago. People were singing and dancing little jigs, sometimes while holding up leather bota bags and trying to aim tiny streams of wine into their mouths. As I neared a long wooden table with benches set out into the plaza in front of a restaurant, I saw a heavyset man with a short white beard seated at one end with several other people. A billed cap shaded his face, which was turned toward a young couple dancing a jota to the sound of a lively flute and staccato drum beat. From what I could see of his features, he fit the image I had of him. Apparently, either no one had recognized him or he had only just sat down.

I approached, program in one hand. "Excuse me, Mr. Hemingway," I said, standing in front of him across the table, "could I get an autograph?"

He turned his grizzled head and looked me over through his tinted glasses. After a moment, he asked me if I wanted a glass of wine. "Sure," I blurted. Then he excused himself from his companions—two men and a woman—rose, and we moved to the other end of the table, sitting opposite each other on the benches. He had brought along a bottle and his glass. A waiter came over with another glass and poured me some red wine.

We lifted our glasses, drank a bit, then he asked to see my program so he could sign it, which he did, writing his name quickly and clearly next to an illustration of two men in berets running ahead of a black fighting bull. Perhaps sensing I was nervous, he asked me my name. "Ronald," I said, "or Ron."

"And?"

"Arias," I said, pronouncing the word as I would in Spanish.

"Where are you from?"

"Los Angeles."

I was surprised that Hemingway would want to know about me, but in a relaxed, scrutinizing manner, he kept up the interrogation for about ten minutes. Like a curious, solicitous reporter, he seemed to have a checklist of questions: what was I doing in Spain, how was the hitchhiking so far, what did I think of Pamplona, the festival, who were my parents, what did I want to do with myself, and what did I want to pursue?

I told him about leaving home, about my Mexican background, about wanting to travel, about staying in a Paris youth hostel and watching the prostitutes of Pigalle, and about being chased off one night by a one-eyed, one-armed drunk who didn't want me to share his tar-paper shack with him. I even professed that I wanted to be a writer and had written for my school newspaper and literary magazine. Hemingway smiled, perhaps amused but pleased.

Finally he paused and nodded as if to say I was now free to fire away. Surprisingly, no one had interrupted us and I still had his full attention. So I asked him what he thought of Pamplona and San

Fermín today, compared to when he was first here as a young man. "Very different," he said. "Not so many damned tourists." Elbows on the table, he leaned forward and explained that the San Fermín he remembered was like a simple country fair. Truckloads of people from the Basque countryside all around, and for this one time in the early morning men could test themselves in the streets ahead of the horns. Same as now but simpler, not with hordes of foreigners.

"What's happening is sad," he said. "I blame myself. I had something to do with it." But the music, he added, had not changed and the wine tasted as swell as ever.

I finished my glass of red, wanting to stay longer but not knowing what else to ask or say. I thanked him for his time and rose to leave. We shook hands, he wished me luck on the rest of my trip, then I backed away into the crowd. That was the last I saw of him.

Two years later Hemingway would shoot himself at his home in Idaho. I would read about his mental problems, his paranoia, his depression. I can only imagine the horrors of mind that would drive him to suicide. I never saw that side, only the interested, wistful side of a man who for some reason wanted to share thoughts with an American kid who had asked him for his autograph. Perhaps by probing the eagerness and innocence of a seventeen-year-old, he was retrieving some of his own lost youth.

As an author he would never have much effect on me—others would do that. But I believe Hemingway affected me in another, deeper way. The quest for my father, for *pieces* of my father, began that summer in 1959. Until then Daddy had been a distant, disciplinary presence in my life, a hero, a protector, more model than mentor. As a child I wanted to be like him. But as I grew older, I realized there were parts of him missing, like an ability to relax and open himself to others, especially his sons. As we moved from place to place and school to school, I compensated by admiring, even imitating other adults. However, until I was traveling solo in Spain, I had never consciously sought the fatherly acquaintance of an older man. In Pamplona, if only briefly over a glass of wine, I felt I'd met that kind of man.

Me with my dad.

Lago di Garda, Italy
July 11, 1960

Junior and me with our dad.

March 1968, Oceanside Calif.

Berkeley

Three years later we were scattered in different cities but at least we were all back in California. My parents and Junior had moved to Travis Air Force Base, east of San Francisco Bay, I was attending the University of California at Berkeley, and Bobby was running a men's clothing store south of Los Angeles in Oceanside. We didn't get together as a family much anymore, but sometimes I'd hitch-hike home on weekends and holidays. If I got lucky with the rides, I could be ringing their doorbell in under two hours.

Mostly I visited for my mother's sake—to "pep her up," as we would say, and make her more like the old "bubbly Mommy" we used to know in her healthier days. Before Korea Daddy would call her "la reata," or whip. But since leaving Germany she continued her slide into a kind of heavy-hearted sadness, going through the motions of daily life as if she were nursing a deep, unhealable wound. She had prayed to the Holy Mother in Portugal at Fatima, and in France at the grotto of Lourdes, but no matter how fervently my mother sought help, her burdens were not lightened.

Now, in California, I would see her on my breaks and just assumed age and illness were to blame for her frequent periods of melancholy—though by her reckoning she was only forty-one in that fall of 1961. Actually, I thought very little about my mother's decline. I was twenty, restless, and so focused on myself and staying afloat academically that I probably dismissed her plight as rotten luck. An unwilling military wife, she blamed the army for most of her miseries. She hated being rootless, hated the gypsy life, hated the cliques and gossip among the officers' wives, hated having her husband taken away to war and imprisonment, hated the army for trying to disgrace him, and hated being forced to live in such god-awful places that she wound up in a TB ward. At bottom, though, I think she mostly hated losing the dream: an adoring husband, a picture-postcard home in the California suburbs, good health, and sons who never strayed far. *Dear Mama,* she wrote from Travis: *When I was little you used to tell me about the crosses you had to bear. I didn't understand. . . .*

If the dream seemed to float away at every turn, at least she had drummed it into us, her boys, and Daddy too. We pretended we were living her dream. We ignored the painkillers and sedatives she took, the trips to special healers for sciatica, earaches, and other problems. Daddy would lecture us about faithfulness and loyalty, about Mommy being the center of our lives—she was the axle and we were the spokes. We said life was grand but we didn't mean it. We dipped our fingers in the alabaster font in the hallway entrance, genuflected with wet fingertips, and stepped outside into the harsh sunlight, pretending we could see. We also attended mass on Sundays, talked of miracles and saints, and avoided touchy topics like belief in God or the possibility of another war, this time in Vietnam. Above all, we tried our best to keep Mommy "peppy" and "perky." Very few things could still rouse her interest, not even the piano or ceramics, both of which she had abandoned for good in Germany. But she still seemed to like cooking, reading, and occasional walks.

One of the best ways to rouse her from the doldrums was by suddenly suggesting we do something together, much like the mornings when we were kids and she'd wake us with the bright-eyed *Let's go to the beach!* battle cry. Now it was our turn to pull her along to a movie, a bike ride, a picnic, a trip to the commissary, or maybe just a drive off base for a chocolate sundae at the Vacaville Tastee Freeze.

Once on a Saturday trip home I offered to show my parents around the university Sunday when I returned. We could have lunch at the student center, walk through the gardens, visit the library, the bookstore, the lecture halls. *Dig the scene on Telegraph Avenue*, I challenged, posturing behind my pitifully wispy goatee and black turtleneck.

My mother squeezed my hand. She glanced at my father, who had just come in from a morning of tennis. "Oh, Daddy, let's go!" she said, playing the little girl. "We can drive him back after mass."

"Fine," my dad said, embracing her with one arm, pulling her to him, "after church." She looked up dreamy-eyed, *tickled pink*, as she would say.

The next day after attending mass we left Junior at home and drove from Travis to a high, barren hill overlooking the north end of the Golden Gate Bridge. My father, still a captain, was in charge of the guided missile unit at the site and he needed to do a quick inspection. Afterward, we headed around to the East Bay and Berkeley. We parked in an unmetered spot just off Telegraph and emerged into a shaggy melange of T-shirts, torn jeans, and sandals—students lugging books and backpacks for the most part but also a mishmash of bearded derelicts, Hari Krishnas with children, folksingers, a flutist playing Debussy over a plate of incense, sellers of beaded jewelry and peace symbols spread out on the sidewalk, and a few people handing out flyers for everything from coffeehouse openings to anti-war rallies.

Into this throng marched my father, a dignified six-foot figure in a dark green uniform adorned with the usual regalia: shiny brim cap, epaulets, gold-colored braid looped over a shoulder, brass buttons, captain's silver bars, name badge, unit arm patch, colorful rows of rectangular little chest ribbons, and a few dangling medals. At best he looked out of place, at worst, a bird of rare plumage, a target for hostile stares and mutterings. If he noticed, he didn't let on. He kept his back straight and his gaze ahead, striding stiffly through enemy turf. My mother, looking quite glamorous in a satiny green dress with matching high-heeled shoes, referred to the assembled weirdness as a collection of "eggheads." Later my father dismissed intellectuals as unnecessary by saying that sometimes "ignorance is bliss."

As we neared the edge of the campus, Sather Gate ahead of us, he must have heard some particularly nasty remark and whirled around to face a young woman in tattered cutoffs and a tie-dyed halter top. She was clutching several books under one arm and a partially filled Coca-Cola bottle in the other. "What did you say?" he asked in a strong but controlled voice.

Her eyes scanned the close-up wall of hardware and ribbons. "Uh, forget it."

"Miss," he said, "I'd like to tell you something."

She raised the bottle to her lips, swallowed, then started to move away. "What are you, a cop?" she asked, pointing at him with the bottle, then swaggered away.

The three of us watched her retreat toward the street, then my father shook his head and smiled. "Must be a nice life," he said. My mother patted his arm and said the girl obviously forgot her manners.

"Welcome to free speech," I said, and we turned and walked onto the campus. Our little tour was supposed to be a pick-me-up for my mom, but it was starting out as a downer for my dad. Still, he should know that many students feared and despised the military and its links with industry. I said as much, and he simply answered that communism was the "real enemy, the real evil."

As we walked between the massive granite buildings of classrooms and offices, my parents gazed up at the gray columns, seemingly in awe. I thought of open-mouthed children taken for the first time to school. Neither of my parents had gone to college, my father dropping out of high school after two years and my mother exiting in her senior year. We wandered through gardens where students were sprawled on the grass reading, taking notes, sleeping, embracing, or smoking.

Further on, we passed an athletic field where I had marched around in army ROTC drills the previous semester. I didn't want to be a reserve officer trainee, but as a transfer undergraduate student I was obliged to take the course. I didn't tell my dad that on the final exam I made the lowest possible passing score in the class. I couldn't keep all the battles and skirmishes straight. And at inspections and drills I either missed polishing a button, left a smudge of oil on the rifle breech, or I'd go left when the instructor barked "Right!"

I also showed them a lecture hall where I had taken Microbiology 101, then took them by another hall where I had The Great Novels class. I pulled open an unlocked door and we peeked in. I explained the routine: classes, notes, books, profs, exams, essays, and the relentless, anxious feeling that you've never studied enough, that you'll never know enough. I wanted to make it clear that memorizing a world of facts and thinking about them was hard work. One class in Spanish followed by another in literary criticism followed by still another in microbiology, then back to my hermit's room where I studied, drank coffee, and smoked filtered little cigars until I fell asleep. I omitted telling them about the girl I had dated twice, my part-time janitor's job in a sorority house, and the one-act plays I wrote.

At the time I was in a Eugene O'Neill phase, eager to somehow "ship out" and taste adventure at sea or anywhere but in the classroom. Late at night, wrestling with invention, I regretted coming from what I thought was a normal family. We were not troubled enough, not *tragic* enough, to give me the stories to write beyond melodrama. My friend Dick would commiserate, then we'd drink our wine, talk about Rilke, and listen to more Monk.

My parents listened politely as I blathered on, perhaps thinking higher education was unhealthy for me. Then my mother sat on a seat in the top row and pretended to scribble words with an imaginary pen. "Professor Ron," she said, frowning, playful, raising a finger in the air. "Do you believe chocolate is better than vanilla?" Daddy, standing by the door with his brim cap tucked under one arm, smiled.

"All right," I said, "I get the hint."

Later, after we were seated in the student center snack bar, slurping at our ice cream, I told them I was dropping out at the end of the semester. The slurping stopped as they waited for an explanation. I said I had applied for a journalism scholarship to study somewhere in Latin America. I told them I thought I had a good chance at it because of my Spanish and reporting on school newspapers.

Mommy's eyes shifted from Daddy to me. After an awkward pause, he nodded. "I'll be back. I'm out of cigars."

We watched him move between the tables, dump his cone in a trash bin, then head out the doorway to find a five-pack of King Edwards. I looked at my mother, then at his cap on the table in front of us. "What happened?"

"He's hurt, mi'jito."

"Hurt?"

"You should have asked him first."

"For what?"

"His advice. He says you never ask him for his advice."

"I don't need it. What can he tell me?"

"He's your father. It's a courtesy. Now go find him."

I said he didn't know anything about my life now. I had been away from home for almost three years. I had lived on my own, first in Oceanside with Bobby, where I finished a year and a half of junior college, then alone in Berkeley. I had hitchhiked to New York once, and I had traveled all over Europe by myself. Now I wanted to go south beyond Mexico.

I pointed out that Daddy wasn't interested in my opinion, that it was always a one-way street with him. The last time I gave my opinion about anything serious he said I didn't know what I was talking about. I didn't tell my mother then, but what I had said to him was that I thought God was dead. I had mentioned Camus and Sartre, humanism, and free will. I was puffed up and showing off, throwing out my new ideas like what I thought were so many jabs to his safe little world of black-and-white rules. He listened until I wound down, then with a hardened look said something about me wasting my time if that's all I was learning.

My mother asked me again to go outside and talk to him. I told her he wouldn't understand. She said I'd be surprised and that he had once told her that of his three boys, I was the one who most reminded him of himself. "He knows you better than you know yourself," my mother said in a lecturing tone, as if to pronounce me naive and disrespectful. I remember thinking I had to get away, escape, pick a faraway spot on the map and go.

We finished our ice cream cones. My mother again asked me to talk to my dad, get his blessing. I said I couldn't, that if I did I might say something I'd regret later on. I didn't tell her that deep down I *did* want to hurt him by leaving him out of my decision. I didn't want him to control me. I wanted to do this one thing on my own.

In late November, a few weeks after their visit to Berkeley and just before my twentieth birthday, I called to tell them I had gotten the scholarship from the Inter-American Press Association and would be leaving for Argentina at the end of the semester. "Oh, Ronnie!" my mother shrieked. "I knew you would!" I made her proud, she said, and they both congratulated me. Two days later I received a four-page, double-sided, hand-written letter from my dad packed with advice and information. The pages were numbered, the margins and paragraphs neatly ordered, as if lined up with a ruler, and the first letters of each word as well as every T were capitalized.

Ronnie –

InvesTigaTion WiTh The Pass-PorT SecTion On Base Revealed ThaT Various LaTin CounTries Require Visas, TourisT Cards, ExiT PermiTs, PassporTs, ETc. In OTher Words, No One DocumenT Will Serve To Gain Your EnTry To All The CounTries Which You Hope To VisiT. I'd Recommend You IniTiaTe AcTion AT The EarliesT PracTicable OpporTuniTy To ObTain Your New PassporT. . . .

Toward the end of the letter he asks me to read an enclosed newspaper article on Latin American dictatorships, then adds:

One Often Wonders How In The World We'll Ever Manage To Do The Right Things Down There. We've Been A Party To The Steady Deterioration Of Several States And Allowed It To Reach Proportions Which Will Be Very Difficult To Overcome.

At the bottom of the last page my mother squeezes in a few lines to wish me a happy birthday, signing off with hugs and kisses.

Several weeks later on Christmas Eve, among my presents under the tree was a small leather-covered "Schedule Diary" for my upcoming trip. On the inside cover my mother had written, "With our love and best wishes for a wonderful and memorable year in So. America. —Daddy and Mommy, Xmas 1961."

I still have the pocket-size notebook. On the last six pages my father had jotted down a dozen or so names and addresses of people who might be helpful to me in the countries where I would stop on my way to Buenos Aires. Other than that, the pages are blank. I know I took the address book with me, but for some reason—maybe rebellion—I never wrote anything on its pages.

Buenos Aires

My father called it right in at least one regard—I was a lot like him in my eagerness to get out and see the world. I was twenty, stuffed with facts, street-green, and not too savvy about people, especially the opposite sex. That is, I was a virgin, a non-rogue. I could have used some pointers but he never had that talk with me. Either it was too awkward for him or he figured I'd learn soon enough on my own.

For years I'd only been teased, probing the possibilities with girlfriends in Colorado and Germany. On my way south, however, in Costa Rica, I entered paradise for the first time. I was sitting on a bench having my shoes shined in the main plaza of San José just before noon, when a young woman surprised me with a wonderful proposition. Without a glance down, I paid for the shoeshine, rose, and followed her to a room in a nearby hotel. After about twenty minutes I found myself out on the street again, floating through the warm, moist air, a helpless, silly smile on my face.

I arrived in Buenos Aires, eager to explore my new home, find a place to stay, register for a class, try the subway and buses, and wander about. The city reminded me of Paris or Barcelona—noisy, sophisticated, a sprawling, hazy place of wide boulevards and sumptuous façades, where most men, if they weren't laborers, wore dark suits and the women kept to dresses and heels, as formal as Berkeley was casual. And just about everyone looked

European—tall, light-skinned—so unlike what I'd seen in Mexico.

During my first week exploring my new home, I had only seen one very dark person. Actually, I met him one morning in the Plaza San Martín. His genes were obviously African, but his speech was strange, something I hadn't heard. He approached and very politely but anxiously asked me in a drawled-out accent where the central post office was. I told him and then he said he hoped I would excuse his poor Spanish but he had only arrived a few weeks ago from Brazil and was just learning to make himself clear.

Edison seemed harmless enough. He had young, lively eyes, a pleasant voice, pressed trousers, and a clean short-sleeved shirt. I told him I was new too. We traded facts about our homes and why we were in Buenos Aires. He explained that he had come to find work, had been hired as a bellhop at a downtown hotel, and would someday like to become a guide and Portuguese translator for Brazilian tourists.

I suggested having coffee and we headed across the plaza to a sidewalk cafe. We sat at an outside table and ordered two espressos, then he apologized for not inviting me first. Normally he would have offered, but he couldn't under his present circumstances. "I have no money," he said with an embarrassed grin.

I sympathized and offered him a few dollars. He wouldn't take it; he said it made him ashamed. I repeated my offer but he wouldn't hear of it—that's not how he was raised. I agreed, saying as long as you could work for money you shouldn't take charity. Edison nodded and assured me that today the hotel would give him lunch and dinner. That's what he was told.

After we finished our tiny cups of espresso, he confessed that his real problem was his mother in Rio who desperately needed medicine for a serious stomach problem. If she didn't get money to buy the medicine she would only get worse. When I met Edison he was on his way to mail a letter to her, explaining that he felt terrible but had no money.

"How much do you need?"

"In American, about fifty."

"What if I loan you fifty?"

He looked stunned, then for the first time since we met he smiled and appeared relaxed. In 1962, fifty dollars was more like five hundred. But I had enough in my wallet because I had just cashed my first check from the scholarship fund. Thanking me repeatedly, he wrote his address on a scrap of paper and promised to repay me from his wages over the next two months. I gave him my address and we embraced. He called me Ronaldo and promised to see me soon. I said I hoped his mother would get better and as we parted, I remember feeling good that I could help someone I now considered a friend, my first in Buenos Aires.

Of course, two months, then three months, then four, came and went, and Edison did not appear. The address he gave me was phony, and there was no one employed with that name at the hotel where he said he worked. Edison was gone. I didn't even have an IOU, so I couldn't even think of making a claim with the police.

I may have been like my father in my thirst for travel, but we were poles apart in gullibility. He could never match me as a sucker, especially after I met Edison for the second time. It was many months later and by then I had almost forgotten my lost loan, but one morning I spotted him on a downtown street. When I confronted him, he gave me an effusive apology, saying he had had to return to Brazil right after I gave him the money. Sadly, he said, his mother's condition had worsened and she had died just before he arrived home. The family had no money to give her a proper burial, so with no father in the picture and as the eldest son, he had to arrange for her to be "tossed" into a field of graves for paupers. "Might as well have been on a garbage dump," he said, his voice cracking slightly. I told him I was sorry to hear all that, but I still wanted my fifty dollars back.

"I promise I will give you the fifty tonight," he said, now speaking with a much more natural accent in Spanish than when we first met. He explained that he had lost my address and had no way to contact me. Then he invited me to have coffee with him. We made our way to the first cafe we saw, sat down at a table indoors, and he ordered two cups. He offered me a cigarette and we both lit up. Edison then repeated his oath: "I swear on the sacred memory of my mother that you will have your money tonight." To this day I don't know how it happened, but that afternoon Edison somehow sweet-talked me into loaning him another fifty U.S. dollars—this time to pay for the cost of giving his mother a proper burial. We even went to the bank together so I could withdraw money from my account. Predictably, I never saw him again. Also, I still can't explain to myself how I had been swindled twice. I must have been lonely.

I never wrote about Edison in my letters home. If I had, Mommy would have kissed me for kindness, while Daddy would have done one of his nasalized chuckling numbers, drawing his head back in wonderment and reproach as his favorite comedian, Jackie Gleason, would do whenever sidekick Ed Norton made a bonehead move. The last thing I wanted my father to think of me was that I was naive beyond help.

Whether I knew it then or not, I was on a mission to become a writer. But first I had to observe, to live in the world with open emotions—naively, if necessary, if that's what it took to meet the truth. In those first days at the Pensión Santa Fe I lived in a cubicle-like room formed by three plywood partitions. I began to write about the men and women I shared my meals with every day. Hunched over my portable Smith-Corona, I produced a string of fumbling, sad portraits: a man who plays tangos on an out-of-tune piano, a landlady who loses her teeth, a cook with no imagination, a truck driver with two families, and an Italian woman looking for a husband.

I also began attending the University of Buenos Aires. My scholarship required me to study for at least one term, so on a whim and thinking it would be easier than taking a class given in Spanish, I signed up for a course in Old English. On the first day of class our professor entered the dingy, darkened classroom with a cane in one hand and a smallish woman at his side helping him along. With seasons reversed from the northern hemisphere, Buenos Aires in January was its usual warm and sticky self. Even so the stooped old man wore a black pinstriped suit and appeared cool and dry. He moved behind the lectern, seemingly oblivious of the six or seven students seated before him. To my classmates Jorge Luis Borges was an eminence, a renowned poet, short-story writer, and librarian with encyclopedic knowledge of world literature and history. But to me at that moment Borges was just another professor in front of a blank chalkboard.

I soon discovered he would never use the chalk nor would he ever read to us from a book or from notes. Borges was blind then, or nearly so, and throughout the classes I attended over the next several months he would recite from memory long passages from *Beowulf* and other works in language that sounded like a jagged, halting blend of German, Danish, and bits of decipherable English. In discussing some word, line, or image, he would only speak to us in English—modern, British-accented English. He would stare out blankly at the room, a distant, solitary figure, following a maze of memory and logic of his own making. Occasionally he would stop and ask a teacherly question. He would wait for an answer, elaborate on a student's opinion, then continue the lecture.

At Berkeley I had been with other men and women who displayed prodigious knowledge. One professor, Carl Sauer, not only could name all the edible plant life from Florida to California, but he had also traced on foot the same epic route taken four centuries earlier by the Spanish explorer Álvar Núñez Cabeza de Vaca. Sauer walked thousands of miles to verify reality. By contrast, Borges traveled everywhere and every place, but it was all in his mind. When reciting he appeared to enter so deeply into the life of the text, into the play of its sound and meaning and into parallels in other ages. Even when you didn't understand what he was saying, you knew that his thoughts at that moment could be located as easily in seventh-century Britannia among tribes of Angles, Picts, and Saxons as they could be wandering the immigrant barrios of Buenos Aires in the 1890s, singing tangos and drinking cheap wine.

Years later, as I felt with Hemingway, I realized that Borges—the person, not his printed stories—possessed the kind of inventive, curious intelligence I often wished my father had. In a way Borges showed me a side of Daddy that could have been but wasn't. At least, I never saw it.

Aside from a brief romance with an intense young redhead who sat behind me in class, I made few friends that year. But I had plenty of colleagues as a reporter, first with the Associated Press, then with the *Buenos Aires Herald*, an English-language daily read by Anglo-Argentines and visiting Americans and Brits. The scholarship people encouraged me to work as a journalist, so I began with a few freelance pieces for AP, which led to my full-time *Herald* work. One of my first assignments was to cover an attempted military coup against the government, which at the time was almost a monthly affair. Coups were events that apparently could be trusted to novice reporters. As it turned out, tanks and tear gas were hardly ho-hum.

When I got back to the *Herald* office, nauseous and still crying from the sting of the gas, I slipped a blank sheet of paper into the typewriter and stared at my scribbled notes for the longest time. Toby, my neighbor seated at the desk next to mine, tapped away at his keyboard with hardly any pauses. Out of the corner of my eye I watched him effortlessly build a story from a single page of notes. Toby was a dapper middle-aged Londoner who invariably wore a bow tie and a cardigan sweater-vest. I learned from Martha, the Irish copy editor, that he was a bachelor, had come to Argentina years ago, and stayed on because he liked his job. Toby covered activities in the Anglo-Argentine community and would eventually teach me all I needed to know about cricket wickets, polo ponies, soccer, and the services of the Anglican Church.

At the moment, though, a bigger hurdle loomed. I squeezed my eyes, knuckling away the tears. Helmeted figures with rifles were moving in my direction. They were ahead of the tanks, and as I peered from behind a tree, young men started tossing rocks at the soldiers. Just then I felt a hand on my shoulder and I opened my eyes. "Trouble starting?" Toby said.

"You make it look so easy," I blurted.

"What have you got?"

I recited my jumble of facts and impressions, unable to provide an overall view of what really happened. He said to write the way I had seen it, though I should begin with something strong. "Remember, in this kind of story, what you write is personal."

I began with the hurt in my eyes, and after that, the story seemed to roll out on its own. Toby read it, nodded, said, "That'll do," and continued typing. It was his third crisp and uncomplicated piece for the day, and after he finished he dropped it in the copy box, rolled down his sleeves, and slipped on his tan seersucker suit coat over the cardigan. Last he placed a brown bowler hat on his head, tapped it down once, and said goodnight to the remaining crew in the newsroom. He left without a glance in my direction.

Over the many months I reported at the *Herald*, Toby sat closer to me than anyone else at the paper. Yet we were never friends. I drank no coffees or beers with him, shared no meals with him. Our closeness was entirely professional. When I needed a word defined, Toby cheerfully obliged. I pestered him for spelling checks, dates, proper punctuation, names and titles of government figures, past and present. Whatever I asked of him, he was always helpful in that upbeat but no-nonsense manner the English affect so well.

I was reminded of Toby when I heard that he had died in Buenos Aires some years after his retirement. No fuss, no extreme emotions at the simple burial. As Toby would have wanted, his exit was quick and efficient. He may have struck others as simply a tidy, unambiguous man, but to me he was my first standard and model of a working reporter.

After my military coup story I went on to report everything from dock strikes to synagogue bombings by neo-Nazis who liked to carve swastikas on the breasts of young Jewish women. As the only gringo on staff, I also played host to visiting American journalists like the bland, Clark Kentish correspondent who appeared one night in an Ivy League suit, button-down shirt, and quiet tie. Apparently, Hunter S. Thompson had yet to transform himself into the wild-man-of-American-letters I would read about ten years later. Off we went to a jazz club for a few drinks and to listen to another future notable, saxophonist Gato Barbieri. Even in the darkened, smoky club, Hunter seemed aloof and dull. It's hard for me to believe it now, but I thought he was a bore. Maybe it was me, my doing; maybe he had something else in mind for evening kicks.

Along with enthusiastic letters, I sent my parents clips of all my stories. I was congratulated in return, but the praise seemed minimal and perfunctory. Something was missing, especially in my mother's letters. There were no squeals, no exclamation points, only *That's good, Ronnie—we're happy for you,* followed by a few homey, mundane facts: a new blender, a drive up to Napa, Mama's Chihuahua giving birth to five puppies, Junior getting so tall. My mother always wrote in beautiful longhand script, masking her low moods with graceful, perfect penmanship that was never tiny, pinched, or cramped. She also had a way of sometimes mixing and changing tone in the span of one or two lines. On the back of an August 1962 snapshot of my parents standing by their new Buick convertible—she in a flouncy cocktail dress and he in his dress blues—she writes,

On our way to one of those eternal Army you-know-what parties. How do you like the Glamor Buick? It turns on a dime, and yes, Daddy drives it to work sometimes.

Several months before this picture was taken my mother wrote me the news that the army had finally promoted my father to major. Again, none of her old exclamatory fanfare, no excitement, no joy. Just the news and the hope that maybe now he would consider retirement.

I look at the three-by-three-inch color photograph, probably snapped by Junior. Our father's hair is starting to thin out in front and he appears relaxed, self-assured, a metal-tipped swagger stick held in his left hand and tucked to his side. The uniform sparkles and I imagine how proud he must have felt when he made major. We all knew the last thing he wanted to do was leave the army and retire. But retire to what? For better or worse, despite my mother's rantings against a monster she blamed for wrecking their lives, the army was about the only master he had ever known. Besides, he truly liked being a soldier.

You would never know it from looking at the calm face in the photo, but at the time it was taken my father already knew the military carpet was about to be pulled from under him. As the adjutant general writes in a letter dated August 6, 1962,

> In accordance with the army's maximum service policy, I must inform you of your release from active duty on 30 September 1963. . . . I hope this early notification will assist you in planning your future.

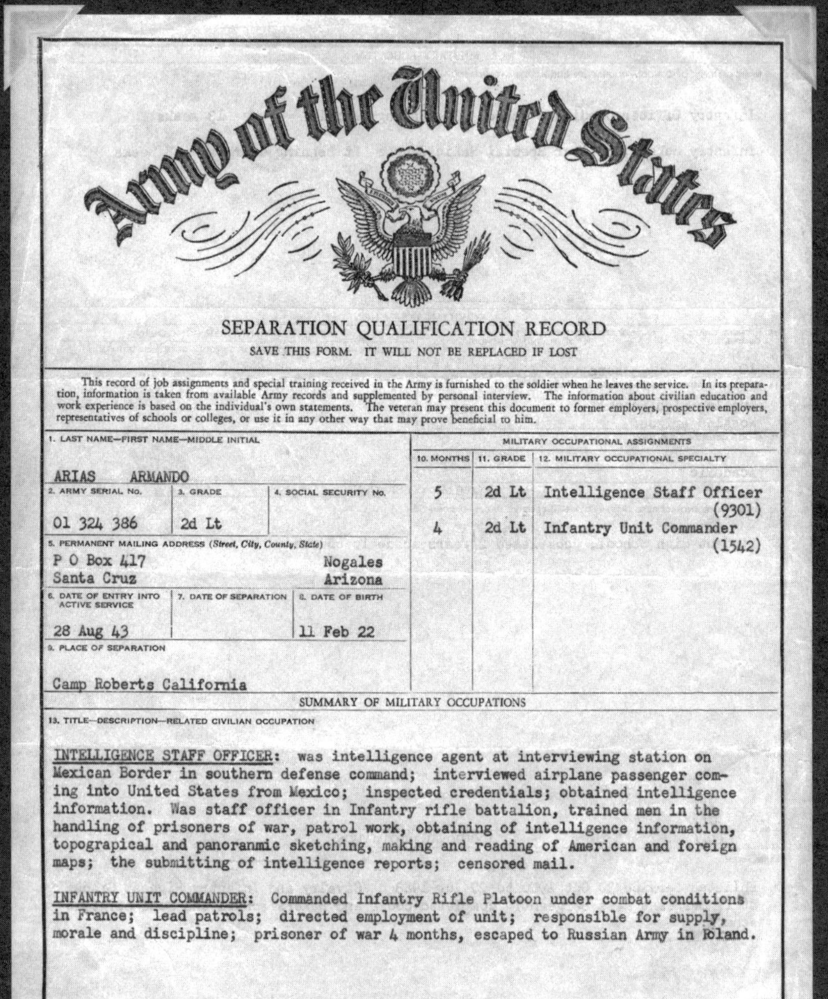

Army of the United States

SEPARATION QUALIFICATION RECORD

SAVE THIS FORM. IT WILL NOT BE REPLACED IF LOST

This record of job assignments and special training received in the Army is furnished to the soldier when he leaves the service. In its preparation, information is taken from available Army records and supplemented by personal interview. The information about civilian education and work experience is based on the individual's own statements. The veteran may present this document to former employers, prospective employers, representatives of schools or colleges, or use it in any other way that may prove beneficial to him.

1. LAST NAME—FIRST NAME—MIDDLE INITIAL: ARIAS ARMANDO

2. ARMY SERIAL NO.: 01 324 386

3. GRADE: 2d Lt

4. SOCIAL SECURITY NO.:

5. PERMANENT MAILING ADDRESS (Street, City, County, State): P O Box 417, Nogales, Santa Cruz, Arizona

6. DATE OF ENTRY INTO ACTIVE SERVICE: 28 Aug 43

7. DATE OF SEPARATION:

8. DATE OF BIRTH: 11 Feb 22

9. PLACE OF SEPARATION: Camp Roberts California

MILITARY OCCUPATIONAL ASSIGNMENTS

10. MONTHS	11. GRADE	12. MILITARY OCCUPATIONAL SPECIALTY
5	2d Lt	Intelligence Staff Officer (9301)
4	2d Lt	Infantry Unit Commander (1542)

SUMMARY OF MILITARY OCCUPATIONS

13. TITLE—DESCRIPTION—RELATED CIVILIAN OCCUPATION

INTELLIGENCE STAFF OFFICER: was intelligence agent at interviewing station on Mexican Border in southern defense command; interviewed airplane passenger coming into United States from Mexico; inspected credentials; obtained intelligence information. Was staff officer in Infantry rifle battalion, trained men in the handling of prisoners of war, patrol work, obtaining of intelligence information, topograpical and panoranmic sketching, making and reading of American and foreign maps; the submitting of intelligence reports; censored mail.

INFANTRY UNIT COMMANDER: Commanded Infantry Rifle Platoon under combat conditions in France; lead patrols; directed employment of unit; responsible for supply, morale and discipline; prisoner of war 4 months, escaped to Russian Army in Poland.

WD AGO FORM 100, 1 JUL 1945

This form supersedes WD AGO Form 100, 15 July 1944, which will not be used.

16—45815-1

Record of Separation from army service, 1946.

Cuzco

My partner Mike rode shotgun that morning, leaving me to fight with the rocky, rutted surface of the dirt road leading north to Cuzco alongside the railroad line. I was trying to keep the right-side wheels high up on the outer ridges of the washboard's edge. That way I could make good speed and save us time getting to the village school we were scheduled to visit. It was dry season in the Andes and the boxy Peace Corps jeep trailed a roiling cloud of dust. Ahead, under a clear, cloudless sky stretched the narrow cultivated valley of the Vilcanota River, winding its way toward Cuzco and the Amazon wilderness beyond.

It was 1963 and I had left Buenos Aires, briefly returned to California, then joined the Peace Corps. I still wasn't ready to return to college, and I was eager to see more of South America. Luckily, after several months' training in the vague, catch-all field of community development, I was sent into the mountains of Peru, far away from big cities and U.S. government bureaucrats. Now Mike and I were about to face our first real test of fear and the hard reality that in Latin America often turns to illusion.

Through the dusty windshield, about two hundred yards off to my left across a flat fallow field, I noticed the hunkered shapes of peasant farmers. We had heard that they planned to demonstrate against an absentee landlord who for years had refused to rent them the land to grow crops or pasture their livestock. The

Quechua-speaking Indians now squatted in defiance of warnings from authorities.

"Check that," Mike said, pointing to what looked like soldiers in the background on the other side of the Indians. As we drew closer we could see the figures in green hurriedly moving to and from several trucks, unloading weapons. Within seconds we began to hear the pop-pop-pop of automatic fire. At the same time I saw the Indians drop to the ground, either hit or trying to stay low.

Our baby blue jeep, with its billows of very visible churned-up powder, was about to enter the line of machine gun fire. I hit the brakes and we skidded around into a harsh, rattling U-turn, then raced back through the dust in the opposite direction. "Keep it floored!" Mike advised unnecessarily. When we could no longer hear the sound of shots over the noise of the engine, I eased up slightly on the accelerator. I'd been gripping the steering wheel so tightly that my hands were numb. "That was close," I said.

"No shit, Sherlock."

In nearly a year and a half in the Andes of southern Peru, we had never witnessed such violence. Driving the twenty or so kilometers to Sicuani, a provincial capital in the Department of Cuzco, we went over what had happened, then grew silent.

In important ways Mike was my double. He had grown up as a military kid, the son of a navy officer, lived abroad in Japan, dropped out of a California college, and joined the Peace Corps with similar motives to mine. Though we were both inspired by John Kennedy's challenge to do something for the world's poor, mainly we were in it for the adventure of living in a foreign place far from our predictable, tepid existence in America. When we found ourselves posted to a remote and poor area about two miles above sea level, we couldn't have been happier. Many months later, even after our well-intentioned do-good projects failed one after another, we still liked our rustic, relatively autonomous life far removed from bosses and bureaucrats.

We were washouts as breeders of better rabbits, fatter hogs, and bigger cattle. We swallowed our disappointment and went on to other ill-fated efforts to help farmers make the jump from primitive foot plows to the Machine Age. My favorite was the donated one-cylinder tractor we got from an Iowa farmers association. Under the eyes of an entire village, we took the shiny red work-demon out for a demonstration on hillside terraces that had been planted with potatoes since before the time of the Incas. Barefoot campesinos in homespun clothes milled around, skeptically eye-balling our small but mighty machine, which was about the size of the average sit-on lawnmower. I straddled the seat and sat down.

A few women in heavy skirts and white stovepipe hats cried out when the engine revved to life. With a lurch, the tractor moved forward. I steered alongside the remnants of an old furrow, pulling the plow behind, its single blade slicing slowly into the hard, dry earth. A few yards into the task, the tractor began to emit a stream of black smoke, then a clanging of metal on metal erupted from the engine. I cut the throttle and turned off the ignition. It took us hours to roll and carry our "gift to the people of Peru" off the hill over a patchwork of irrigation ditches and narrow fields. Right there, with a few tools we opened up the engine head and discovered we had broken the single aluminum piston arm, which we later learned was unavailable in Peru. The little tractor was too small for the job, so the project died. Not long afterward somebody planted flowers in the engine block.

Now, as we approached Sicuani, I was wondering how many of those people had been hurt or killed by the machine gun blast. I slowed the jeep at the northern edge of town, stopping at the small one-story hospital located next to the rail line. Inside I told the lone doctor and several nurses what we had seen. The doctor immediately alerted the police. Hours later Mike and I sat in the plaza finishing our beers, still shaken but wondering why we had not seen anyone rushing out of town toward the site of the shooting. In the afternoon we headed back to the hospital and there, piled on a single flatbed car, were the bloodied, clothed bodies of the campesinos who'd been shot—men, women, and a few children. I counted seventeen, plus one live baby an orderly had lifted out of the tangle of victims.

Mike may have volunteered to help the hospital staff—I don't remember—but I stood dumbly at the scene, helpless to do anything else but watch. Locals called the hospital "el matadero," or the slaughterhouse, because of the high death rate among patients. I didn't know if that was true, but I knew conditions inside were primitive. Mike, as game and good-natured a friend as I've ever had, once volunteered our services to help clean up the "surgical waste" in back of the hospital. What we found were stenchy clumps of organs, tumors, and other body parts dumped on the ground near a fire pit, a feast for flies and other insects. We incinerated what we could and left with our noses raw. I had never returned to the hospital until the day of the massacre.

It was evening by the time I walked back across town to our place on the other side of the river, which at that point was only a wide stream thirty miles from its headwaters. We lived on the second floor of a two-story adobe building with a good view over the high brick wall of a small prison next door. Most of the male inmates looked like the Indian squatters who were shot that morning—with the difference that these campesinos probably had been convicted of theft, murder, assault, or rape. Every morning at dawn they would emerge from their cells, line up in formation on the concrete basketball court, and sing the Peruvian national anthem. It began with the rousing lines "Somos libres, somos libres, seamos, seámoslo siempre!" (We are free, we are free, we will always be free!)

The irony of the prison inmates being safer than their brethren on the outside struck me as tragic but normal for a place with such great inequalities between rich and poor, powerful and powerless. Crossing the creaky old bridge over the Vilcanota, I stopped and leaned over the metal rail, listening to the rush of shallow water but still hearing the pop-pop of machine gun fire. Behind me under the dim light of a lamppost bulb someone padded by. All I could make out was a barefoot woman carrying something on her back, most likely a baby or a market-bound sack of potatoes, corn, or coca leaves. I remembered the women I saw across the field. Figures in layers of skirts, they looked like tiny parachutes collapsing in little heaps on the ground.

With donated American bulgur wheat and powdered milk, Mike and I also ran a lunch program for rural schools in the Indian communities, one of which included the people who had just been killed. So probably I had seen the little barefoot victims on one of our visits to the area's bare-bones, dirt-floor schools.

I wondered how Daddy would have reacted to the killings. In two wars he must have seen death many times, killed others himself, and faced his own impending death. But of course he never talked about the wars or told us what he'd done or seen. All I could remember was the afternoon sometime in the late forties, when I came home from school and found him sitting on the curb in front of our Coolidge Avenue house. His dog, a Chihuahua, had just been hit by a car and now the bloodied little body lay open-eyed and motionless in his hands. I forget its name, but this particular dog owned Daddy's affections more than any other pet our family had over the years, including a menagerie of dogs, parakeets, canaries, goldfish, turtles, roosters, and hamsters. The brown-and-white Chihuahua, he said, was the only thing he had ever had that was completely his. Tears dripped off his face as he spoke. Then he sent me on into the house. Later he buried the dog in the backyard next to a newly planted peach tree.

I never wrote to my parents about the massacre, probably because I was stymied by what happened the next morning as Mike and I walked around on our usual stops—the hole-in-the-wall coffee and pastry shop in the main plaza, the post office, the nutrition program office for the schools, the bakery that made the buns for the kids' meals, then to the lady at the train station who sold our favorite local meal—anticuchos, or skewered chunks of beef heart and sirloin slathered with hot sauce. Wherever we went we brought up the killing of the campesinos. Incredibly, no one could recollect any news of a shooting. It simply had never taken place. Even when I asked a nurse I had seen the day before at the hospital attending bloody survivors, she shrugged and said she didn't know what I was talking about. Not a peep about the killings. Apparently, Mike and I were the only ones who had avoided amnesia.

Several years later, I read of a similar massacre in Gabriel García Márquez's *One Hundred Years of Solitude*. The setting is coastal Colombia and dozens of protesting banana plantation workers are killed, loaded onto a train of flatcars, and taken away.

Afterward, the inhabitants of a nearby town fall under the spell of fear-instilled silence. The deaths had never occurred, and the citizens of Macondo continued life as if nothing more momentous than a cleansing overnight rain had swept over the town.

My own Macondo provided other doors to a different, more visceral reality than what I'd known in my pre-Peace Corps days. On certain Sundays we caught the cockfights and bullfights. And once we witnessed a battle between a bull and a captured condor. The legs of the massive bird were tied to the bull's back, and the two animals, fought for hours in a dusty arena until the condor pecked out the eyes of the bull. I was told this victory symbolized indigenous revenge over centuries of subjugation by the Spanish colonialists and later ruling elites. Other times Mike and I would rent horses and ride up into the higher mountain valleys to look for wild vicuñas and mountain lions. At 16,000 feet in altitude, we would escape the snow by staying the night with shepherds, eating mule meat and drinking shots of a homemade brew that sent our frontal lobes into throbbing thin-air orbit for most of the next day.

I was now about the same age as my father was when he was a prisoner of the Nazis. Yet I had always pictured him older, already in his thirties, fully mature, a soldier of derring-do escapes and night treks behind enemy lines, a hero rescuing captive comrades. But at twenty-two who was I in Peru? I didn't realize it then, but all my adventures, my discoveries among the poor, my dusty swagger through mud-walled villages, even the khaki trousers, *Indiana Jones* hat, and combat boots I wore—all of it probably derived from my attempts to imitate my father's eventful young life. More accurately, I was competing with him, trying to impress him with what I had done, where I had gone, the people I had met. By contrast, Mommy had boundless, often unjustified, confidence in me. I never felt I had to perform for her, accomplish the incredible. It was enough to know she received and gushed over my news stories or my letters home.

As for Daddy, applause for anything I did was invariably muted and measured against what I imagined to be some impossible military code of conduct. When he lectured to us about honor, self-respect, and loyalty, I used to think these words were like commodities, things or habits you choose and acquire. Once you had them, *that was that*—you were loyal, honorable, full of self-respect.

Then I moved through puberty and into the swamp of Catholic guilt over any number of sins, from masturbation to my petty theft exploits at the Fort Sill gym. But once into college, my reading of St. Thomas Aquinas, the existentialists, and a few books on Zen Buddhism destroyed whatever faith I professed in idols and rituals. In Peru, Mike and I—both fallen-away church-goers—even had ongoing disputes with a zealous group of American and Irish priests working in Sicuani. They kept trying to yank us back into the fold, but none of their arguments ever weakened our apparent steadfast lack of principles. We drank too much, hurled too many profanities, befriended prostitutes, and in the end the Carmelite missionaries gave up trying to save us.

The authority I could not escape, however, was my father's drumbeat of moral and military *rectitude*, one of his favorite cautionary words. Even in Peru, at a safe distance from his disapproving gaze, I could hear the voice admonishing me to behave myself.

My sojourn in the Andes ended in late 1964, exactly a year after John F. Kennedy was assassinated. It was early morning and I was mixing up one of my huge omelettes on our Primus burner. Just about everything edible that we had went into the frying pan—onions, potatoes, quinoa, garlic, tomatoes, and slices of canned wieners. Mike was sitting at the table in his white boxers, waiting to feast and reading a paperback. Suddenly, a high-pitched voice called up the stairwell from the first floor. "¡Senor Ronal! Te llaman por teléfono desde los Estados Unidos. Es tu madre. Urgente dicen."

I paused then, as if in a trance, and continued stirring the omelette with the fork.

"Earth to Ron!" Mike shouted. "It's your mom calling. *Urgente*, man!"

By the time I reached the telephone company office with its three booths for long-distance calls, I was sweaty and gasping for breath. The connection was bad, so I called her back. Her first words were, "Ronnie, mi'jito, I need you." In a choking voice, she said she wanted me to help her and could I come home? "Yes," I said, *"of course!"*

I listened to her crying recitation of my father's infidelity, coldness, and abuse. She said she even had to call the police after he pushed her on the basement stairs and she fell, dislocating a collarbone. (Later I heard another account that has her accidentally falling off their bed and onto her shoulder.) He moved out and she tracked him to a beach apartment where she found him with another woman. I was exulting as I listened. *Yes! The man's not perfect.* "Moral turpitude!" she said. I could hear the hurt and anger but more than anything, the loneliness.

Earlier in the year, after my father retired from the army, the family moved from Travis to Van Nuys, then Glendale, and finally further south to Oceanside. I knew my parents' marriage had soured, but I figured the change to civilian life might help them both. It didn't. In fact, for reasons I didn't know then, his departure from army life doomed whatever appearance of marital peace they had managed to keep in recent years.

After my mother's call for help, I telephoned my boss in Cuzco, described the crisis, and was allowed to leave for home immediately, two months shy of finishing my two-year tour of duty. Mike and another Peace Corps volunteer saw me off at the airport. We embraced and joked about my missing the national anthem wake-up call every morning, then I skipped up the ramp of stairs and waved good-bye. I was sorry to be leaving my friends in worthy excess, but I was excited about going home in a time of emergency. I was glad to be needed. Zorro to the rescue.

Propellers spinning, the airplane taxied away from the terminal, turned, and began its noisy roll down the runway. Lifting off, it climbed steeply, then tilted westward toward the coast over the snow-draped peaks of the Andes cordillera. As Cuzco retreated beneath a sprinkling of puffy white clouds, I turned away from the window, adjusted my seat backward and closed my eyes.

Oceanside

By the time I arrived in Oceanside, a semblance of domestic order had been restored. My father had returned, and my mother, while not entirely forgiving him, had accepted him back. I was never clear on how the truce came about, but by December 1964 the drama at 415 South Horne Street seemed to have leveled off into a period of ponderous gloom. It was as if we were characters with predetermined roles, speaking rote lines. We knew how it had been, but now we were trapped in a grim, grinding plotline, helpless to improvise and break for the sunshine.

Daddy played the breadwinner, a civil servant in a job placement office, strong and stoic, although his good looks and Old World formality would continually provoke suspicion and jealousy at home. For a time he even worked as the commandant of a military school, which seemed to suit him perfectly, except that he was now leading around boys with dummy rifles.

Meanwhile, Mommy played the long-suffering victim-wife, smoking a lot and taking too many pain pills and sedatives to cope with her sciatica, earaches, bad teeth, depressive tailspins, and a dislocated shoulder that was never properly treated. Junior and I had strong supporting roles, though mostly we would be seen running for cover whenever the lopsided fights erupted. That is, a hysterical Mommy would be given to hurling plates and other breakable objects at a calmly impassive Daddy, who, she would shriek, behaved "no better than a dog chasing a floozy bitch in heat!" As for Bobby, he was not present, since he had followed my lead and joined the Peace Corps to work in Colombia.

Nearly as tall as Daddy, Junior now loomed over me, spoke with a deeper voice than mine, and was called Armand by everyone but his family. At home he would escape to his basement bedroom and crank up the music to smother the noise and nastiness upstairs. I would do the same by waiting it out either in my bedroom or on the back-porch steps. Sometimes we'd commiserate together, but generally we were miserable in our separate ways—and because of our confused feelings toward our parents' problems, we never did blame or castigate Daddy for his extramarital liaisons. Incredibly, perhaps because we feared him, we never discussed his indiscretions. In fact, we tried our best to ignore what was happening, tried to skirt the sadness and the hurt, tried to pretend we were happy.

In quieter times, when Daddy was at work, I assumed the role of Mommy's main crutch. I listened to her rail on about his indifference, even—and this was a first-time shocker for me—his *barbaridades* in bed with her. She no longer seemed to care about propriety or masking from her sons the most private side of her life. Though she was never explicit with us, Mama, whom we'd visit from time to time in Los Angeles, once told me that Daddy's sexual insistence was just a man's normal physical drive at work. Still, she would spit it out: "horrores y barbaridades," although in English "horrors and barbarities" fails to carry the weight of contempt Mama saved only for the devil himself.

Not long after I returned from Peru, I started writing in a journal again, something I hadn't done in years. A stitched hardbound book with lined pages that I'd bought in Germany, the journal became a friend. In it I wrote for solace and maybe to make sense of what was happening to us. On December 28, 1964, echoing Dickens, my entry begins: *I think of good times in these, the worst of all times.* The rest rambles on philosophically without specifics. But near the end is a passage I have crossed out, probably because I was either embarrassed by the pompous tone or because I refer indirectly to my mother:

For her there is no tomorrow. I will never know the anguish that lives next to me. To comfort, to understand, is my only part.

The entry ends with a nostalgic wish to relive

the good days of freedom within, days of Peru, of Argentina, of climbing mountains, descending to jungles.

I escaped into memory because the present was so listless, boring, uneventful. We were each going through the motions of dull routines—Junior to school on his skateboard, Daddy to the employment office to work the front desk in a suit and tie, Mommy to the doctor's at Camp Pendleton or to the cushioned lawn chair on the patio with a novel or to her bed and the fragile sleep of the wounded. Daddy seldom played tennis, and Mommy long ago sold the piano. But both relied on the old Gründig—she for her Mexican rancheras and the tango and Peruvian folk records I brought from South America, and he for his classical composers. She would end up sitting on the living room carpet next to the console speakers, crying for hours at a time. When he had his turn, he'd sit back in his Naugahyde recliner, eyes closed, lit cigar in hand, and listen to his symphonies at full blast, driving us from the house or at least away from any communication with him.

Needing money, I had begun a string of grunt jobs, from dishwasher and short-order cook to mail carrier during the Christmas season. One night I moonlighted—literally—doing back-killing stoop labor on a farm down the coast in Encinitas. That night another guy and I, working in tandem, caught and artificially inseminated hundreds of female turkeys. Conditions for conception, I was told, were best under a full moon.

Even Junior—or Beebe, as we still called him—got a job. This pleased us all, especially me. Not much else could excite us, as my journal entry for June 25, 1965, confirms.

Today has been a better day than most. My brother worked on a job, the first in many years (since his paper route). It was a great moment for all of us. He worked hard all day in a cactus nursery. Afterward, riding home and retelling what happened to him during the day, he was never so triumphant or proud as then. We're all extremely proud of the once "leadfoot" Beebe.

July 11

House alone, the wind coming thru the rooms, Tuffy lying out on the back porch, Ciao quietly playing with his feathers, and our great-grandfather clock from Germany, its pendulum swinging ceaselessly from side to side.

For the most part we ignored the beauty of our location—the panoramic ocean view from the big picture window in the dining room, our stately, tree-lined street, the mild and breezy coastal weather. Of all of us, Daddy probably best appreciated our pleasant surroundings. If he wasn't outside watering the surrounding lawn and flowers, cigar in hand, he was cleaning off the bricked-in grill and patio in back. Maybe it was his way of escaping the heaviness inside the house, but on at least one occasion his yard work urge took him over completely. In my journal I fretted about not understanding people, but I'd have to be blind not have noticed one Saturday morning that Daddy was operating on the edge.

He said the tree out front needed a little trimming. So he started with the pruning sheers. His target, I believe, was a medium-sized ficus with a full bounty of lustrous green leaves. The tree grew in the grassy strip between the sidewalk and the street curb, and he wanted to cut back some of the overhanging branches. At first he climbed an extension ladder to trim the higher, outer leaves and smaller branches. Then he tackled the lower portions, piling up the cuttings below on the ground. Every so often he would stand back and inspect his work. We watched him from the living-room bay window, rolling our eyeballs and wondering when he would stop.

After clipping off most of the leaves and smaller branches, he then retrieved a handsaw from the garage and attacked the upper branches. They were about as thick around as a man's arm. This took about half an hour. Again he stood back to survey what now looked like a big sculpture of blunted deer antlers. Finally, he spent himself sawing the two main branches growing from the trunk, each about as thick through as a man's thigh. What remained was basically a tall stump.

"It'll all grow back," he said cheerfully as we helped haul away the leaves and limbs to the back alley for the trash pickup. Since he appeared to feel so good about finishing his chore, none of us said anything about the recent butchery. We could live with the naked, limbless tree.

Twice that summer I got other peeks into his mind. Once was when I asked him to read a library book I found riveting. It was Slovomir Rawicz's *The Long Walk*, which is an account of the Polish author's escape from a Siberian gulag and his trek south across the Gobi Desert and over the Himalayan mountains to India and freedom. My father read the book, but offered no opinion when he returned it to me. "I thought it would remind you of your escape through Poland and Russia," I said, knowing at least that much about his World War II experience.

"Yes," he said, "a little." When I asked him about his own escape, he put me off with "There's not much to say. That was a long time ago."

On another occasion he was just as terse in commenting on the movie *The Wild Bunch*, which Junior and I took him to see. For its time, this western was the most visceral, bloody depiction of repeated killings of people ever put on the screen for public consumption. I knew our father had been an avid horseman, liked westerns, and of course had witnessed much violence and death himself. With oddly twisted logic, I thought he would enjoy such an escape.

Afterward, we walked out of the theater into sudden, blinding daylight, got our bearings, then crossed the street to our parked car, now a third-hand Peugeot sedan. I asked him what he thought of the movie, and all he would say was, "It's OK if you like that sort of thing." I remember thinking that he probably thought the film was close to being a cartoon, that the real thing could never be captured in film because it would always be a fake recreation. Whatever suffering he had seen and felt in war, these were private memories, locked away, harmless to anyone else.

The only other activity we did together—Mommy included—was attend mass on Sundays, usually at the San Luis Rey Mission east of Oceanside. I would have found an excuse not to go, but I liked hearing the Franciscan friars sing Gregorian chants in the old adobe church. We would all spruce up for our weekly respite from the doldrums, us in our best suits and Mommy in heels, elegant dress, and one of her lacy mantillas artfully draped over her shoulder-length hair. I didn't notice it then—at least not enough to puzzle over—but oddly for such a religious person, Mommy never took communion, never knelt up front at the railing for her wafer. But then I hadn't confessed my sins nor swallowed a communion wafer in years, either. I didn't know it then, but I would soon know why she could not take communion: that the sacrament was forbidden to divorced women.

Toward the end of summer I was poised to leave home again. With the war in Vietnam growing, I had registered for the draft and although I had no qualms one way or another about joining the military before they recruited me, I wanted more creative stimulation than what soldiering would give me. Years of watching men drill and prepare for combat, of nearly flunking out of ROTC myself, of being kept to an unquestioning yes-sir, no-sir discipline throughout my childhood, convinced me that the military did not foster intellectual growth. At the time, Vietnam was simply a faraway destination, another Korea in the making, another chance for a young man to risk his life for patriotic adventure. At least that's how I saw the conflict then. Also, I had been out of the country for three years, only to come home to a family mired in a domestic war of its own. I was pathetically distant from just about every political and moral cause then brewing.

Since I'd left Berkeley, I'd been reading a lot of stories, novels, and poetry by Latin American authors. Following the path of least resistance, I enrolled at UCLA for the fall semester, changing my major from English to Spanish. Two weeks before I registered on campus my mother woke me in the morning after my father had left for work. Junior, too, had gone off to the beach with friends. "Ronnie," she said, nudging my shoulder, "can you come with me, drive me to Los Angeles?"

Normally, at eight in the morning, she was still in her night robe and slippers, or even still in bed. I slept late because of my night fast-food job. Even so, I would still be up before she was. I'd brew some coffee and take some to her bed, rousing her with the clinking of the porcelain cup and saucer. The reason she slept late was that she was a natural night owl and wouldn't fall asleep until three or four in the morning. At night, if I'd get up to go to the bathroom, I'd sometimes see her shuffling around phantomlike in the kitchen or living room, wearing a brown alpaca sweater I had bought her in Cuzco, smoking one cigarette after another.

This morning, though, she was fully dressed in slacks, blouse, and flat shoes. Her hair was combed back under a kerchief tied under her chin, and she wore dark glasses. "Sure," I said, thinking my grandmother or uncle might have called and needed help for something. "What's up?"

"Never you mind. Just get dressed. I'll explain on the way." Her voice sounded strangely abrupt. She was practically speaking through clenched teeth.

I quickly put on a pair of Levis, shirt, and shoes, swallowed a glass of orange juice, and grabbed a banana and the slice of toast with peanut butter that she had ready for me. We got into our second-hand Volvo, me behind the wheel. In minutes we were heading down Main Street, passing the welcome sign for visitors coming into town from the north: *Tan your hide in Oceanside!* The Norman Rockwell style of illustration on the billboard showed a blonde sunburned little girl, a toddler, whose bathing suit was being yanked from behind by the teeth of a small white dog that looked like Tuffy, Fluffy's replacement since the older one's recent death.

On the highway leading to San Clemente my mother began to speak in a serious, at times deadpanned, voice. It was as if she did not want to tell me something, yet she was powerless to stop her words. With an impersonal, hardened expression that barely concealed her anger at having to reveal a long-held bitter secret, she said, "I'm taking you to see Frank. Your father, your real father."

I was speechless. But there it was, bannered in front of me like an open wound. This revelation was actually something I had repressed from a dim image of an evil presence from my mother's past. The image appeared one afternoon when my mother had driven us out to West Covina to visit her friends Victor and Cecilia Giner. Daddy was in Korea and we were always eager to make the trip to our "Uncle" Victor's citrus ranch—always a great place to play. Actually, he really was my uncle, being Frank's older brother. And on that particular day the short black-haired man who stood at the top of Victor's driveway as my mother drove up the narrow incline *was* Frank.

I only caught a glimpse of him, but as soon as she saw him it was as if she had seen the devil. Without a word, she slammed the Chevy's power-glide gears into reverse and the car jolted backwards down to the bottom of the driveway and into the street. Then she shifted again and floored the gas pedal, tires squealing, rubber burning as if she were fleeing hell. In a way, she was, but she never explained what happened. We just knew that Frank was somehow evil, was someone she hated so strongly and with such anger that his name never needed explanation. As we rode home that day, we knew not to talk of the obvious. Yet Bobby and I knew we had just seen the unmentionable.

My own inability to dwell on who he really was and what had just happened came from my mother's steadfast pretense that we only had one true father, and that was Daddy. She clung to this idea so convincingly that we also believed it. To question her belief would have been a sin. In this way I was complicit in keeping the lie going. Throughout my childhood, even into my early twenties, I never really wanted to know the truth because I was convinced it would upset the entire artifice of the Hallmark family she had created in her mind. And this is what she lived for.

Now, about fifteen years later, I focused on the freeway north, weirdly excited that I was about to meet my birth father. I was curious about what he would be like, but mostly I was glad that at last something shocking was about to shake up our depressingly pathetic drama at home, something that would yank us out of our funk. Before I dared to ask why we were going to meet Frank, about halfway to Los Angeles Mommy matter-of-factly explained that she needed money and was going to see if she could get it from Frank, who owned a nightclub in West Covina. At the time I remember thinking not so much of this new father in my life but of the possible end to my mother's awful situation in her marriage and with her health.

I see now that she was so obsessed with her own crisis that she showed no concern for me or my feelings about meeting a father I had never known. She didn't even ask me if I wanted to see him. After so many years of hiding his existence, I felt awkward to just be talking about him.

Since I could remember, she had always covered up the details of her first marriage, even cutting away offending parts of pictures in photo albums. She would blot out Frank's name or abruptly change conversation topics. She was protecting me, of course, and until I was a young adult it worked. I was two years old when Daddy adopted me, so I knew only one father. Like the stray duckling parented by a dog or cat, I was attached to Armando Arias. Biologists call it imprinting, and I discovered it's a stronger bond than a genetic link between father and son.

Eventually, we found the nightclub, I parked the car, and we got out into the sunshine for the short walk to the entrance.

Inside, once I got used to the dim light, I followed my mother to the bar. "Frankie," she shouted, approaching the square-jawed man with the receding hairline who was rinsing glasses behind the counter. He looked up and after a moment of surprise, smiled and said, "Hi, Emma!"

No kisses, handshakes, or embraces. My mother didn't even bother to sit. Instead, all business, she stood and motioned to me. "I want you to meet your son," she said in a flat voice.

"Ronnie?"

"Yeah, it's me," I said.

"Jesus Christ!" Frank blurted. "Let's have a look." He came around from behind the bar to kiss me on one cheek, then squeeze me in a bear hug. "Hey, guys," he shouted to a few customers at the bar, a waitress and the chef peering out from the kitchen. "This is my boy, Ronnie!"

I felt oddly self-conscious, even slightly embarrassed, because I didn't feel some attachment, some instinctive connection with him. Shouldn't I feel a bond? In my mind I had rehearsed the moment. It would be emotional, maybe tearful. So why was I unmoved, thinking he was nice enough but still a stranger?

"Frank," my mother interrupted, "I need your help."

"Money?"

"Yes."

"What's the fucking problem?"

My mother glanced at me, then said to Frank, "Your mouth hasn't changed."

Frank lowered his brows. "Why should it?" he said, then laughed. I could see Bobby's prominent ears and thick eyebrows. As he stepped away and back behind the counter, I also saw the hitch I had in my own stride. And I heard my own thin, raspy voice. Beyond that, even as my mother rattled off her request while he listened, I felt only a mild friendliness toward the man I most looked like.

Mama had stayed in touch with him and it was she who encouraged my mother to visit Frank, whose Mexican name was Bonifacio Giner. Desperate and friendless, my mother probably thought that some extra money would help pull us out of debt and maybe brighten things in her marriage. But I don't think Frank offered anything big. He had a wife, a daughter, and other obligations. "Armando should be taking care of you," he said, and Mommy could only agree. Her voice softened and she appeared as if she knew all along that he would turn her down.

At the time, it didn't occur to me that my mother might be using me to get Frank's sympathy. Then again she just might have needed the company, or simply someone to drive the car. Frank told me he had deeply missed Bobby and me all the years we were growing up. "Too bad, but you know"—and here he glanced at my mother— "Emma wouldn't let me see you." Then, as if to explain their breakup, he said, "We fought a lot. She had a mouth too, and I had a temper. So I hit her. What could I do? I don't like what I did, but I did it. Hey, what're you drinking?" Frank was likeable and easygoing, as gregarious, open, and candid as Daddy was solitary, reserved, and guarded.

Before we returned to Oceanside, we gave each other hugs, and again I felt an unreal sensation of guilt for not being touched by him emotionally. I was role-playing, watching myself in a movie, going through the motions, expecting drumrolls and trumpets, but there was only practical conversation and cheerful mutual curiosity.

Frank wanted to know what kind of work I did, where I had gone to school, and what my plans for the future were. I told him about my newspaper work, about my Peace Corps service, and my vague, unsettled notions of seeing more of the world. For his part, Frank said he had tended bars most of his life, had done well enough at it that with his wife's help, he could buy and run his own classy restaurant, live in a big house, and play golf at a quality country club. Only when he mentioned his daughter did I feel some surge of emotion. Her name was Linda and she was years younger than I. Linda, my half-sister. I think the idea of having a little sister is what most moved me the day I first met Frank.

We visited him one more time a few years later, and I heard that he had a mild heart attack after we left him. He was certainly emotional, something in my own nature that must have come from him and my mother. But again, just as when I first met him,

I felt no close filial connection on this visit, either. For my part, it was only a social friendship.

Several weeks later I began classes in Los Angeles. On visits home, whenever I was alone with my mother, we stayed clear of talk about her tumultuous, brief marriage to Frank, who I got to know better in later years—though never with the emotional fireworks I had with Daddy. As for Daddy's adoption of me and Bobby, my mother never discussed that, either, nothing beyond a perfunctory statement of fact. Nor did she ever explain Junior's sudden appearance as a newborn in 1948. Explanations would only keep us from innocently playing our parts to fit into her dream of the happy family. Like the citizens of Macondo, she liked to erase one truth in order to invent another more to her liking.

In early November my parents flew to Colombia to attend my brother's wedding to a young woman from a coffee-growing town in the Cauca Valley. Bobby recalls a high point of the visit:

> *I wanted Daddy to meet with the military commander of the small garrison protecting the town. Knowing that he was a retired army major, they gave him a military welcome and asked if he could review the troops. Colombia was the only country in Latin America to send troops to Korea, and they lost hundreds in that war. So while he was reviewing the troops, an older non-com stepped forward and identified himself. He reminded Daddy that they had met in a POW camp where Daddy was taken to help translate for a few of the Spanish-speaking POWs. You should have seen the reaction and response from the two of them. It made my day, and Daddy's too. The non-com said that Daddy had saved his life!*

Los Angeles

Four years later, in August of 1969, I was fighting boredom as a public relations hack for an international bank in Washington, D.C. I was also married and the father of one son with another on the way. My wife Joan and I had just returned from my parents' place in Oceanside and I was still stewing, angry at myself, and at my mother.

I had taken my old journal with me to California, the hardbound German one that I occasionally used for story ideas and personal ramblings on just about anything. One day Joan and I took Michael, our year-and-a-half old son, down to the beach with my father, who pampered and played with him as if he were a kid himself. But my mother, now thin, frail, and heavily dependent on medications, stayed behind. I think she was also miffed that Joan was so protective of Michael. Just about every time we left him with my mother, who was usually in a maudlin, drugged-out haze, she'd neglect him in some way, once even letting him wander off toward the street. "She's sick," Joan would say. "How can I leave Michael with her?"

So while we were all at the beach, my mother found my journal and must have been reading it, especially the parts about her written several years before when she was most deeply depressed. At the time, I had just emerged from my own period of gloom and loneliness. What changed me was having loved and married someone who was as straightforward and honest as my mother was roundabout and deceptive. Joan, my bride, was also smart, cute, and confident. In the two years we'd been married, she had helped me see my parents with more objectivity. This refreshingly clear-eyed view of them also helped me sever my mother's grip on me and my future. I never thought, for example, that their cloying behavior as a couple in public was abnormal. They would fawn over each other, trading affections in Spanish, both of them calling each other "Mommy" and "Daddy," my mother batting her eyes and playing the coquette, my father responding like a lovestruck teenager.

"Doesn't that seem weird?" Joan asked. "It doesn't seem normal." I had to agree the displays were odd, but I'd lived with it for so long that the coy girl-solicitous charmer routine seemed as normal as my own amateur attempts at love poems for Joan. Needless to say, she and my mother never did get along. After some early skirmishes, my mother retreated from trying to influence my life. Now the message was clear that she would have virtually no controlling part in her grandson's upbringing.

The harshest journal entry I wrote about my mother had been prompted by what I saw during one of my weekend trips to Oceanside from West Los Angeles, where Joan and I had been living as graduate students. I was feeling particularly impatient with my mother's inability to improve her health. I was also frustrated because I couldn't distance myself from her unrelenting neediness and the stagnant, gloomy atmosphere at the house. Finally, with a rush of meanness, I exploded over the space of five pages.

1/10/67

I hope, & yet maybe I don't hope, she never sees this. But why not? To someone I'm beginning to hate, I think, shouldn't I want to punish? No, no, no. I just want to get away at this moment, to forget, to leave my "obligation." Am I sick? Maybe I am if I think I or she should have departed or deceased long ago. How does he continue with her? As a master would with a crippled, dumb animal. But animals aren't pitiful because they do not think, are not responsible for their actions and influence over others. She, on the contrary, oozes and excretes sickening self-pity. Worse, she begs, it seems, for more hurt by complaining to everyone in her every utterance. I can't talk to her. There's absolutely no dialogue. If we speak, I agree to whatever she says or suggests. But even with nodding agreement she incites me to her own aims and wishes. She knows what is truth sometimes. So why does she continually want to be hurt by it? No one loves her. At least not her husband. How can he? How? Now, she says—almost with pride, or why bring it up?—he bathes her. He does everything for her. But impassively, as a kennel-keeper with a dog. Both had seen a psychiatrist, having reached another impasse. On the suggestion that she be interned in a mental sanatorium, she immediately called the man a fake—or thought so, for how could <u>he</u> be right?—and sought quick solace by telephone with one of her sympathetic doctors. Of course! A quack, nothing but a 30-year-old "embryo" doctor! She no longer continues a rational line of talk. Any subject digresses into the personal and usually ominous. Death has to pervade all. At least suffering. Yes! See the open wounds. Here's the salt. Yes, yes. Have pity for me. Then you can love me. Like the Virgin, my queen, with swords—ten, twelve silver swords—through her chest and heart. Pure coincidence having to bear the sufferings of mankind. Having infested <u>all</u> sons, not just one, with a hypocritical stoicism (really just a plea for more and more and more love, which in the end is non-existent) and having sought comfort in these 3 lives because hers is so empty, she now attempts to control their emotions and demand love. So absurd. She is sick, I told Jr., and he would not believe. In any case, it's too late.

Today received another 1-A Draft notice from State Appeal Board. What a warm appetizer after a choice purgante (her), which makes me write this.

What to do?

I once thought how terrible and nasty it was that sons & daughters left and separated from parental protection and foresight. I was then on the controlled side, a kid. I understand why the split occurs so often in American urban families. Traditional, professional and financial controls are down & a natural, willing separation of generations takes place. Doesn't have to be violent, traumatic. Relations can continue in separate houses. But no. My mother won't have it. A stubborn, convinced woman, she's a threat to my sanity unless I do something.

This same entry is probably what she read while my father, Joan, little Michael, and I were at the beach. When we returned, my mother appeared woefully sad and forlorn. She was standing by the big dining room window, wearing her stretched-out alpaca sweater. She was staring at me as if I had just kicked her. Then she came up to me when Joan and I were feeding Michael in the kitchen. "Ronnie," she said in a weak voice, "how could you write those horrible things about me? Am I really such a monster?"

It took me a moment to realize she must have found my journal. What had I written? Suddenly, I remembered all the frustration and anger I felt at having to watch her hopeless decline.

"Why, mi'jito?" she said. "Why did you write those things?"

I began to explain the entry as my own harmless ravings, as an outlet to let off steam. But Joan interjected that maybe mothers should not read the personal diaries of their sons, that they had no right to read them. My mother looked doubly wounded. Then she accused me of betraying her. In a breaking, barely audible voice, she said, "Do you really hate me so much?"

After a lame apology to calm her down, I left the room. Reading the harshest part of the journal entry today, I admit I overdid it, although I wouldn't change a word. That was me then and those were the grim circumstances that briefly aroused a self-destructive impulse. Naive, desperate, and politically ignorant, I was even thinking of joining the army in order to escape. Why wait to be drafted? Enlist, grab adventure by the neck. Vietnam, here I come!

I can't change what I wrote about my mother. However, I will forever regret the pain I caused her—and the cataclysm in our lives that my scribbled desperate sentiments precipitated. What happened to our family was probably inevitable, with or without my contribution. I only wish it hadn't been so brutal, so final.

By early the next morning, September 8, when we were walking out the front door for the San Diego airport, my mother was still looking weepy and wounded. She pleaded for me not to leave, not to abandon her. In the living room, after I kissed her goodbye and turned to step away, she fell to the floor and grabbed my leg. She was clutching my trousers. "Mommy," I told her, "we're going to be late. Junior's waiting. We've got to go now." Finally she let go as I started to step away. Then my father and I helped her up and she remained standing next to the grandfather clock by the front doorway. Joan and Michael were waiting on the sidewalk while my father helped Junior load our luggage into the old cream-colored Peugeot. It was parked at the curb next to the tree that Daddy had rendered limbless a few years prior. I gave him a quick hug, then opened the door on the front passenger side and scooted in next to Junior.

As he shifted out of neutral and we started forward, I waved to my mother, who was still standing in the open doorway, Tuffy at her side. She was leaning for support against the doorjamb, looking as dejected as I've ever seen her. As the tiny figure receded from sight I felt a knot of guilt in my throat for leaving her in such a pathetic state. But I was also annoyed that she had read the journal in the first place.

I can't say what my mother was really thinking as we left for the airport. I had surprised her with my journal confession and stunned her. She didn't even wave to us, just stared ahead, sinking back into the darkness of the deeply wounded. And Daddy remained next to her, giving us a jolly smile while waving his right hand and tilting his head. I look at the photos I have of him, and in many of them he's smiling and making the same head and hand movements. He's doing it even in a grainy picture taken by an Associated Press photographer visiting the POW camp in North Korea. I assume the jolly gesture was habit, no matter what the circumstances.

In Washington, D.C., when Joan, Michael, and I were entering our brick duplex, the phone was ringing. I answered. It was Junior calling. "Ronnie," he said in a practically whispered monotone, "Mommy died."

"What?"

"She died in bed sometime after you guys left this morning."

"No!"

In the same flat manner he told me that she appeared to have died just before our father found her in her bed. He became very upset, crying and unable to do anything. Junior called my uncle and the police, and an ambulance came to take her away. Tuy said he'd drive down from Los Angeles to help take care of things. I told Junior I would fly back immediately. I didn't even unpack my suitcase. All I remember of the return trip is that I smoked a pack of Marlboro Lights, pacing and fretting at O'Hare during an hour layover in Chicago.

When I entered the house the first thing I noticed were all the framed family pictures, plaques, and diplomas hanging in the dining room. Tuy and my cousins had just left, Daddy was outside in back emptying a wastebasket in the alley trashcan, and Junior had slipped downstairs. So I was alone a few minutes with Mommy's posted record of our family—our faces, our degrees, our promotions. I looked around, past the dining room table, scanning the lace-covered credenza, spotting the brass bell ringer somebody sent my parents from Turkey. It was usually on her night table. She would ring it for attention or help if she needed it. I peeked into their bedroom. I had just seen it the day before—the wrinkled covers on the bed, sunlight blasting in through the uncovered windows, and she, sitting in bed, her black beret tilted jauntily to one side.

It was not a big bedroom, and was actually somewhat cramped because of the big four-poster bed, which along with a chest of drawers occupied most of the wooden floor space. Yesterday there were several of her novels on the bedspread and on the German night table with the gray-and-white marble top, which also had room for an electric clock, a small lamp, a cup and saucer from her China set, an ashtray, her combs, her glasses, her cigarettes, and her stainless steel lighter with a map of Spain and Portugal etched on one side.

Now everything had been removed from the marble surface. All that remained of hers was a round white knitted doily under the lamp base. The bed was made; nothing was out of place. Sunshine still entered the empty room, but somehow—maybe because of my mood—it seemed dark. I imagined Mommy propped up against two pillows, a book in one hand and a pair of eyeglasses resting on the bridge of her nose. I bent down to kiss her hand, saying "Mano" as I used to say as a kid before going to bed. Then quietly, as if she were still present and alive, though sleeping, I backed out into the hallway.

Just then I heard Daddy enter the kitchen, the back screen door banging shut behind him. His eyes looked tired and the skin of his face seemed to sag. With a somber spectral expression, he said, "Welcome home," then quickly embraced me. I asked if there was something I could do, and he shook his head slightly. Then he went to the bedroom and stretched out on the bed with his slippers on. He stayed like that for about an hour. I felt bad for him, but I thought there was little consolation I could give.

A few days later we buried Mommy in Holy Cross Cemetery on a hillside plot overlooking the MGM Studios in Culver City. It seemed perfectly appropriate given her infatuation with movies and Hollywood. The group by the gravesite was small and included Daddy, Mama, Tuy, his two daughters, me, Junior, my aunts Helen and Lore, and Bobby and his wife Gloria—both back from Colombia where he was now a Peace Corps director. Joan, pregnant with our second child, had remained in Washington with Michael.

We stood solemnly on the slope next to the unlowered coffin, listening to the priest's last words. Mama and Helen cried, and when the ceremony ended, everyone but Daddy, Junior, Bobby, and I remained by the grave. I remember thinking how unreal the setting seemed—traffic on the 405 streaming along in both directions, the Santa Monica Mountains barely visible through the haze, the relaxed gravedigger partially hidden behind a tree, sitting on his yellow backhoe munching a sandwich. I was thinking that Mommy's suffering was finally over after years of unanswered prayers. In a sense, she died of a broken heart, the result of a process started years ago. Yet the anchor of guilt I carried around my neck told me otherwise. Did my angry, ugly words somehow push her over the edge? Yes, I'm convinced they did, but at the time I could no more halt the inevitable than any of us could change who we were. My mother's course was set years before I even came along.

I also remember my father's wistful words, spoken to no one in particular, as he stared blankly at the coffin: "She was a spunky little lady." For a while the words hung over the bright green, fake-grass carpet covering the mound of freshly dug dirt. There were no tears, no more words. Just our silence after that spontaneous, flat-voice summary of Mommy's whole personality. Spunky. But she hadn't been spunky in years.

A few weeks later my father tried to kill himself near her grave. Accompanied only by Tuffy he drove the Peugeot from Oceanside to the cemetery, and there he took an overdose of sedatives. Somehow while still conscious, he then drove the car several blocks away where he crashed into a bank of oleander bushes near a freeway exit. The driver of a car behind him notified the police, and by the time they and the paramedics arrived my father was unconscious and barely breathing. They performed an emergency tracheotomy, then rushed him to Daniel Freeman Hospital, where he remained in a coma. The attending physician said that he would have died if he had remained without help in the car another few minutes.

I made plans to fly back from Washington again, but three days after his suicide attempt, he began to come out of the coma. Junior remembers:

> *I've tried to reconstruct that time, but maybe I've subconsciously blanked it out. But now it's bubbling up. Number one, Tuffy got out of the car and we never found him. Also, Daddy was one of the first patients in the new ICU ward at Freeman. I remember holding his hand and being there when he came to. He looked at me, recognized me and then started to cry. He never said anything, obviously he couldn't because he had tubes in his throat, so he couldn't say anything. But he looked at me and started crying, and I have always interpreted that as his saying that he was a failure, that he didn't complete it. A sign of weakness. I don't think he ever wanted to show a sign of weakness. He was a prototypical officer and a gentleman, with a Latin or Spanish heritage to boot. But he woke up, saw me and started crying. He realized that he was not dying and he had failed.*

And Bobby:

> *Gloria and I went to see him every day. Once during the second week when we were there, he was in a semi-conscious state. Because the doctors and nurses were all Asian, he thought he was in the POW camp. He saw Gloria, but then grabbed me by the hand and in a very low voice said, "We have to break out of here. We've got to get out of here." And I didn't understand what he meant. Then he said, "Don't let them do this to me." And then it suddenly dawned on me, and I remember telling Gloria in Spanish, "It's the Chinese. He thinks he's back in Korea."*
>
> *I went to a pay phone. Don't remember who in the Army I called, a recruiter or someone, but within two or three hours they*

had whisked him out of Daniel Freeman and had placed him in a special ward for former POWs at the veterans hospital in Long Beach. I wanted to talk to the doctors there about him, but they wouldn't discuss anything with me.

Joan was now close to giving birth, so I remained in Washington. My brothers and uncle gave me updates on my father's recovery, which appeared to be amazingly fast for someone who had almost died only a few weeks before. Most of the other patients, however, were much younger and were being treated for delayed-stress problems from their combat experience in Vietnam.

Junior, who was then attending Long Beach State, recalls:

It was a lot like some of the scenes from Cuckoo's Nest. *Open wards, men just sitting or shuffling along. Then there was Daddy, who I thought looked perfectly normal. He was shaved, showered, clothed. He had a little bandage over his throat. He could walk a little, and we would walk around. But I kept thinking he shouldn't be in here, not in a VA psych ward.*

If we talked about anything, it was about how I was doing in school, about me playing tennis. But we never talked about what had happened or about Mommy. Very superficial. Just tried to keep things up, like we always do, zippy and peppy.

After a few more weeks my father was released from the vets' hospital and moved into an apartment in the Los Feliz area of Los Angeles. Around Christmas of this same year, 1969, he wrote to us that he had recently married Yvette, a woman he had met some months before at the Griffith Park public tennis courts. We knew he had been dating her because Junior, who had met Yvette, had told us. I called to congratulate Daddy, and he sounded like a changed man, upbeat and cheerful. "That's one happy man," Joan said after chatting with him. From the picture Daddy sent us, Yvette's expression looks worshipful. A tall, attractive brunette, probably in her mid-thirties, she is holding my father's hands in hers, her face inches from his, staring into his eyes. She seems so different from Mommy, especially in her last years when she had become so sick, stooped, and shriveled.

I talked to my father one more time, and we sent them a Japanese tea set as a wedding gift. We even invited them to visit us in Washington.

Then, a few weeks after we mailed off the tea set, the strangest thing occurred. As I usually did every year, I sent him a card for his February 11th birthday, but it was returned unopened. Across the front of the envelope he had printed the words

Return To Sender. Cease Communication.

I called his number, but his line was no longer in service. Joan and I couldn't figure out why he might have returned the card. I checked with Bobby, who was still in Colombia, and he also got an unopened card returned. Junior, now busy with his studies at Long Beach State, managed to visit them a few more times but had no inkling why he chose to cut contact with me and Bobby. Finally, Junior told us Daddy and Yvette had moved away from Los Angeles, probably north to Ojai, but he never pursued further contact with our father.

We spoke about his absence, wondered how and where he was, and then just figured he would someday come back and reconnect with us. The years passed and we believed he was happy. That's what seemed important at the time, though my brothers and I were puzzled and hurt by his silence. Even so, we decided to respect his wishes to be left alone.

Only my uncle and grandmother believed something devious was behind his disappearance. They suspected him of having killed my mother by tricking or coaxing her to take an overdose of barbiturates—and apparently there were some pills on the night table by her bed, along with a partially filled glass of Ovaltine, which Mama believed my mother never liked. Tuy recalls:

> *Right after your mother died he went to see Father Prohens in Colorado Springs. I think his conscience was bothering him and had to confess to the priest to relieve his conscience. I remember he didn't want anybody in the room where she died. Why? When he came back from Korea he wasn't exactly himself like before.*

He was like two persons. He could be lovable to your mother, like he was really taking care of her. Go to the kitchen and fix her some coffee and toast. Oh, Mommy, would you like something else? Very sweet to her. That was one personality. The other one was the one we knew through your mother. She told Mama everything. Your mother and Armando used to have violent arguments, and he would beat her up. One time in the basement she thought she was a goner. She said he had hit her head against the cement floor, then quit and went upstairs. His mind wasn't right.

Then there was the dislocated shoulder. She was so small and he was a strong man. Maybe that's why he didn't want her to go to an orthopedic surgeon to get it fixed. If she did, the truth would all come out. I just remember he didn't want anybody in the room where she had died. He asked me to leave the room. Obviously he didn't want me or anyone else looking around. Why? I was her brother, not some stranger.

After her death, I thought of going to the authorities. But what for? You can't prove anything. There was no autopsy, no tests or anything. The death certificate said she died of a coronary thrombosis, which is what we suspected. Coupled with her weak condition, down to ninety pounds, we thought maybe her heart gave out. But there were drugs, though I don't believe she killed herself. As much as she was suffering, Emma was not suicidal.

Also, there was the birthday card I sent her. All the cards to her were in the living room the day she died, all except mine. But a few days later I get the top half of the card I sent her, and it's torn in half. The writing is on the bottom part, and it looks like she had written something. Maybe she was trying to tell me something. And why would he send me back the card? Torn in half. I asked him, "Gee, what happened to my card?" But he never did explain it.

It stands to reason that later, after he left us, that maybe he was thinking that if he disappeared, he'd never have to explain anything to anybody. There'd be no one to answer to. He'd be free.

PART 2
1985–2000

My father with Yvette Veilleux, newly married in 1970. Ventura, Calif.

Me with my grandmother and my sons, Jonathan, left, and Michael. Los Angeles, 1972.

Waves

For years I've wanted to cross to the far shore. I've been warned against it, but this morning as I set out into the light chop, I can clearly see the other side, a thin, dark line beneath a tiny ribbon of white cliffs. My map shows it's about eight miles away. There and back is sixteen. How far can I go? How long will it take? Can I do it?

With each wave, each pull of the paddle, my rhythm settles in, until I'm moving my little boat on instinct and muscle alone, conscious only of the breeze, the cool wetness of the spray, the thin blue sky, the sunshine reflected all around, the slap of water against the rubber hull, the steady swells lifting and lowering the kayak, tilting it upward and downward, me in my rocking chair, tilting up, then down, up and down.

Out beyond the last reef, past a few head-bobbing sea lions, I see my father holding me in one arm. I'm three, and it's early in 1944, just before he went overseas. Khaki uniform, dark glasses. The image I have is from a snapshot my mother kept in a family album. I don't remember the moment in the picture, but I'm thinking that my parents' problems must have begun around that time. Or maybe before, long before they met, before I was even born, before she married my first father Frank, long ago when they were all children themselves, eager, playful, sensing each moment newly, innocently, like the waves coming at me now, each one new and changing, all motion, motion all around, everything cool and salty and blue, all of it new, every moment new.

The earliest memory I connect to my father is of dark men and urinals, probably in a train station or bus terminal. I don't remember the circumstances, only that my father took me there. I can still smell the cigar smoke mixed with body odors, shoe polish, soap, and cologne. I see the row of men lined up against a wall of white porcelain basins, other men moving around behind, coming and going. I see their long suit coats, broad-brimmed hats, long pleated trousers, everything mostly gray or brown except for the white shirts and wide ties with patterns and flowers in reds, maroons, yellows, and greens.

It's a pleasant scene, nothing stinky about it. I don't even remember standing at a urinal myself. The men were tall, big-handed, dressed-up. In my three- or four-year-old mind, I remember that as the real world of men, a place of cufflinks, gold rings, smells of stuff slapped on faces, the mirrored look of shiny, slicked-back hair, of combing, pissing, zipping up, brushing off, straightening out, washing up. And me standing in this dark, smoky forest of suits, feeling warm and protected.

I look behind me, pausing in my strokes, gauging how far I've come and whether or not I should continue. I don't measure distance in time but by what I see and how I feel, by what I sense the conditions ahead will be. Wind, wave heights, currents. Now that I've stopped paddling, I can sit and survey everything around me. A few sailboats, five distant smokestacks, a passing tugboat, bobbing seabirds, floating patches of oil mixed with twigs, seaweed, plastic bags, and tangled strands of fishing line.

I grip my paddle, bring down the spatula-shaped blade through the water, then do the same with the blade on the other end. Slowly, with efficient, windmilling strokes, I move ahead and reach a forward-moving speed that I can maintain without spending myself completely. The swells rise higher now, and the oncoming breeze has more bite, the spray more sting.

After a long stretch of this, I estimate that I'm halfway across. The cliffs ahead seem bigger, brighter, the shore looks less like a long dark line, more jagged now. I see tiny trees, rooftops, a water tower and glints of windowpanes.

Time to stop. With one hand I pull back the spray skirt from the forward lip of the cockpit. The waterproof fabric cinched around my waist protects me from wave blasts and a dripping paddle. Underneath, from between my legs, I find my plastic water bottle and unscrew the attached cap. After several long swallows, I recap the bottle and set it down again under the canvas deck. Then I stretch the spray skirt's elastic drawcord tight around the combing and paddle on.

This continuous physical effort is the closest I'll ever come to innocence. No matter how regular and similar each wave feels, all are different and infinitely varied. I'm thinking that the search for my father and the reasons behind my family's collapse are also a matter of innocence, of stumbling on one unexpected fact after another.

I pick my course into the shore and head for the water tower. What happened the morning my mother died? Who or what was to blame? Why did he try to kill himself? And why did he leave and walk out of our lives? Was it something we did or didn't do? Was it something he did, maybe in the two wars?

When we were young, we held him in such fear. Yet somehow in our separate ways we loved him as much as we could, which was difficult since he was absent so much of the time, absent even when he was present, ever quiet, secretive, enigmatic, a mystery even to my mother. "Armando," I once heard her say, "who are you? I don't know you."

I sometimes wonder what I would be like if Frank had raised me. He was excitable, open, a drinker who said whatever popped into his mind. By contrast, Daddy was a serious, sober gentleman soldier, seemingly always in control of his emotions. But what's the point here? I'll never change the past. Besides, on the whole I'm OK with myself, with what I've become. To some degree, Daddy had a hand in this, and for that I thank him.

After almost three hours, I reach the shore, easily scooting onto the sand, tired but exhilarated. I'm actually on a sandbar that's connected at low tide to a wider beach. I see no one, no moving creatures, only sandpipers and overhead a lopsided V of Canada geese. Slowly I stand up, step onto the sand, then start whooping and hollering, doing a little dance around the boat as if I'd just crossed an ocean. "I did it! I did it!" I shout. After more dancing, I trot off to celebrate by pissing next to an off-limits tern-nesting area. Returning to the boat, I pull everything higher up on the beach, drain a water bottle into myself, eat my turkey sandwich, and lie back on the warm sand. Yes! I'm fifty years old and I did it.

After a while, I turn over and sit up, running my fingers across the sand. I imagine my father as straight lines, or lines trying to become straight. Clear-cut, no curves, nothing uneven, nothing in between or ambiguous. Then I draw my mother. She's a tangle of circles, spirals, and little knots of emotions. Maybe this mismatch was the root of their problems. Straight lines, circles. I don't know. I smooth over the sand, erasing my marks.

I'm here, triumphant on the far shore. Returning should be a cinch. The wind has risen, spitting up whitecaps. No worries, though, because it should be blowing at my back. The paddling will be easier. In the distance, in the sky beyond where I began, I see the dark shapes of rain clouds billowing up. I'm thinking that I'll beat them to where I'm going. I rise and pull my boat down to the water's edge and into the shallow oncoming froth. I get in, quickly adjust the spray skirt, then plunge ahead into the first real wave.

Mexico City

I waited until she stopped crying. The cheeks of her thin face were streaked and a paper surgical mask dangled from her neck. We were standing behind the police barrier in front of a toppled thirteen-story apartment building in Tlatelolco. Dust and stench was in the air, which is why so many people wore masks. My mask, white and cuplike, also hung from my neck. "Do you live here?" I asked her in Spanish. No answer. "I'm sorry, but I'm a journalist. I just want to know why you're crying."

She shook her head and gestured for me to go away. Normally, I would. Invading someone's privacy is arrogant and presumptuous, but this was my first big assignment on a new job and I wanted to write about more than the number of casualties or the dollar figure in damage. I could have wandered away looking for another promising survivor. Instead, instinct kept me at the young woman's side. I waited a while longer. Then I told her my name and politely asked her for hers. Samantha, she told me, and we shook hands.

In silence we watched the searchers and rescuers pick over the jumble of death before us. Every now and then they signaled that another body had been found. Other reporters, sensing Samantha had a tale to tell, approached and also tried in vain to pry out a few comments. Eventually, they left. Finally, I asked about her family. Still no response. Parents? Brothers? Sisters? Someone there in that building? Then I mentioned children, thinking she might be married. There was a nod. A son? She held up one finger. "But he's fine," she added. "He's with my husband, and the two of them are fine."

"I have a son too," I said. Then without thinking I blurted words that seemed to well up from some deep pool of repressed emotions: "I used to have another son, but he died."

For the first time, Samantha looked at me squarely, this time with sympathy in her wet eyes. "How old was he?"

"Six."

"My son is seven months old."

"What's his name?"

"Jonathan."

I caught my breath. "What?"

"Jonathan."

I didn't grasp the coincidence until I had it out for her to hear: "That was also my son's name. Jonathan Carlos." Samantha seemed to wince, but after that she spoke freely of her own losses in the collapsed building—her mother, brothers, sisters, aunts, and cousins, thirteen people in all. They had been living in two apartments on the third floor. "I think they're all dead," she said. "I don't know."

I returned to New York and the magazine editors liked the story so much that they sent me back immediately to find them another good story. I did and from then on I was mostly assigned to the "death beat," covering stories of disaster, destruction, and dire diseases. The D Man, as a colleague put it. Summoning gut senses I hadn't used since my years scrambling about South America, I took to such reporting like a caged bird to freedom. I became a parachute journalist, dispatched to spots around the globe to write about earthquakes, hurricanes, floods, famines, wars, plane crashes, shipwrecks, suicides, and murders. I specialized in human misery, stalking emotion, dropping briefly into people's lives, then stealing away with portraits of pain like Samantha's, like mine the day my son Jonathan died, freakishly hit by a car while walking with Joan on a sidewalk in San Bernardino, California.

That was in March of 1976, six years after my mother had died and my father had disappeared. For a long time Joan and I, having moved from Washington and now teachers at small colleges, functioned like programmed zombies, hearts ripped out of our chests, going through the motions of living. And poor Michael Luis, he and his brother were like twins. To say the least, it was a very difficult, fragile time for him and for us. Joan sought help from a grief specialist, and after two years I saw the same therapist, who after three visits uncorked from me a torrent of wrenching, sorrowful sobs that I'd been unable to release. In this and other ways—like traveling for distraction—we coped with our loss, each of us keeping our own separate, indelible images of Jon, my favorite being that of the scruffy kid gliding by on a skateboard, big smile, tummy out, balanced, serene.

I bring up my mother's and Jonathan's demises because by 1985, when we had moved east in pursuit of new careers—in Michael's case, a college degree—death was still very much on my mind. In the interim Mama had died, too, prompting me to write a short novel with death as a theme. Then there was Frank's death, which I took in stride, because I had never felt emotionally connected to him the way I had with Daddy. However, at the funeral, I was amazed to see such a large crowd on hand for the graveside service. I counted 142 cars. Obviously Frank had many admirers. But to witness such an outpouring of affection for the man who, in a sense, I had only just met and yet who fathered me, provoked a touch of regret that I had missed out on knowing the lovable bartender and nightclub owner everyone else remembered. At least before he died, Frank and I briefly became friends in a bantering kind of way. But it wasn't the same as it was with Daddy, with a man who, even after many years of absence, still held me enthralled.

So death and grief invaded my life. At the magazine, feeling quite natural about it, I began *hunting* death as a story subject. My interest may have appeared morbid, but I was actually obsessed with people who made it through deadly events, people who struggled closest to the edge, survivors of calamity and great suffering. I reported on victims of cancer, AIDS, torture, starvation, amputation, imprisonment, homelessness, extreme poverty—whatever the cause, I would find the survivors.

I also intensified my reading of survival tales that wrestle with the meaning of such torment, works like Primo Levi's death camp narratives or Wallace Terry's *Bloods*, a book of oral histories by black Americans who fought in Vietnam. And I bought my first kayak, ostensibly for pleasure and exercise but really for some physical challenges in my normally deskbound life. It soon became my own survival vessel, a means to move offshore and explore unfamiliar, potentially dangerous waters.

Coincidentally, about this time I learned from Bobby, who got it second-hand from an uncle on the Arias side, that Daddy may have died a few years back, possibly in 1980 or '81. In California, maybe Glendale. There weren't many details. Not how, not really when nor where. The report we got was vague and sounded like a rumor. "I doubt it," Bobby said. "Something's not right." My younger brother, Armand, was just as skeptical. "I find it hard to believe. We still don't have a body. I've read enough spy stories to know you can fake your own death. Leave it to him to pull the final Houdini act."

I agreed. He was probably up to something clever and sneaky. He was too good at surviving close calls to die so soon. We thought that he might be using his military skills. Bobby suggested he was a mercenary. I thought the army might be sending him on secret missions in Latin America, leading special forces in Colombia or El Salvador. Hell, he could do that. He's a warrior, a soldier, hard-core to the end. Strangely, reluctantly, I felt an odd sense of pride that he might have given everyone the slip, for whatever reason eluding detection one more time.

He may have retreated from our lives, but he wasn't gone from our minds. The spiral that occurred in my parents' marriage stayed with us like a fog that never quite lifted. For us, the sixties, that worst of times for my family, weren't what they were for most of our generation. Instead of Woodstock, Vietnam, and demonstrations, we were either fighting on other fronts outside the country or we were mired in the scene of sickness and lassitude at home. My brothers both did short army stints, luckily at the beginning and end of the war, so they missed Vietnam duty.

As for me, Daddy, the army careerist, had surprised everyone by encouraging me in plans to emigrate to Canada. "You'd be the first to be killed," he told me in all seriousness. "I know you." He did, of course. He knew what we'd be capable of in combat, knew that core of survival instincts and skills in us better than we did ourselves. Certainly he knew how well we could follow orders quickly and cleanly, without confusion or distraction. That he didn't think I was good soldier material never bothered me. I took it almost as a compliment, smugly thinking of myself as the creative free spirit in the family. Actually, what kept me out of the military was my marriage to a persuasive, raving pacifist, a fatherhood deferment after Michael's birth, and finally, my twenty-sixth birthday, which popped me out of the draft lottery.

Daddy always said he knew us better than we knew ourselves. More accurately, he thought he knew our breaking point. Years of holding him in fear and respect would not allow us to question if he was right or not. We just assumed he was. And then later, after my mother's death and his suicide attempt, we discovered he wasn't so unbreakable himself. The way the sixties played out for our family unsettled us, and by 1985 my brothers and I were still ambivalent about that time and about him. Mostly we tried not to think about what happened, about the questions left dangling.

"I admire him, if you can call it that," Armand said, "for putting up with Mommy's illness and all. I mean, a lot of guys would have walked. It certainly wasn't the best of circumstances. Most guys would've bailed." Like Bobby and me, Armand also harbored some resentment or defensiveness over Daddy's unexplained, sudden departure. "About him going off, truthfully I never thought about it much. I just packed it away. I figured, fine, it's his choice, he's happy—at least the last time I saw him he seemed to be. He was retired, playing tennis, had a young wife. I guess he was happy with that. So he chose his lifestyle, fine. So be it."

"I'll find him," I told Armand. "I'll find out what happened."

"I don't know," my brother said. "What's going to happen is that you're going to be really frustrated if you don't get to the root."

"I'm a reporter; I can do this—before it's too late."

I didn't tell him that ever since we had heard about our father's supposed death, I'd been having dreams of him living in a shabby second-floor room somewhere out of the pages of a Steinbeck novel. In my dream he was always alone. A lit cigar, a bottle of grape juice, a few cockroaches foraging along the baseboards. Dressed in workpants and a long-sleeved shirt, he appeared stretched out on a swayback mattress, his head propped up on the pillow. In the dream he was quietly smoking the cigar, but one time he rose and walked over to the grimy closed window and looked down on the traffic and people below.

I told Armand that someday maybe I could write about our family. I asked him if I did, how much should I get into his adoption? How much truth should I tell?

"All of it," he said. "It's about time someone did."

"You sure?"

"Everything."

A while after that conversation, I flew down to Mexico City to cover the earthquake aftermath, hearing Samantha's story and returning to New York. On my turnaround visit for my second earthquake story, I remember one sad but ultimately fortuitous moment. I was standing on a restaurant balcony overlooking the Zócalo, the city's huge and ancient central square. From my first visit to Mexico years ago with my parents, I thought of the Zócalo as a place of constant, vibrant movement, alive with cars, bicycles, motorbikes, trucks, horse-drawn wagons, and all kinds of pushcart vendors, men and women, selling everything from tacos to homemade toys. It was a feast for my thirteen-year-old eyes.

However, now, in the late afternoon, the giant square was almost empty and quiet. Through the dusky, hazy light, I could see the darkened arches of government buildings, the tilted basilica, and in one corner, the light-drenched stones of an Aztec ruin. Occasionally I glimpsed an ambulance streaking down a side street. With so many buildings down and so many thousands dead and injured, life seemed to have left the city's heart. I thought of my father, and suddenly the idea of writing a book on survival, *his* survival, emerged and floated out into an awesome, eerie silence. That's when I scribbled my first notes of things to do.

Write Pentagon
Chk Glendale obits
Glendale mortuaries
Chk Nogales
Ojai
His brothers
Friends?
Wife?
Find him.

Taken while I was watching a body being removed from a building in the Mexico City earthquake of 1985

Photo by Ben Martin—*People*

Me in front of trailer where my dad lived. Chorro Grande pack station, now abandoned, in Los Padres National Forest, Calif., 2001.

New York

My new job kept me scrambling on one tough story after another, so that more than two years would pass before I could start tracking down my father. My brothers and I still weren't convinced he had actually died or if he had encouraged a rumor to cover his tracks after he exited for parts unknown. "Where's the evidence that he died?" Armand asked me somewhat rhetorically. "Show me something that's proof."

"Give me a little time," I said. "I'll find the proof."

"You won't find him. Nobody will find him. He has it all figured out. Whatever he's up to, wherever he went, you'll never find out. He's too good."

I assured him I'd get to the bottom of things. If our father had died, there had to be records, a death certificate, hospital bills, a mortuary document, witnesses, something or somebody that would verify his death. Armand was skeptical. "Don't you remember? Daddy used to try out his Russian on us. He was always saying words to us. Where'd he learn that? He was in Russia during World War II, you know. They could have used him as some kind of spy."

When Armand's wife, Betty, said he'd been reading too many espionage thrillers, my brother asked us, "Haven't you ever seen *The Manchurian Candidate*?"

We had. I had even read a book on the so-called brainwashing ordeals that took place in the North Korean POW camps.

"Well," Armand continued, "doesn't it make sense that Daddy could be what they call a *sleeper?* That is, when they need him, they trigger that other personality that will follow orders. He could even be a double spy."

"You mean," Betty suggested, "like a split personality, one side disassociating with the other?"

Armand smiled at her logic. "He's probably alive and well and living in Europe, probably in Lago di Garda. Has a place on the shore and is using another name."

"But where's the proof of that?" I asked.

Armand, the voracious reader of international intrigue novels, added that was precisely his point: a good spy can disappear for good, can fake his death, and walk away from his previous lives. "He could have faked everything," Armand said, "Who's to say he didn't? We'll never know, unless we find him by accident somewhere in the Italian Alps walking his dog."

Betty and I agreed the picture was far-fetched, and days later, when I had returned from California to New York, I wrote about my brother's spy theory in the first of many "Armando"—or "A"—notebooks, including the above dialogue. I intended to approach my task like any other reporting project, filling a notebook with facts, quotes, names and references to check. At the time, I figured I'd need one or two of the four-by-eight-inch wire-ring reporter's notebooks I normally use on assignments.

As it turned out, over the next fourteen years I would end up with a desktop pile of many more notebooks, journals, diaries, and memo pads of many sizes, from legal length to tiny booklets half the span of my palm. I suppose I became the notebook fetishist only my mother could have appreciated. But whether I was anchored to my mid-city cubicle shaping stories from other people's reporting files or off reporting and writing my own pieces for the magazine—be it famine in Ethiopia, poverty in Haiti, death in El Salvador, or war-wounded kids in Nicaragua—wherever I might be when an "A-book" fact or idea struck, I would always have my bound and lined paper pad tucked into a pocket or backpack, ready to receive information before it floated away.

Sometimes my entries on the subject were directly germane, other times I might ramble off the mark into impressions about human loss or my own struggles as a writer, especially one groping for a style and structure I could use for the much bigger story I was beginning to see take shape. Years before, when the process began, I thought this story was mainly about my father. Reporter that I was, I thought I had no business intruding in the spotlight. I felt I should remain outside the story. But over the years as I went about my research, I saw myself gradually become very much a central part of the story. There were the years I lived with my parents, then came the years in which I saw a transformation in their marriage. And finally, much later, as I tracked down people and documents, I gained enough emotional distance from my parents so that I could write about myself then and now.

Despite suggestions by friends that I just turn known facts of my father and the family into a novel, inventing what I didn't know, I began to envision the story as my own quest for a father. In a practical sense, I was searching for the truth about Daddy as soldier, prisoner, husband, and father to three adopted sons. But in a more universal sense, I was also searching for the true nature of fatherhood, envisioning Daddy as only one of my many fathers, though by far he was the main male presence in my life. And in discovering him as a flesh-and-blood person, defects and all, I was gradually discovering myself. His story was becoming my story.

The more I peeled the proverbial onion, the more trouble I had accepting his decision to close the door on me and my brothers. From the beginning, my efforts to find and understand him grew from the questions surrounding my mother's death and his disappearance. I also liked the chase. But now, as I glimpsed pieces of the man, I felt a growing need for closeness to him. It was a yearning, not for answers about marriage and fatherhood—I knew he couldn't help me there—but for the embrace of the father who defined much of what I was. I wanted to get inside of him, be him, if only to see myself through his eyes. At bottom, even as I grew into my gray years, I wanted his approval of my existence. Like a kid, I simply wanted him back.

I started stabbing at narratives, once completing a commissioned article-length story for the *Los Angeles Times* Sunday magazine. "There's too much here—it should be a book," the editor said, returning my piece. So I quickly wrote three chapters of a proposed book and promptly had my labored, reticent effort sent back with the admonition by a previously interested book editor that I "open a vein."

Actually, in those first fact-gathering years, I was opening more notebooks than emotional blood vessels. As a middle-aged adult with less than adequate hindsight, how could I respond to what happened if I didn't know the truth, or all that could be construed as truth? No wonder my early jottings ranged from telegraphic, cryptic lists to reminders and meanderings of the moment.

4-12-86

Man in the streets
Son's search
Go to logical spots
Why did he escape?
How?
Portrait of a survival artist
Only glimpse the man
Hints, clues, a closeness, an expectation and tension throughout.

5-10-86

Coming on 11 months at the mag. Ups and downs but still the best work I've had in years. Joan still finding her way in IBM, but mostly likes it. Michael finishing his 2nd year at Wesleyan and plans to transfer to UCLA in fall. Good guy, good son. Eventually he'll land on something he loves and then he'll cruise. Right now it's all about music.

I've been so privileged to live this long, have known so much. Yet it could all be over anytime. The end, the shell of what I am, is not so abstract as it once was. Maybe seeing so much death over the past year has done this to me. My own skull, my flesh and frame, all seem like carriers of the inert end, as if I were already stretched out, my tissue beginning to decompose.

Morbid me tonight. Blame it on my headache and overdoing it outside on the water. Sometimes I feel like writing far away, creating a place and story as distant as my dreams and good sense will take me. Letting go, if only I could.

12-2-87

Called Capt. Schmidt at the Pentagon for "paper trail" info. Out, will return call Thursday.

Tomorrow call repository of military records in St. Louis with S's SS #.

Today in Grand Central, 3 black guys doing jiving harmony for tips. Reminded me of A, of that early memory of so many men, some whistling and singing, real low in loose, easy rhythms and melodies, clenching their cigars, maybe talking to the shoe-shine man. So many men in the big restroom. Was it at the train station? He took me there. And he took me to my first basketball game, the Globetrotters, and my first football game. The Rams. It was a scrimmage. When? 46? 47?

Ironically, my job was actually taking me to very distant *real* places, usually in foreign countries to write about one case of human awfulness after another. But even on such trips, invariably loaded with dramatic, deeply moving experiences, my father always seemed to be lurking at the edge of my vision. At the Mekele airstrip north of Addis Ababa, for example, I was watching a pair of Soviet tanks race back and forth on the other side of the runway. I had finished my reporting duties and was waiting for my plane to arrive so I could leave the area, which was surrounded by anti-government rebel troops.

I couldn't help thinking that if my father were here he might cross the runway to talk shop with the drivers for a while. He would find out, as I did, that the men were recharging the tanks' batteries by running the engines. He would discover that the tanks and machine guns propped up in several foxholes were there to protect Soviet and other cargo planes ferrying food and medical supplies to the sick and starving refugees from the drought. I was certain Daddy would laugh when he found out the tank drivers were really just racing each other out of boredom. Standing by the dusty airstrip in the midday heat, I could even hear that familiar nasal-sounding laugh, as if he were watching *The Honeymooners* or Groucho Marx.

But there were other times during my first years as a parachute journalist when my father seemed to speak through the stories themselves. The first occurred in El Salvador during that country's civil war. The contracted photographer who met me in San Salvador, the capital, was a French-born war photographer who had covered the battle of Dien Bien Phu in Vietnam during the fifties. Thin and gaunt, with short, gray hair, he seemed distracted and often irritable as we went about gathering the words and images of the first war tale we came across: the death of an innocent elderly woman caught in one of the city's daily outbursts of cross fire. She was mopping her kitchen floor when a government bullet struck her in the face. The photographer and I arrived at her home minutes after the shooting had ended.

We peeked into the kitchen and glimpsed the body and the puddle of blood on the ceramic tile floor. Only a six-year-old grandson had been in the house during the shooting.

"Let's get to the morgue," the photographer said. "That's where the family will show up."

I finished my spot interviews with neighbors, the grandson, and a police officer, then we left for the morgue. There we learned that the sixty-two-year-old grandmother's body would be taken for burial to Usulután, a provincial city reached only by a dangerous, uncertain ride through guerrilla-held territory. We heard that two bridges recently had been blown up and we would have to cross on the railroad tracks, as well as negotiate several treacherous, muddy detours. Also, many stretches of the potholed highway were further damaged by mortar round explosions.

Once we were on our way in a dilapidated, much-dented Ford taxi, I soon realized our sweaty young driver was a maniac. That is, he drove like one, egged on by my camera-laden companion next to him in the front passenger seat. "Come on, go faster, hit the holes at top speed!" the Frenchman instructed in Spanish. "Less damage that way." He explained that the idea was to "fly" over the holes. From my spot in the back, I braced myself and waited for one of the bald tires to blow each time I heard a jaw-jarring thunk.

About halfway to our destination, with the taxi swerving and galumphing between walls of sugarcane plants, the photographer turned to me and gravely said, "You don't see them, but they see you."

"Who?"

"The guerrillas."

"Great," I said. "And they're aiming guns at us."

"Of course."

The rest of the trip I was as nervous as he was calm. In this he reminded me of my father—fearless, relaxed, surveying the oncoming pitted asphalt ahead as if he were studying a flower. I asked what his last assignment was and if he usually worked in war zones. He said this was his first assignment in more than ten years. Before that, he had covered many wars, going back to the French war against the Viet Minh. "But ten years ago," he explained, "I wanted to disappear, just go off and start something new. Leave the past behind. And I did. I found my island where I could do that."

"Why'd you leave?" I asked.

He looked at me with a smirk, then turned away and laughed. He never answered me. In fact, he told me I talked too much and should button it. After all, we were exposed and in danger. I kept quiet, on the lookout for the slightest movement amid the sugarcane on both sides of the narrow pitiful excuse for a highway.

After about two more hours, we reached Usulután without incident, found the church where the woman's body was displayed in an open coffin, and went to work getting quotes and taking pictures. Months later, in New York, I heard my testy partner in El Salvador had died of inoperable cancer. The story I did with him was his last. He knew he was dying, and maybe whatever pain he might have been feeling had produced his edgy behavior and his cavalier attitude toward possibly being picked off by a rebel sharpshooter. The cancer prognosis also may have pushed him to leave his island—that is, to die among people taking pictures, doing what he could do best.

Did my father also want to start over by disappearing? What drove him to sever all ties to his past, to his life as a soldier, husband, widower, and father? Like the French photographer, would he have come back to what he knew before, back to us, if he had known he had a fatal disease and only had months to live? I wanted to believe he would do just that.

Another time, on assignment in São Paulo, Brazil, I was reminded of how easy it was for even the famous—or infamous—to change identity and take up another life with new friends and neighbors. My story target was the newly discovered bones of a disinterred body purported to be that of Josef Mengele, the concentration camp doctor at Auschwitz-Birkenau who came to be known as "The Angel of Death." I spent a long afternoon with a Brazilian forensic anthropologist, who methodically walked me through all the identification work that had been done: a microscopic examination of the skeleton's every part, as well as the perfect matching of Mengele's known injuries, diseases, and abnormalities, such as a hip fracture, a broken right thumb, osteoarthritis of the spine, and a small hole in his cheekbone caused by a tooth infection. Even without the match with Mengele's dental records, which the Brazilians had requested from Mengele's son in Germany, consulting scientists all declared that the remains of the notorious doctor who had eluded capture for four decades had at last been found.

Josef Mengele had been living under the alias Wolfgang Gerhard and had drowned at 67 in 1979 when he suffered a stroke while swimming at a beach near São Paulo. However, he spent his final years living comfortably in a quiet suburb of the city, enjoying a reputation among neighbors for being kind to children and working happily in his garden.

At one point during my afternoon visit to the forensic anthropologist, I was alone in a room with Mengele's dark, earth-stained bones—all painstakingly lined up on a table to form a proper skeleton. I picked up his right pinkie, just the tip or end bone. For a moment I had the urge to pocket this grim souvenir. I looked at it closely, wondering how many monstrous acts it had been a part of, how many thousands of victims it had touched. Then, before my host returned to the room, I replaced the gnarly piece of digit on the table, neatly aligning it with the finger's last knuckle.

I thought of the concentration camp in Poland and wondered if my father had seen it, perhaps only days or weeks after it had been liberated by Allied troops. After all, the prisoner of war camp my father escaped from—Oflag 64—wasn't all that far from Auschwitz. In those last days of the war, Josef Mengele also escaped, disappearing in South America. Like many Nazis, he created a new identity, a new life for himself. Yet he was still a hunted war criminal, facing a trial and certain execution if he were ever caught, all of which were strong motives never to resurface again. But my father? What were his motives? What were his reasons, his demons?

Nogales

I went to Nogales to find my father, not the one my brothers and I knew but the much younger one, the boy Daddy had been. I was between magazine assignments, free for three days. So I flew from New York to Arizona to interview my father's eldest brother, Julio, now a retired foreign service officer. It was all prearranged, as were my visits to two of the other brothers. Richard, the youngest of the four brothers, refused to talk to me in person. On the telephone all he would offer me was, "I'm sorry, Son. He was a good man. That's all I can say. I can't tell you anything more. Goodbye."

Julio, however, was gracious and helpful. We had never met, yet he welcomed me into his stylish, modern condo as if I were a son. A UC Berkeley graduate and lifelong bachelor, he was the most educated and refined of the Arias brothers. He had worked in various consular posts abroad and eventually rose to become head of the State Department's passport office as well as the U.S. Consul General in Guadalajara, Mexico. For a balding man just into his seventies, he looked trim, healthy, and ten years younger than his actual age.

We sat down at the dining room table. It was Julio who in 1981 told my brother Bobby that our father had died the year before. He said a Ventura, California, mortuary had notified him of Armando's cremation, prepaid because my father knew he was dying of lung cancer. Julio said no one was on hand at the time to gather his effects or arrange a service, but assured me, "Yes, he did die. In 1980."

I told Julio that my parents' marriage had gone sour after he came back from Korea, but that after my mother's death he tried to kill himself. Julio said he hadn't known about the suicide attempt, and it surprised him because it seemed so out of character. I turned on the microcassette recorder. "Tell me about him growing up," I said, and Julio began to speak in a deliberate, thoughtful manner, sometimes using quaint or antiquated words that made him sound like a gentleman from a hundred years ago.

As a kid he was wild, rebellious and mischievous. Always up to something. On one occasion when he was about twelve but looked older, he went to a second-hand automobile dealer. He said that his father wanted to try out an automobile and had asked him to pick it up, to test it. And Armando went off by himself or with some of his comrades and made it to Tucson and back in that car. He was always doing things like that. When my dad found out, he was of course angry. My father was the old-fashioned, Spanish type. Stern. He tried to bring us up the way he had been brought up in Spain. But of course it was difficult in an environment like this, and Armando was never one to take things lying down. Very rebellious, travieso. I think it was he and Florencio who would get a belting from my mother for their disturbing activities. We lived on Elm Street, and Armando had a lot of friends in the neighborhood. He played on the streets and in the hills, and sometimes they would go into people's orchards and steal fruit. Typical little boy pranks. Never got caught.

"But your mother found out?"

Father wasn't around much and wasn't as likely to fly off the handle as Mother would. I don't know what kind of childhood she had. I think she was bewildered by the responsibilities of a wife and mother of four sons and a daughter. She would sort of lose control. She went only up to the second grade in school in Mexico, and in all her years in Nogales, Arizona, she didn't learn English. During World War II, when she was applying for citizenship she was test-

ed for English and knowledge of the Constitution. The man testing her went up to the judge and said, "Your honor, Mrs. Arias can't speak English." And the judge said, "Well, the the mother of four boys who are in the forces of the United States doesn't need to speak English to be a citizen. And he waived that requirement.

"When did your parents pass away?"

My father in 1972 and she several years later, maybe in '76, I don't remember. We all saw Armando after the death of my father. Armando and I were never very close. As kids we all just fought among each other. But that time he was a very self-possessed person. I remember we went to eat at a Chinese restaurant. He didn't talk much about Emma. He'd come with his new wife and it was just polite talk, nothing serious. My mother was always very proud of him. He had such a dashing appearance. He was her favorite. First it was Richard, then it was Armando. She had her heart set on him marrying Barbara Wilson, and who knows? It might have happened. But he married your mother. You probably know that my mother didn't take to your mother.

"I knew that, but I never knew why. I always thought it was because my mother had been married before and had two kids at the time."

Maybe that too. But when he returned from the Army, all the attractive girls, girls from good families, seemed to be atwitter over him. Maybe they hadn't met him but saw his picture in the paper and had heard about him and his exploits in the war. I knew a few of these girls, on both sides of the border. Well, Barbara Wilson was a very pretty brunette. A sweet, well-bred girl. Her father was a tomato grower and broker. Had everything. One of the richest men in Nogales. They owned a hacienda in Culiacán and a big house in Nogales up on Crawford Street. Barbara and Armando knew each other, I don't know from where, but as you know he was very handsome and just drew the girls. People used to compare him to Gilbert Roland, the actor.

"Did they ever date each other?"

I know he was once invited to their hacienda in Mexico. I remember this because of the story that went around afterwards. These very macho ranch hands thought they'd put one over on the dashing dandy from the north. They offered to let him ride one of their best horses, they gave him an unbroken stallion. What they didn't know is that Armando was an expert horseman. He'd been trained in the mounted cavalry. So he got on this wild, bucking horse, and to everyone's amazement he succeeded in taming him. The Mexican machos couldn't believe it. Like out of a Hollywood movie. From then on, he was like a legend.

"When did he go into the army?"

He was 14 when he enlisted. He told them he was 18. I was three years older than he was, so that means he was born in February of 1927 and enlisted in 1940. He went to Ft. Huachuca first, then Ft. Bliss. I wasn't surprised when he left high school and ran off to join, although I was surprised he got away with it. But my dad, the stern disciplinarian, took it philosophically. He accepted it as his son's irrepressible rebellious nature.

At this point in the interview, we paused and I believe Julio offered me some tea or a soft drink. When we resumed, he looped back to their industrious nature when they were kids during the Depression.

We started doing things to earn pocket money, which we had to turn over to Dad, and then he would give us spending money. We delivered papers, sold magazine subscriptions for an agency. Saturday Evening Post, Ladies Home Journal, *and* Country Gentleman. *We used to sell those door-to-door. For a while we even tried doing business importing leather goods—ladies' handbags, wallets, things like that. And Armando was very good at that. He was the best one of us at selling. I was pretty good myself but I remember Armando was the best. Thinking about it now, I suppose none of us was able to acquire as strong a raison d'être—that is, something to live for, to stimulate us—as your father. He liked being useful. It gave him great satisfaction.*

I showed Julio some of the news clips about my father that I had collected, even one story from a Nogales newspaper about his brother in Korea. The story includes a sentence about "Lt. Arias's wife and baby" arriving to visit the family, the baby being my brother Armand. When I told him that my mother had returned from her trip saying Julio's mother had "spurned her," he understood completely.

Did you know that Armando and his second wife were divorced? She moved away and left him living by himself up on the side of a mountain near Ojai. That's all I know. Maybe when it came to a close, intimate relationship with a woman it was difficult to give of himself. For a time, yes, but there was no long-term closeness.

Suddenly, I wasn't really listening. Even though my eyes were open, I was watching the man in my dream stretched out on a sagging bed, alone in an empty room. I glanced at my tape recorder; Julio's words were still being recorded. Then my thoughts returned to what I had just heard. Where exactly did he live? What was it like? Did anyone know him? Where was Yvette now? Vaguely I heard Julio mention his father being away most of the time, working as a clerk for the Southern Pacific railway.

. . . long hours, especially during the tomato season. In those days there was a lot of transportation of tomatoes and other vegetables across the border from Mexico. And he also played the piano at the local cinema, for the silent movies. He was the church organist for 25 years in Nogales. He learned to play in a seminary in Sonora. An uncle of his who was a priest had him sent over from Spain to be placed in the seminary. But instead of becoming a padre of a church, he met my mother and became a padre of five children. . . .

Later in the day, I finished the interview and we said our goodbyes at the front door. Julio was cordial, but shook my hand stiffly. I don't think he was used to visitors intruding on his solitude, but he seemed curious and maybe amused that I was looking for my father and planning to write about him. "Good luck on your quest," he said. When I told him I was now going to meet Gene, the eldest Arias brother, he only nodded, as if to say, "Fine, do your work." I knew the five brothers had had little if any contact with each other over the years and that elusiveness seemed to be a family trait.

Gene, or Eugenio, was a true cowboy. Though he was retired and now managed an apartment complex, he had herded, roped, and lassoed steers for most of his working life. A thin, angular octogenarian with a clean, stiff Stetson and a smoker's cough, he corroborated Julio's description of the brother they obviously admired but hadn't really known since they were all children. "I called him Hank," he said, "a good cowboy name. Affectionate, if you know what I mean." In his laconic way, Gene was hospitable but he didn't provide me with much. No stories, no intrigue, no telling facts. But I did feel that he had some deep feeling for his kid brother.

After leaving Gene, I then met a third brother, Florencio. He said he used to call my father "El Rata," or "The Rat" in Spanish, "because he was so good at pinching things from the store—nothing big, but he was real clever, very sneaky." Like my talk with Gene, my interview with Florencio produced little more than surprise at my retelling of his brother's checkered career and life. It was as if he were listening to the tale of a stranger, which was understandable, since my father had run away so young, never returned to live in Nogales, and over the years had little contact with his family. Yet Florencio admitted that with a father who was distant and authoritarian and a mother who was a static influence on her sons, "Armando went looking for that warmth and direction a strong family gives you to succeed in life. My dad wasn't around much to do this, and my mother didn't do anything. She didn't show us how to behave. If we learned anything, we had to pretty much learn it on our own."

In 1940, the First Cavalry Division's mounted units, the army's last, were stationed at Fort Bliss, Texas. Although the army would phase out the horse cavalry in 1943, there were about 8,000 horses when my father's unit was posted at Fort Bliss. Horse shows and polo matches were popular, and the men of the Eighth Cavalry Regiment—my father's unit—would often participate in parades in downtown El Paso or could be seen riding to their patrol positions along the border. The cavalry troopers would usually wear the standard-issue riding jodhpurs, long-sleeved shirts, knee-high boots and stiff, wide-brimmed hats or World War I-style steel helmets.

I have no pictures of my father dressed like this, but as a greenhorn private most of the time he was probably wearing dungarees and T-shirts for slopping out stables, cleaning corrals and feeding and grooming the horses.

For years Fort Bliss had provided Ciudad Juárez with an abundant supply of young men bent on drinking, gambling, whoring, and doing all the unbridled hell-raising they might not get away with in a less tolerant El Paso. For generations the bordellos and cantinas of Juárez had welcomed these men, as well as the armies of Mexican troops encamped in and around the city from time to time.

As a lanky, robust fourteen-year-old who could pass for seventeen or eighteen, spoke Spanish, and was up for most challenges, my father must have plunged into this rambunctious prewar border scene as if he'd been born to it. Hungry for new excitement and adventures, most likely he held his own physically and learned to ride well. Of the little he told me of his early army career, I remember he did say he liked his nights and days on maneuvers, patrolling the desert scrublands, sleeping out in the open under the stars. From late 1940 through 1941 he actually served as a mounted border agent. Given Germany's friendly overtures toward the Mexican government, he was mostly on the lookout for suspicious or subversive activity rather than illegal immigrants.

Border duty also gave him his first chance to be accepted as a man by other men, even though in some ways he still must have been a boy. I can only imagine how a fourteen-year-old, even one as physically mature as he apparently was, might have confronted the challenges of early manhood. Given the reserved and taciturn adult I knew, I would guess that my father quickly developed a quiet, observant, good-natured demeanor around his new buddies. It would be his armor as well as a way of learning how to be a man fast.

Max Medema, an Arizona native who knew my father as a fellow POW in Poland, also served in the horse cavalry during its last days. Medema, now a retired telephone company executive in Los Angeles, didn't know my father at Fort Bliss, but he gave me an idea of the raunchy, rough-riding men my father had joined.

At that time, just before the war, cavalry troopers were the meanest, roughest, toughest guys in the Army. The Army was filled with drifters, misfits and cowboys. And the cavalry was filled with an even bigger bunch of cutthroats you'd ever want to meet. It was a rough, mean place, and I imagined your dad would have had a similar experience to mine. We'd put on civilian clothes, but the locals could spot us because of the chin-strap streaks where we weren't tanned. They hated the soldiers because of the many real bad types, roughnecks who couldn't read or write, just a mean, tough bunch of horse-breakers. We swore a lot and drank this raw alcohol. If you were new, you found a way to make yourself acceptable. Knowing your dad, he probably kept his mouth shut and impressed them with hard work and horsemanship.

Coincidentally, my uncle was also working at Fort Bliss during this period, only as a civilian in the army finance office. He and my father would not meet until after the war in 1946, but Tuy remembers the cavalry troopers as something quite different from the lowlifes Medema describes.

It was an exciting place, and whenever I see From Here To Eternity, *I think of the barracks across from the parade ground, just like in the movie. Seeing the cavalry was a big thrill. I always enjoyed watching the mounted soldiers on those wonderful horses, sometimes going by right in front of our house. Who knows, one of those men might have been Armando.*

Tuy explains something else: while stationed at Fort Bliss my father was dating a girl named Julieta, who was the sister of one of my mother's friends. After my father came back from the war in 1945, he returned to Nogales, then went to El Paso to see Julieta. At the same time, my mother, who had been living in Los Angeles since before the war, happened to be back in El Paso visiting Mama. "I wasn't there," my uncle says. "I was still in Germany. But I received a letter from my mother telling me about Armando. He was at Julieta's house when Julieta's sister and Emma dropped by. That's when Armando and Emma probably met for the first time. You could say that was the start of their romance."

Chorro Grande

From behind the steering wheel I leaned my head to the left and sucked in the smell of sage and pine. More than a century ago the high country above the Ojai Valley was home to the Chumash Indians, who inhabited what is today Los Padres National Forest. My father must have come here not only for the mountain smells and wilderness but also for the solitude and connection with some greater, more ancient past than his own life of wandering from home to home. At least that was my hunch of how he got to Chorro Grande, a pack station from which riders on rented horses could explore and camp out in virtually uninhabited mountains less than a hundred miles from Los Angeles.

I turned the car to the right, leaving the highway for a dirt road that snaked through some pine and fir trees to emerge in a clearing the size of a football field. To my left was a low wooden cabin, to my right two small, shabby houses, and straight ahead at the far end were several old unpainted sheds, a corral, and, in the shade of two scraggly oak trees, a house trailer on cinder blocks. I parked the rented Baretta in front of the cabin between an aging, dusty pickup truck and a big, floppy-eared mongrel sprawled on the ground snapping at flies. I collected my notepad, pen, and manila folder with the pictures of my father, plus some faded newsclips about his return from Korea, then walked up to the front door. I knocked and moments later the door opened and a broad-faced young man with sandy hair and a full beard smiled and cheerfully said, "Good morning."

"Uh, hi," I said with a nervous catch in my throat. Beyond his shoulders I saw a blonde woman and two small children seated at a kitchen table.

"Can I help you?" the young man said.

"I'm looking for someone." I hesitated and he quickly looked me over, as if I might be the bearer of bad news. "My name is Ron Arias and I'm looking for my father, Armando Arias."

For a moment the young man looked perplexed, then stepped aside and nodded for me to enter. "Hey, hon!" he called inside, "you'll never guess who's here."

"Who?"

"Guess."

"I don't know, the Lone Ranger."

"Close. It's his son."

"What?"

"Armando's son."

The young woman left the kids and welcomed me warmly. Her name was Veronica. The man, who I assumed was probably her husband and the kids' father, ran the pack station and went by the appropriately cowboyish name of Pardner. We shook hands and Veronica asked me if I'd like a cup of coffee or some orange juice. "Coffee'd be nice," I said.

She went into the kitchen while Pardner and I sat at the big table by the window. The children hung around for a while, then became restless and left. The cabin's low ceiling, stone fireplace, and wooden floor and walls reminded me of a bunkhouse or hunting lodge.

I explained that I had talked to someone in Ojai this morning who said my father had died up here. Pardner pointed toward the open front door and said he had lived in the trailer. "But he didn't die here. That was down in Ojai. One night he just left and he never came back."

"How long did he live here?"

"Oh, five, six years. His wife was with him for a while, but then they split up and he lived there by himself. Sort of like a hermit."

Pardner, who looked about thirty, said my father kept an old brown mare named Rusty that he used to take on the trail a lot. He also had a motorcycle and a "little pickup" for trips to Ojai to play tennis or go shopping. He said he first met my father behind a supermarket in town. "He was digging in a dumpster, putting stuff in a plastic trash bag. He said he was scavenging for veggies to feed Rusty."

Pardner looked out the window at the pine trees. "He knew horses. Even taught me a few tricks. We rode a lot together. He was a fine rider. He loved it up here, loved the loneliness and the beauty." For a moment Pardner was silent, then said he'd met all kinds of people, "but Armando was different. He was unique, a gentleman, very European and cultured. He was genuine. No phony. You just knew he wasn't playing a role. He'd really done it all."

As Pardner spoke, I realized he knew things about my father that I had never known until recently, things like his cavalry days at Fort Bliss and patrolling the border on horseback.

Veronica came with the coffee and Pardner continued. "There wasn't much he didn't know how to do," he said, then described how they used to catch and wrestle goats together for branding. "He taught me a lot."

Listening to the bearded packer, I began to feel envious of all he knew that I didn't. I wanted to interrupt and say he was *my* father, not yours. He taught *me* first. I wanted to tell him my dad belonged to me, that he was mine. At the same time, I was also angry that my father had left me and my brothers for the company of men like Pardner. Finally, I asked, "Did he ever mention his sons?"

"He did," Pardner said. "He talked about his family. 'They're doing their own thing and I'm doing mine' is all he said."

I was puzzled. Why would he think we were just doing our own thing? "Anything else?" I said.

"Not really. We didn't want to pry. Your dad was very private."

Pardner said sometime in early 1978 my father went to Europe for about a year. "He sent us postcards and all, then came back already feeling sick. They told him he had cancer, but your dad didn't want chemotherapy. He went to Mexico, probably for treatments, I don't know. Then he came back and stayed here. Self-sufficient, never gave up."

I asked if I could see the trailer. Pardner said a man named Clay was living there now, though he probably wouldn't mind my looking around. I left Pardner at the door and walked past the dog. He was still snapping at flies.

Crossing the clearing, I kicked some of the fallen pinecones that were scattered on the dry grass. As I neared the trailer, which was maybe twenty-five or thirty feet long, I noticed it was tilted slightly backwards and the green aluminum siding was dented and faded. A few lopsided pieces of metal appeared to cover damaged spots. Signs, I thought, of my father's slapdash, rascuachi fix-it efforts. I slowed down, wading into the yellowing weeds, moving from the rear of the trailer to the front, feeling his presence in the bent television antenna, the duct tape on the broken window, the rotted two-by-fours propping up the rusted propane tanks at the front end. His touch was here and I didn't want to lose it.

Finally I stepped around to the side door. I breathed deeply and slowly, trying to calm down. After I knocked twice on the narrow door, I heard footsteps inside, then the door opened. A grizzled middle-aged man with faded tattoos on his arms gave me the once-over and said, "Yeah?"

I introduced myself as the son of the man who used to live here. Instantly, the face creased into a smile, and Clay invited me in. "Welcome to Armando's trailer! *Mi casa es su casa.*"

As I stepped up and inside, he said he had never really known my father, but that it was an honor to meet me. "I feel your dad's spirit is still here. That's why I call it Armando's trailer."

We sat down at the small table in the front part of the trailer. Here and there the linoleum covering the table and the floor were all worn to their plywood base, the windows were grimy, and the wood-burning stove smelled of old, damp charcoal. Pardner had told me Clay was a recluse, an "end-of-the-roader" who read religious books and followed the spiritual teachings of an Indian yogi. This would explain the poster-size portrait of a bearded, long-haired guru thumbtacked to the side of a cabinet. Clay kept repeating the words "your dad," telling me how everybody admired him. He showed me to the rear of the trailer, past the hanging beads and into the cramped bedroom. "I don't change a thing. It's just like he left it. But the books are mine. Place was empty when I moved in."

Then Clay opened the rear door and led me out to a patiolike enclosure with a plywood floor and a table and chairs, all painted white and shielded by a tall wooden fence. He said my father had built it, then told me to check out the "bunker Armando built." We walked about twenty yards from the trailer down a weedy slope shaded by a scrub oak. The bunker was made of piled-up rocks and earth and sheltered an electricity generator. "It's noisy," Clay explained. "That's why he put it out here. It gives me the juice for my TV and lights."

I stared at the bunker, peeked in at the generator half-buried in the earth, at the crooked two-by-four supports, the lopsided tin roof, the frayed black wires that stretched droopily from a pole to the trailer roof. I could see my father hurriedly pounding in nails with little thought to design, piling on rocks, using whatever wire and wood scraps were available. The generator itself was most likely scrounged from a junkyard down in the valley.

I thanked Clay for his time, then hiked up the trail a ways, past the horses in the corral and the goats munching in the brush before turning back.

A year later I drove up from Los Angeles to Chorro Grande again. Everyone I had met on my previous visit had moved away. The place appeared deserted. No horses, no goats, apparently no people. Then I saw two men emerge from behind the old green trailer. As they walked toward me, I thought I should retreat to the car while I still had some distance between them and me. They were big fellows. They had dark skin, were dressed in jeans and white T-shirts, and both had their black hair pulled back in single braids. The shorter, stockier of the two carried a long-handled ax on his shoulder; the other had his hands in his back pockets. They were looking directly at me. Too late.

I smiled and said hello. They stopped a few feet in front of me and the man with the ax frowned. His face was deeply pocked and he glanced past me as if he were searching for other intruders. "Yeah?" he said.

"I was looking for Pardner or Clay."

"Nobody here but us," the ax man said.

The taller, thin-faced man, who appeared to be Mexican or Indian, asked who I was. I told them, with a few details about my father ending his days up here. The two men glanced at each other, then the ax thunked to the ground headfirst and the shorter man asked, "Would you like to join us in the sweat lodge ceremony?"

"Sure," I said, curious.

He introduced himself as Bill Two Feathers, and he seemed pleased. "You came today," he said, picking up the ax. "There must be a reason why you came today. Come on. We'll do this one in your father's honor, in honor of his spirit."

For the next two hours or so I helped Bill Two Feathers and Paul Skyhorse chop logs into two-foot lengths, later arranging them in a latticelike fashion over a shallow pit. Then we piled melon-size stones on top of the wood. The lodge itself was a low, rounded structure made of bent tree limbs and covered with layers of old rugs and blankets. When the fire was lit, we sat on rickety metal fold-up chairs and waited for the stones to heat while we drank cold beer poured into paper cups from a thermos.

The two men were Ojibwas, originally from Minnesota. Bill said he had lived in the state of Washington, then moved south until he found the packing station, which he described as "a good place for the sacred ceremony." The area was once used as a campsite by a now extinct California tribe. Rent was cheap, so he became the Chorro Grande caretaker, living with his wife and two children in one of the shabby houses by the clearing. He never met Pardner or Clay, and now his sole mission was to spread the old spiritual tribal ways among Indians and whites alike.

Paul lived by himself in the trailer. "I got into some scrapes, and that wasn't working," he said. "So I decided to go the peaceful route." He explained he had just finished serving time in prison, or "the iron house," as he called it. "I'm even in a book," he added. "*In the Spirit of Crazy Horse*. It's by Peter Matthiessen and he tells the whole story. Wounded Knee, the shootout—it's all there. He doesn't make me look too good, but I'm there. Page 112. You'll see my name."

Later I would check the reference at a public library and sure enough, starting near the bottom of page 112, Matthiessen writes of a "young Ojibwa named Paul Durant 'Skyhorse,' " who was active in the American Indian Movement and with another man was charged with the murder of a white cab driver at an AIM rest camp south of Ventura. But in 1978, after a year-long trial and much clamoring from the liberal community, both defendants were acquitted and the murder eventually was pinned on two other men. Matthiessen also writes that Paul had a criminal record for robbery, "a reputation for hard drinking," and "a history of mental instability."

I talked about my father and his prisoner-of-war experience, his growing up on the border, his joining the cavalry at fourteen. Bill and Paul listened intently. I told them I was now finding pieces of the puzzle, that if I couldn't find him alive, maybe I could someday tell his story.

After a pause, Bill rose and suggested I check the storage shed that tenants had been throwing things into for years. "Maybe you'll find something of his."

Paul tipped back in his chair. "Go for it," he said, filling his cup again.

I headed for the dilapidated wooden shed, which was about the size of a double-car garage and seemed to grow out of the weeds. I swung open one of the big doors and entered a darkened, cavernous space filled with dusty beams of light coming from several small windows and holes in the planks of the walls. At first I could only see shadows and jumbled shapes. Then I began to see machinery parts, tires, hanging chains, a toilet bowl, scraps of lumber, broken tables, and piles of cardboard boxes—all of it thrown together, caked in dust, and draped with cobwebs.

Once my eyes grew used to the gloom, I started picking my way through the piles at likely spots, poking into one box or crate after another, pulling things into the light, moving them aside, amazed at the jumble of items: mildewed clothes, curled and crusty shoes, stiff, stuck-together magazines, ruined books, a stack of 1978 Los Angeles telephone directories, broken toys, a torn mattress, cans of rusty nails and screws, bolts, an old car battery, plastic jugs of motor oil.

I brushed away an overhead swatch of spider web. Normally phobic about spiders and scorpions, I ignored whatever creatures I might be disturbing and plunged on. Despite the midday heat, the dust and the sweat soaking into my clothes, I dug down, an archeologist of human randomness, sifting, fingering, reaching down through the detritus of years. Why toss a perfectly good sealed ream of typing paper? Why store here a handful of frayed and used toothbrushes, all neatly bound in red wrapping ribbon?

And the owners of these things? I assumed they were people like my father or Clay or Paul Skyhorse, people who came to escape cities and towns and enjoy the mountain life. Or maybe they were just passing through long enough to dump a trunkload of telephone directories they were supposed to deliver to homes.

Until now I had pursued this search for my father only in spurts between my magazine assignments, collecting scraps of information, writing notes to myself, calling, mailing, shooting in the dark. Mostly I had been interviewing my family about what they remembered of him, of my mother, of the day she died, and of the days after my father was found comatose. When I wasn't busy at the magazine, I gathered what scraps I could surrounding my father's story. Not the story itself, but pieces, ideas, moments of where *I* stood in the process.

All along I had been keeping notebooks I called my "A"—or "Armando"—notebooks. In those first years of my search I couldn't say, much less write, the word "Daddy." I still resented his position as the family boss and law for everything in my childhood, all that yes-sirring and no-sirring, hand-kissing, butt-whackings, forehead-thumpings, punishments, and anything else he could dream up. But as I began to flesh out the facts of his life, the image I had chewed on for so long weakened. Finally I could say and even write the word *Daddy* again, naturally and without pause. Not so difficult, I thought. Just another middle-aged guy referring to his pop, his dad, his father.

Strange to keep examining Daddy's life with only glimpses of different periods. How fair would it be for any of us to have our lives reconstructed this way? How accurate?

A few notebooks later, when my enthusiasm for writing a book about him was coming in fits and starts, I scribbled almost illegibly, as if I were muttering.

Affection, yes. Love? No. More like empathy. Wish I could share myself with him now.

Waited long enough. He was, what—53, 54, when he died? Me, now 48. Almost Daddy's age.

Today finally talked to mortuary that cremated him. Daddy had it all arranged. Even talked to the man who did the cremation. Ashes taken out to sea by boat & scattered, he said. No survivors present. Jesus, that's a sad, cold end.

Death certificate being sent. Called Bobby, left Jr. a message. He's still skeptical.

It had been more than eight years since Daddy's death on July 28, 1980, which meant that I probably wouldn't find anything of his near the top of the piles. I dug deeper, concentrating on the area with most of the boxes and crates of papers and assorted small junk. The whole uneven mass stood about four or five feet high and in about an hour I had finished all the stacks except one, having worked my way down to the dirt floor each time before moving on to the next heap of boxes.

Until that day, uncovering the truth about my mother and father had been an almost perverse source of excitement I would share with my friends, family, and colleagues. This stream of revelations—*died of lung cancer . . . Mommy would beg him for pills . . . he joined the infantry at fourteen*—each new fact or quote would be added to my trove of artifacts in the story I would someday tell. It was as if finding the scraps of a life were my only goal, not finding the man or knowing what happened and why. So far I had nothing tangible, only scattered memories and words teasing me. I had become a collector of snippets. I even developed a patter, relying on clichés and labels, referring to my father as a Latin Great Santini, the soldier with the Gilbert Roland looks, an escape artist, an enigma, a stranger, the womanizer who broke my mother's heart.

I was thirsty and dirty. My grimy duty had produced nothing. But only one more stack of boxes remained. Then finito—I'd leave. I uncovered the last cardboard box at the bottom of the pile. As I flipped open the top flaps, I caught sight of the name *Armando Arias*. "Yes!" I shrieked. "Yes-yes-yes!"

The name was typewritten on a smudged, carbon-copied sheet of gray, tissue-thin paper, which appeared to be a receipt for an eyeglass prescription. I slipped my hand along the inside to the bottom, touched what felt like a book and some objects in a plastic bag, then pulled my hand out and picked up the entire box. After a glance around to see if I had missed looking into any other boxes, I rose and carried my discovery into the raw noontime light.

I sat down on the dry weeds and grass, placed the box between my outstretched legs, and waited a moment. Slowly, I opened the flaps again and saw his name. Then I proceeded to work my way down through various pages of his medical and dental records, bills and receipts for X-rays and lab work, college lists of courses and grades, and income tax forms from 1970 to 1979. In this last year, only months before his death, he lists on his tax return his yearly retirement income as $12,740. Stapled to another tax form is written a statement explaining a transportation deduction for medical reasons. This would have been during the time he was still married to Yvette. The handwriting is unmistakably his: clean, meticulous strokes with the initial letter of almost every word capitalized. As I read the paragraph, a strange sensation came over me: I was listening to his voice.

ITEM 6c:
We Live In The Mountains, In The Middle Of The Los Padres National Forest (25 Miles from The Nearest Telephone). The Various Trips We Had To Make To Ojai, Ventura & To The Hueneme Naval Base for Medical & Dental Attention, A Round Trip Distance of 50, 100 & 120 Miles Respectively, Added Up to 1800 Miles X .06 Per Mile, for A Total of $108.

Further down, after Item 25, he tells me what happened to the big family car he and Mommy bought new when they lived in Oceanside. It was the feel-good, fancy car my mother preferred over the Peugeot he drove.

On A Trip Through The State of Vermont, I Overheated The Car, Causing The Block To Crack; Thereby Releasing Water Into The Crankcase, Causing Motor To Burn Up. Car Was A 1966 Pontiac (Bonneville). Dealer Allowed Me $400 On It. Blue Book Price Was $1250.

I continued flipping pages, mostly forms, military records, shopping lists, and more itemized hospital receipts. Several medical forms mention the diagnosis of what eventually killed him: squamous cell cancer in the left lung.

I dug further and came across a typewritten twenty-page speech in Spanish that he wrote while at Travis Air Force Base in 1962. It was to be presented before a visiting group of military officers from Latin America and would explain how the Nike missile system defended the San Francisco Bay area. I remember it because my mother helped him prepare it. I was home for a weekend from Berkeley, and they were working hard on it together. But he was never able to give the speech because the Latin Americans unexpectedly cancelled the visit. He and my mother, I remember, were very disappointed.

I placed the topmost papers aside, then continued picking my way to the bottom. I found three paperback novels—Westerns—a French grammar book, an illustrated guide to France, five pairs of bifocal glasses, grocery lists, and an address book filled mostly with unfamiliar names in Los Angeles and the Ojai-Ventura area. The only names I recognized were that of his brother Gene Arias and, alongside an outdated address, that of my younger brother, Armand. Bobby's name and my name were nowhere in the book.

I figured the report of his death had originally spread when someone spotted Gene's name and notified the old cowboy that his brother had died. Gene then spread the word to his brothers in Arizona, and by the time Julio passed the news on to Bobby in Washington, D.C., several years had passed and some of the facts had changed, like when and where my father died.

At the bottom of the box, a plastic bag lay scrunched in a corner. I reached in, picked it up, and shook out the contents. A gleaming set of pink-and-white dentures dropped out onto the grass. I picked up the plasticky clackers and raised them, Yorick-like, before my eyes. I opened the rows of teeth into a frozen chuckle, then closed them. On the palette I noticed tiny black letters. I removed my glasses and brought the upper teeth closer. Neatly printed in some kind of indelible ink were the thick capitalized letters

A. ARIAS

Startled, I stared at the letters for a moment, thinking I had somehow invaded his privacy but that this time maybe he would overlook the transgression. Then I began to cry.

Later, after I had wiped my face and cleaned my eyeglasses with my shirt, I put back the dentures and everything else I'd taken out of the box—all except my father's California driver's license, which had dropped out of an envelope stuck in the address book. It was issued on December 20, 1977, and would have expired on his birthday, February 11, 1982. I did the calculation based on the birth date of 1927 that Julio gave me. Even though my father had added two years to his age when the ID picture was taken in 1977, he would have been fifty-one years old. Yet it shows a sad and grim man who could pass for seventy.

I couldn't reconcile his age with his appearance. I couldn't entirely believe what I was seeing. In the color photo he's nearly bald, his face is thin and deeply lined around the mouth, his ears are large and elongated, and the skin at the front of his throat hangs loose. What happened to him?

I heard a rustling noise coming from over by the trailer. Looking up, I saw Paul walking toward me along the dirt path. I slipped the driver's license into my wallet, closed the box, and stood up.

"Found somethin', eh?"

"Yeah," I said, "a few things."

I lifted the box and was about to carry it to my car, when Paul asked me if I was ready to do the sweat lodge. I told him I'd like to, but I was running late for some appointments in Ojai that afternoon.

"Hey, no problem. We'll still smoke the pipe and sing for your father's spirit."

"Thanks," I said. Later, I concluded Skyhorse was an all-right guy, whatever Matthiessen might have thought of him.

The five visitors—three men and two women—had already arrived for the ceremony. One, a light-skinned, neatly-dressed woman, could have been an attorney or real estate broker taking a day off from her usual grind. I felt bad about not staying, but I think Paul correctly guessed I wasn't up to it emotionally. Actually, I felt I was running away from an event that would have me sharing my discovery, my moment with my father, and I didn't want to do that.

Holding the box with both hands against my chest, I said good-bye and walked back to my rental car. Minutes later, as I drove out of the clearing and onto the highway, I lowered the windows and could hear the drumbeats over the sound of the car engine. Then the chanting began, loud, insistent, rolling at me in deep, rhythmic waves, finally growing softer, fainter, until all I could hear was the rush of wind and my own dribbly voice trying to sing the song.

San Diego

Oct. 12, 1989

I remember him standing naked in the bathtub, covering himself with his hands, sort of hunched over and trying to hide his privates. My mother had opened the bathroom door, and for some reason I was standing in the hallway outside. So I got a good glimpse of him as she walked in.

In my memory I see him with a slightly frightened, embarrassed expression, wet and shivering, vulnerable. She closed the door and I think I heard her laugh, or giggle. I was about eight years old, and in all the years I knew him, that was the only time I saw him naked, the only time I saw him helpless and without pretense.

I wish I had seen more of this kind of man. What is it that compels me to think of him so much, to want him back, to embrace a man who preferred a handshake and salute to a hug and kiss? I'm tired of looking, of reconstructing, of piecing together this episode or that adventure. The *names and addresses and phone numbers are fading, some people are dead or have disappeared. Will I find them here?*

I was in a third-floor hotel room in San Diego, about to go downstairs to meet 60 or so survivors of Oflag 64, a German prison camp for captured officers located near Schubin in the western part of Poland. For nearly a year I had been in touch by letter and phone with a number of these men, asking them all the same question: Did you know an Armando Arias? Only a few recognized the name. In late 1944, when my father was a prisoner, there were more than 1,500 American POWs in the camp. From all I knew, after the war he never kept in touch with any of them. So now, 45 years later, I was about to attend a reunion of Oflag 64 alumni, hoping a few of the seventy- and eighty-year-olds might remember the slender young lieutenant from Arizona.

I took the elevator down to the lobby, then followed the signs to the Hospitality Room, now filling up with the old warriors, their wives, and companions. Eyes squinted at my name sticker as I moved about, heading in the general direction of the bar. The itinerary listed cocktails and dinner, so I got my glass of cabernet and started to roam the room, nodding and introducing myself as an ex-POW's son. I'd mention my father's name and wait for the headshake or the apology for not remembering him. Around me I heard random talk about grandchildren, golf scores, cruises, medical problems, and the planned tour events for the next three days—the zoo, the harbor, Balboa Park, Old Town. Everyone was polite and gracious to me, but it was obvious this first-day gathering was catch-up time. War stories could wait.

I asked my host, the reunion's organizer, if he knew of an army dentist in the camp whose name I thought was Palmer. This was all I could recall of what my father had told me of his German prison camp experience—that he had escaped with a Jewish dentist from New York by the name of Palmer. Or so I remembered. My host, who said there was no dentist Palmer listed on the camp roster, offered to let me address the group at dinner. Maybe some of what I had to say would stir up a few useful recollections.

Earlier that day I had visited another retired octogenarian, a friend of twenty-five years who came closer than anyone to being my all-time writing mentor and model. Bill Johnson and his wife, Liz, a cookbook editor and agent, were then living in a condo complex only a few blocks away from the harborside hotel where I would meet the ex-POWs. When I had last seen him a year or two before, emphysema had forced him to use an oxygen tank, so I expected to see him worse this time.

As the author William Webber Johnson, Bill was not only a former *Time* and *Life* magazine war correspondent and at one time their top man in Mexico and Argentina, but he'd also published a half-dozen books about Latin America. I had attended his magazine-writing class at UCLA, and once we discovered we had similar mutual interests, a real friendship began. He was especially fascinated by the Terrazas side of my family and my grandmother's tales of Pancho Villa and how our family fit into the Mexican revolution.

Over the years Joan and I would visit Bill and Liz, and Bill would invariably treat us to stories of the "old days" in his career: sharing a desk with an intense young James Agee, introducing Ernest Hemingway to his future wife Mary in a London hotel, or meeting the elusive B. Traven on location in Mexico for the filming of his most famous novel, *The Treasure of the Sierra Madre*. Again, as with other older men who captivated me with their humor, knowledge, and storytelling ease, I found in Bill some of the pieces my father simply lacked. I also just liked being in his company. I respected him as a writer and was thrilled whenever he liked something I had written. It was always an enormous compliment because I knew he could be a tough judge.

After I had begun searching for my father, Bill repeatedly nudged me to keep hunting. As my project gathered steam, Bill repeatedly encouraged me to write a book about my family. "You have to write it," he would say, "and I want to read it."

Well, here I was at his doorstep again, still in a muddle, still with little more to show than a handful of letters, interview transcripts, and a box of my father's effects from Chorro Grande. I knew my visit would be brief, since Bill had a nap schedule to keep. I pressed the doorbell and Liz let me in. Bill rose from a sofa and greeted me with an avuncular arm and pat on the back. A tall, frail figure in his trademark blue shirt, chinos, and penny loafers, he shuffled back to the sofa and sat down next to the oxygen tank, where he reconnected himself to a plastic tube.

"I've got some pictures to show you," he said, pulling out some snapshots of his new kites. He'd recently taken up kite flying and informed me with a laugh that he was a "card-carrying member of the North American Association of Tethered Flight." He talked about the kids at the harbor park who had become his new fans. Then, changing the subject, he asked how my family project was coming along.

I told him about the delays. The magazine had me chasing after all kinds of stories during the past two years, stories that would consume me emotionally for weeks. I named a few, which he recognized because I always sent him copies: a family living in Haiti's worst slum, kids losing limbs in Nicaragua's war, a woman called the "Jane Goodall of three-toed sloths" living in a tree in the Amazon, a medical relief mission to Moscow, and even Jane Goodall herself.

As I spoke, I knew I was making excuses. But the delays were legitimate. The year before, I had to leave the magazine for six months so I could research and write a sea survival book about five Costa Ricans who drifted halfway across the Pacific in a leaky wooden boat. Bill liked the account but was still more interested in reading a book about my family. I said there was so much I still didn't know. As always, Bill and Liz said I had to keep at it.

After our good-bye abrazos at the front door, he removed the tiny plastic tubes from his nostrils and slowly nodded. No smile, just a single nod and a quietly anxious look in his eyes that seemed to say, "Hurry up; get to it. I don't have much time left."

He would die three years later, followed by Liz in 1994. I would regret that they would never be able to see anything I had written about my family. As some consolation, at least I had Bill's books and especially his letters to me. In one of the last, written not long after I had seen him when I was in San Diego for the ex-POW reunion, he writes:

. . . Enjoyed your last visit. Wish I could have taken you kite flying. I'm sure I can convert you. It is the ideal diversion for the contemplative man. Even better than fishing. Come back and we'll attend to all that.

How goes the book? Well, I hope, and not, as our neighbors in Mexico say, por los huevos . . .

I'm sure that as a writer *and* contemplative man, he knew that everything has its time, that my quest had a pace of its own, and that certain work pursues us no matter how many excuses we have.

That evening at the Oflag 64 dinner I stood up and addressed the gathering, all the while thinking that, like Bill, few of my listeners had much time left, either. Of course, I excluded myself, thinking stupidly that the clock ticked only for *them*—the balding, gray guys with oxygen tanks, walkers, wheelchairs, and hearing aids. As the youngest person in the room by decades, I also blithely assumed I was the healthiest, still jogging, playing tennis, or kayaking at every opportunity.

I described my father as a six-foot-tall, medium-build man with black, curly hair and a quiet manner. Then I passed around a 1945 snapshot of him and recited a few facts: he was from Nogales, Arizona; he arrived in France in July of 1944 as part of the replacement forces after the Normandy invasion took place; he was a second lieutenant and rifle platoon leader in the 137th Infantry Division; his military specialty was intelligence; he'd been captured three times by the Germans, the last time on October 9 while he was reconnoitering a river crossing south of Nancy; that's when he was sent to Oflag 64.

"You said *three* times?" one of my listeners asked.

"That's what's in his military record," I answered. "Guess he was unlucky."

"Or very lucky he lived," someone said.

I mentioned the New York dentist named Palmer that my father had told me about. I said the two had escaped when they were all being evacuated and marched westward to Germany only days before the arrival of Soviet troops from the east.

"You sure it was Palmer?" a stout man in the back of the room asked. "I believe there were a few Parkers in the camp, but I don't think they were dentists."

I explained that was correct. The list of camp prisoners shows at least one surviving Parker—Richard B.—with a current address, and I'd already been in touch with him. Unfortunately, he couldn't recall ever knowing an Armando Arias.

After I sat down, a Franciscan priest blessed the chicken, fish, and pasta that was being served, then said that just as men "bond in foxholes, they bond in prison." As he spoke, I was thinking that this bonding never really took with my father. I had yet to find an ex-army buddy he ever remained close to. From what I had discovered of the pattern, he would bond tightly with someone for a while, then drop the friendship, as he did with his Arizona pal Max Medema and others I had tracked down. Henry Ackerman of Hunt Valley, Maryland, for example, for a time felt quite close to my father.

Calling Ackerman. Maybe get lucky—
Ringing—Answers!
"Your dad and I we were together a lot—bunkmates at OCS—same class at Ft. Benning—wonderful person—knew him well—played cards—best of friends really—wondered what happened to him after the war—tried to find him—no luck—sorry to hear he's gone. A great guy. He was the handsome Spaniard!"

The next morning I finished several separate interviews with men who told me they knew or might have known my father. One was an arthritic ex-paratrooper who nervously tapped his aluminum cane on the floor the whole time we spoke. He said he could understand my father not ever saying much about his war experience. "A lot of us won't," he said. "There were things I saw, things that happened that I still won't tell."

Another former prisoner had no such reticence remembering the camp, especially his escape with my father and many others from the main bunch of evacuees leaving the camp. He recalls my father as "someone who never spoke much. But if he did, you listened. I don't know why, but he kept wanting to go south, off to Yugoslavia and the Balkans. We didn't."

Finally, I spoke to George Herr, who told me he had known my dad and remembered that there was a Dr. Julius Parker in this same group of escaped prisoners. "Initially, there were about 120 of us," Herr said. "I don't recall seeing your father. But I saw him later, when some of us were hiding in a barn and in the straw. He was elusive. They couldn't get out of him why he wanted to go through the Balkans. He just kept saying we should escape through the Balkans." Herr added that he believed Parker said his wife had originally come from Brooklyn but that he was practicing medicine in Tennessee. "He's probably the man you're looking for."

Back in my room, following another Herr suggestion, I made a call to Nebraska to a former POW who had worked for the camp's senior commanding officer and known my father. The phone rang and Manley Dotson's wife answered. I explained who I was and what I was after. "Oh, my," Hazel Dotson said, "he can't speak. He can't do that. He had a stroke. Sometimes he'll whisper a word or two, but that's about it."

I said I was sorry to bother her at such a time, but would she mind writing my father's name on a piece of paper and holding it up for him to read? Maybe he knew him. Mrs. Dotson agreed and asked me to wait on the line. Minutes later she returned. "He read the name," she said. "He seemed to get excited, trying to say something. But all he could do was whisper one word in my ear—spy!" I said I hoped he would get better and regain some or all of his speech. Maybe he might talk to me then.

I was thrilled. The notion that my father was into espionage would explain a lot about his secretive nature. But I'd have to wait to see if Manley Dotson would recover enough to talk to me either by phone or face to face. Unfortunately, after I spoke to Mrs. Dotson, I learned by letter that her husband had passed away. I was sorry for her and disappointed that he hadn't told me more. All I could do now was to keep trying to find someone on the Oflag 64 group's active membership roster who knew about the spying.

Then the army's military archives office sent me a bombshell—a registered package that soon had me doubting my father was a spy for the good guys. With the help of Senator Christopher Dodd, I had requested whatever was in my father's army file. I was told that part or all of it had been destroyed by a massive fire at the archives storage facility in St. Louis. So I hadn't expected much, certainly not fifty-two declassifed pages of an investigation I didn't know had taken place. On the cover page was the following explanation:

I N V E S T I G A T I O N

of

Irregularities in connection with 2d Lt Armando (n) Arias, Company "K", 137th Infantry, being Missing In Action 3-times and twice returning to duty.

The date on the second page is November 8, 1944, and the transcript of the investigation is addressed to the commanding general, Thirty-fifth Infantry Division. Conducted by Lieutenant Colonel Jack Tingle, the division's inspector general, the investigation begins with the following history of my father prior to joining the division in France. Apart from his birth date, which according to his birth certificate should be February 11, 1927, *not* 1922, the facts appear to be correct.

He joined the Army in October of 1940; went to Cook and Bakers School at Fort Bliss, Texas, in 1941; this same year joined an Eighth Cavalry mounted troop at Fort Bliss; attended mess sergeant school at Camp White, Oregon, in 1942; completed Infantry Officer

Candidate School at Ft. Benning, Georgia, in 1943; became a border agent in military intelligence at Fort Sam Houston, Texas, also in 1943; served as a drill instructor at Fort Benning in early 1944; and began overseas service in France in July of 1944.

The transcript's next section reports that he joined the thirty-fifth division's replacement pool July 17 and was assigned as a platoon leader to Company K of the 137th Infantry Regiment's Third Battalion. On July 31 he was reported missing in action near Torigni, south of the Normandy coast. On September 13 he returned to duty at Crenechamps, again assigned to a platoon, this time with I Company of the 137th. Three days later, on September 16, he was reported missing for the *second* time, at the Meurthe River near Nancy. On September 25 he returned to duty at Buissoncourt, back to K Company. Then on October 9, in the village of Fossieux, he was reported missing in action for the *third* time and subsequently did not return to his unit.

According to the investigation, what triggered suspicions by his commanders were three factors: the number of captures, his bypassing of the usual debriefing procedures before returning to frontline duty, and his failure to give satisfactory explanations and accounts of his absences. Before his first capture, for example, just as his company was about to go into battle, he left his platoon, heading by himself down a road toward the rear of the American front lines. When asked where he was going, he replied vaguely that he had to look for some more men. He never returned.

Major Budd Richmond, the battalion's executive officer, was one of the last persons to have seen my father before he went MIA.

The last I saw of this officer in question he was standing in the center of a crossroad of a sunken road and the main road into St. Jean. This was approximately around 1600. This officer was standing out there in the open with absolutely no covering and quite some distance from where his platoon was supposed to be, and I called to him and told him that if he did not take cover he would get hit.

Other soldiers, men in my father's platoon, testify that he then walked away toward the rear. That was the last they saw of him until nine days later when he rejoined his original unit, K Company, near Nancy.

The second time he went MIA, he was leading three men to look for possible shallow routes across the Muerthe River. The investigation reports that when they arrived at the near bank:

Lt Arias next ordered the 3 enlisted men of his patrol to stay where they were; informed them that he had orders from the battalion commander to cross the river; gave his billfold and field jacket to these enlisted men with the remark that, if he did not return, to turn them in. Lt Arias then swam across the river with great difficulty and much noise, being described as almost drowning in his crossing; reached the enemy side of the river and walked straight up the riverbank into the hands of German soldiers. This looked suspicious to the enlisted men of his patrol and after waiting some little time they withdrew and were fired upon by the Germans while so doing. The above events were in broad daylight and the enlisted men of his patrol on the near side of the river could clearly see German soldiers running around and fires burning on the opposite bank. Not a single shot was fired by the German soldiers in the capture of Lt Arias . . .

Answering the question of when his suspicions were first aroused, Lieutenant Colonel Albert Butler, my father's battalion commanding officer, testifies that this occurred after he heard eye-witness accounts of the second capture:

. . . he swam the river and had considerable trouble in doing so, floundering and going under the water a couple of times; he arrived at the far bank and his strength seemed completely spent. He staggered and seemed to flounder around trying to regain his strength. He finally did so and started walking north in the direction of the enemy toward the woods they were in, and as he neared that section of the woods he was seen to halt and to reach down and unhook his belt and then walk with his hands up in the air into the woods, and that was the last they saw of him. They pondered the next move as they didn't know whether to go after him and try to give him some help, or to move on.

Q: Did you hear the approximate time that Lt Arias was seen to enter the woods with his hands in the air?
A: Around 1730.
Q: Was it daylight?
A: Yes, sir.
Q: What time did you hear this?
A: Approximately 2400.
Q: When were your suspicions aroused?
A: The next afternoon we actually made the river crossing and on completion of the crossing I found a location right below the dam approximately 300-yards from where Lt Arias swam the river—the personnel could have crossed on foot by wading.

Staff Sergeant Glenn Hewson also testifies that he talked to one of the three men, a private who witnessed the river crossing and capture. The private told him "it looked damn suspicious to him."

Q: After Lt Arias returned to duty on 25 September 1944, did you ever hear him asked the question of how he escaped from the Germans?
A: I had heard a couple of men ask that question and he would give an answer that evaded giving an answer.

Another sergeant, Gerald Jones, was also asked what conversation he heard or had with my father about his second escape.

```
He was awfully close-mouthed. All I asked him was how
he managed to do it. I said, "Sometime I might need
to know myself." And he just laughed and said, "I
just got away." He didn't say how or anything.
```

And Staff Sergeant Robert Kaufman, who was the last noncom to see my father before he went MIA the first time, makes the following comment about seeing him again after his second capture and subsequent return to his original unit, K Company:

```
I had no conversation with him during these few days
with reference to his experiences as a German prison-
er of war or as to his escape on either of his two
occasions. However, one evening I was sitting with Lt
Mullens and Pvt Veillon, who was in his platoon that
first time. Well, when Lt Arias came in, Lt Mullens
said to him, "You remember Sgt. Kaufman," and I turned
around and before he could answer I said, "Sure, I
remember you. The last time I saw you, you were going
across the road to find a couple of your men and you
disappeared. What happened to you?" And he looked over
to Pvt Veillon and he said, "Veillon, what did happen
to me?" and Veillon said, "Yes, what did happen to
you?" And nothing  more was said.
```

As for the third time my father "took off" and went MIA, as one of his men remarked, there are only two testimonies in the investigation, that of Private Glen Kirk and Captain Hubert Stephens. Kirk states that on October 8 in the late afternoon he was in my father's platoon at the edge of the town of Fossieux.

Q: What was Lt Arias doing at that time?

A: He came down to get someone to knock out a machine gun nest.

Q: Could you see the machine gun nest he was going to attack?

A: No, sir.

Q: Did you know that there was a machine gun nest?

A: No, Sir.

Q: How far away was the enemy at that time?

A: There were some in the first house not over 50 or 75-feet away.

Q: At the time you last saw him, who was in command of the town?

A: The Germans were.

Q: Have you anything further to testify about this matter?

A: No, sir.

Captain Stephens adds that about that time . . .

a Polish prisoner of war told me that five or six German officers were in a house near the center of town sniping. I know this sniping was going on. About 1700 Lt Arias came to me and told me, "Captain, I ought to go after those men." I told him to stay with his platoon. Company "A" of the 134th was cleaning out the town. About 2230 that evening he came into my command post and handed me a pistol he had taken off a German PW and asked if I wanted it. And that is the last time I saw him. The next day the Germans counterattacked with approximately five tanks and overran the positions of Lt Arias' platoon.

My father never did give a clear and satisfactory accounting of his captures and escapes. Nevertheless, he did reveal some clarifying details to his commanders. Captain Lloyd Friedman gives this account of his conversation after the first escape:

```
He told me how he had been captured below St. Lo and
that he had been taken by the Germans through various
enclosures, etc.; how he had escaped from the Germans
while being taken on a railroad train supposedly into
Germany somewhere between Paris and the German border,
and he had jumped out of a boxcar and had escaped
alone and filtered back through the lines somehow
or other.
```

Captain Friedman's testimony also includes my father's account of his second escape.

```
He said he had been captured right after he crossed
the river and that he was taken to several towns in
that area, and he didn't know which ones they were.
He escaped while he was being held in a building and
the guards were not watching him very closely when he
went to the latrine. He made one statement which I
thought was odd and that was that he said one of the
guards that guarded him this time was the same guard
that guarded him the other time he escaped, and that
the guard recognized him.
```

Captain Gerald O'Connell, the CO of the Third Battalion's Headquarters Company, talked to my father after both escapes. O'Connell gives the version of the second escape he heard:

```
He told me he'd been a prisoner of war, and I said,
"How on earth did you escape this time?" And he said,
```

"one of the guards recognized me." He said it was a rainy night and the guards were not very alert and were standing around and he just walked off and worked his way to a Frenchman's home, where they kept him in a room until the American troops came into the sector where he was. And then he worked his own way back in through the lines. . . . The last remark I remember making to him is that, "You are either awful clever or have a lot of guts."

Q: After Lt Arias went MIA the second time on 16 September 1944 at the Meurthe River crossing, did you come into possession of any of his personal property?
A: Yes, sir, his personal billfold was delivered to me.
Q: Did you examine the contents thereof?
A: Yes, sir.
Q: What, if anything, did you find unusual therein?
A: I found a slip, a form paper from the IPW, or Intelligence Personnel, with Lt Arias' name on it, and it was the slip which designated the fact that he had come through there and been interrogated. This slip had this printed on it: "Destroy this slip after interrogation."
Q: This interrogation would have had to be after his first escape and before his second MIA?
A: Yes, sir.
Q: Do you have anything else to testify to in connection with this matter?
A: No, sir.

The investigation shows that after both escapes, my father reportedly said that he was helped by members of the Free French Forces and was once hidden by a French farming family just east of Paris. As I read this, I immediately thought of my family's "secret," something I had heard during one of my mother's screaming assaults on my father and instinctively knew not to mention to anyone. The secret concerned my father's alleged affair with the daughter of a French couple who hid him in a room or barn after one of his escapes. Later, after she gave birth to a baby girl, the daughter wrote him a letter with news of the birth, informing him that he was the father. The letter apparently arrived sometime in late 1945. By then my parents were already married and Bobby and I were legally adopted.

When my mother read the letter, she went berserk. Even though he had been unmarried during the war, she had already fallen hard for him. They had even talked about getting married when the war was over. My uncle believes the letter's news about another woman and the birth of his daughter put my mother into an emotional tailspin. It ended in a nervous breakdown, for which she was treated by her doctor as well as by a folk-healing curandera in East Los Angeles.

I was too young to remember any of this, but my mother eventually recovered. What I do recall from the years before the two wars were her swift and often violent outbursts against my father. But then these explosions could just as easily be followed by sweet shows of affection, complete with public kissing, hugging, and professions of love and eternal faithfulness.

In early 1995, I would also receive a letter with echoes of that time. The letter was sent by an Arizona World War II vet who was forwarding to me an article from the French magazine *Le Parisien*. There, under the headline ***Elle n'a jamais oublié l'aviateur de l'Arizona*** (She has never forgetten the pilot from Arizona), a studio photo of my father in cap and uniform appears next to a picture of 86-year-old Hélène Duru. Translated, the article from the August-September 1994 issue gives me a less sinister, more human view of my father than the one he offered his fellow soldiers.

> For Pierrette it is fifty years from the time of the liberation but the memory is still fresh of her American pilot hidden in May en Multien after his escape from a prison train, and also in the memory of her mother Hélène, today 86 years old.

"I was harvesting with my mother when my father arrived in the field with a conspiratorial look. 'I have hidden an American pilot and we need to give him something to eat,' he said to me.

"Imprisoned in 1940, my father had returned from Germany in 1943 and was responsible for watching the railway. That is where he found the pilot, a prisoner of the Germans. He had jumped from the train. We waited to feed this young man, whose name was Armand Arias, until nightfall. Then, to avoid detection, we crossed the wood for some kilometers to bring him something to eat. Mainly sweet potatoes, some biscuits and some cigarettes that my mother had sneaked from the back of a truck on the Hannibray Road."

Conversations were also difficult, because of the language problem. So Hélène, mother of Pierrette, did not hesitate to purchase an English dictionary. "What? Are you going to take English?" was the comment of the village baker to this strange acquisition, as he had accompanied her to Mieux. The baker later said to her, "Why didn't you tell me the truth? You must have needed help to feed him."

"But during this time everyone distrusted everyone," Hélène explained. She knew the danger of hiding and helping Allied pilots. Armando stayed two or three weeks and had left with some members of the liberation army.

"We had a warm relationship" Hélène said. "Two days earlier he had met up with a group of FFI with whom we were in contact. The same day that he was due to leave, the group had been taken and they had all been shot."

When the Americans passed through he kissed the mother and daughter and hitched a ride on a tank. "We never saw the good-looking Arizona pilot again. The only news that we had about him was from his brother Julio some months later. He told us that his brother had been taken prisoner again by the Germans.

Since receiving the letter and article, I have written to the family, but for whatever reason have not received a response. Perhaps this is as it should be, because I have all I really need from the facts presented in the article. And for all I know, my family's particular hush-hush secret about a youthful affair in France may have been a matter of confusion, invention, and intense jealousy on the part of my mother. As for the "pilot" error in the story, that's the part I most like. Why not pass himself off as the *Aviateur Armand*? As a dashing eighteen-year-old, surrounded by war, Nazis, and suspicion everywhere, why not a touch of style?

When my father failed to reappear for duty after his third MIA, the army suspended its investigation into his "irregularities" and the matter was never continued, not even after his repatriation and the end of the war. His actions were condoned because after both escapes, the record shows he reported only to the regimental commander for debriefing. In this way, he bypassed the normal debriefing procedures for returning MIA troops, who were usually sent to the rear for medical and psychological checks and for debriefing by an army intelligence officer.

After my father's sessions alone with the regimental commander, instead of being sent to the rear for more debriefing and perhaps some rest and recuperation, he was ordered immediately back to the front lines. From what the testimonies reveal, only the regimental commander knew what my father's mission was. And the only written proof of this unusual debriefing procedure was the slip of paper found in my father's billfold. He was supposed to destroy the form after receiving it, yet he kept it in the wallet he gave his men before crossing the river.

Perhaps this was his way of informing his immediate commanders that he was reporting to someone and that person was their regimental boss. He would only talk specifics with the commander. That's why, as one fellow officer said, "it was like pulling teeth to get something out of him. And what you got wasn't much at all." Of course, my father's reticent nature, his "clever secretiveness," as his brother Julio puts it, made it easier for him to keep silent about his missions.

I have spoken to researchers at the Military History Institute in Carlisle, Pennsylvania, and they patiently listened to me give an account of my father's captures and escapes. I said it seemed as if he had been gathering intelligence on the movement or treatment of POWs, or he might have been connecting with the French underground forces for some purpose. And all of this he would communicate to his commanding officer after returning to his unit.

Essentially, I was told that official, accurate confirmation of any such missions was virtually impossible. "Family stories are family stories," one librarian told me. "Who exactly was he working for? Was it intentional? Was it accidental and then developed from there? Spy? What does that mean? There are many, many kinds of spies."

After corresponding with military espionage specialists, I realized the librarian was right. The byzantine world of espionage allowed for a whole range of spies, from shadowy, rumored operatives who supply tips for a price, to the people who sell state secrets to foreign governments. Suffice it to say that everyone—especially combat veterans—I contacted on the matter of his repeated captures and escapes agreed that such missions were quite possible. However, what specifically he was up to is anyone's guess.

I once asked him how he escaped from the train. He said he jumped off. "No," I insisted, "how exactly did you get out?" Then, reluctantly—even though it was twenty years after the fact—he explained how he pried off a slightly loose board near the vent at the top of the boxcar. After he wriggled his body out through the hole, he waited until he saw a clear spot and tumbled out away from the tracks. "No broken bones," he said. "That was it."

What passed between him and the regimental commander is not on record, and both men are now deceased. I can only conclude that my father was gathering intelligence about enemy troop movements or prisoner shipment routes. But to what purpose for the army, I don't know. However, he was trained to do this kind of work. Unlike other such missions in which men were air-dropped behind enemy lines, my father had apparently volunteered to get himself captured. Then through stealth, luck, and moxie, he would escape, hide, and with the help of local anti-German militia, return to American lines. Then he would repeat the process.

L'ILE-DE-FRANCE LIBEREE
SEINE-ET-MARNE

Petites victoires et grandes trahisons

Heures de gloire, mais aussi heures de drames. Les héros de l'ombre ont souvent réussi à déjouer la surveillance allemande. Comme à May-en-Multien où, malgré la menace du peloton d'exécution, un aviateur américain a été caché par des villageois. Parfois, c'est la trahison qui l'emporte. Quatorze habitants de Chelles seront ainsi massacrés dans le bois de Boulogne après être tombés dans un piège.

Dossier : Nathalie Kovarcik Frédéric Choulet

PIERRETTE avait treize ans au moment de la Libération. Mais le souvenir de « son » aviateur américain, caché à May-en-Multien après son évasion d'un train de prisonniers, est précis dans sa mémoire, et dans celle de sa mère, Hélène, aujourd'hui âgée de quatre-vingt-six ans. « J'étais en train de glaner avec ma mère, quand mon père est arrivé dans le champ avec des airs de conspirateur. *J'ai caché un aviateur américain, il faut lui trouver à manger*, nous dit-il.

» Prisonnier en 1940, mon père était revenu d'Allemagne en 1943 et était affecté à la surveillance de la voie ferrée. C'est là qu'il a trouvé cet aviateur : prisonnier des Allemands, il venait de sauter du train. » Restait à nourrir ce jeune homme, du nom d'Armando Arias. « Ce que nous faisions la nuit. Pour éviter de tomber sur des importuns, nous traversions le bois, long de quelques kilomètres, pour lui apporter à manger. Surtout des patates. Et des biscuits et des cigarettes que ma mère avait subtilisés dans un camion qui s'était renversé sur la route d'Hannibray. » Les dialogues étaient assez difficiles, à cause des problèmes de langue. Alors, Hélène, la mère de Pierrette, n'a pas hésité à acheter un dictionnaire d'anglais. « Quoi, tu vas te mettre à l'anglais ? » s'est étonné le boulanger du village qui l'avait accompagnée à Meaux faire cette étrange acquisition. Boulanger qui lui dira plus tard : « Pourquoi ne nous as-tu pas dit la vérité, nous t'aurions aidée à le nourrir. » « Mais à cette époque, tout le monde se méfiait de tout le monde... » explique la vieille dame qui connaissait le danger de cacher et d'aider des aviateurs alliés ; Armando est resté deux ou trois semaines et reparti avec ses compatriote la Libération. « Il avait chaud, et nous avec. De jours auparavant, il dev rejoindre un groupe de F.F avec lequel nous étions contact. Le jour même où devait partir, le groupe a é pris, et ils ont tous été fusi lés. » Quand les Américain sont passés, il a embrassé mère et la fille et a sauté sur u tank. Elles n'ont jamais revu bel aviateur de l'Arizona. « Le seules nouvelles que nou avons eues de lui, c'est par so frère Julio, quelques mois plu tard. Il nous annonçait que so frère avait de nouveau été fai prisonnier par les Boches. »

Elle n'a jamais oublié l'aviateur de l'Arizona

Hélène Duru, qui, en plein été 1944, n'a pas hésité à acheter un dictionnaire d'anglais pour pouvoir parler avec un aviateur américain caché chez elle.

A 1994 article in *Le Parisien* about the woman in France and her memory of the American "aviator" Armando Arias she hid from the Nazis in 1944.

July 3, 1989

Dear Joe,

I asked Manley if he knew
and he said he
remembered him. He seems to
know something else about him
that he wanted to tell me but
he can't get it out of course.

He is beginning to say a little
more all the time so some day
he will be able to tell us It
is very slow though

I asked him questions about
what he may have done in the
camp as he says no & yes but
I didn't hit on the right thing
so will just have to wait.

Best Regards
Hazel Dotson

Letter from the wife of a former American World War II POW who knew my dad in Oflag 64. Manley Dotson knew of his spy missions but could not elaborate because he'd had a stroke.

Map showing location of World War II German POW camp

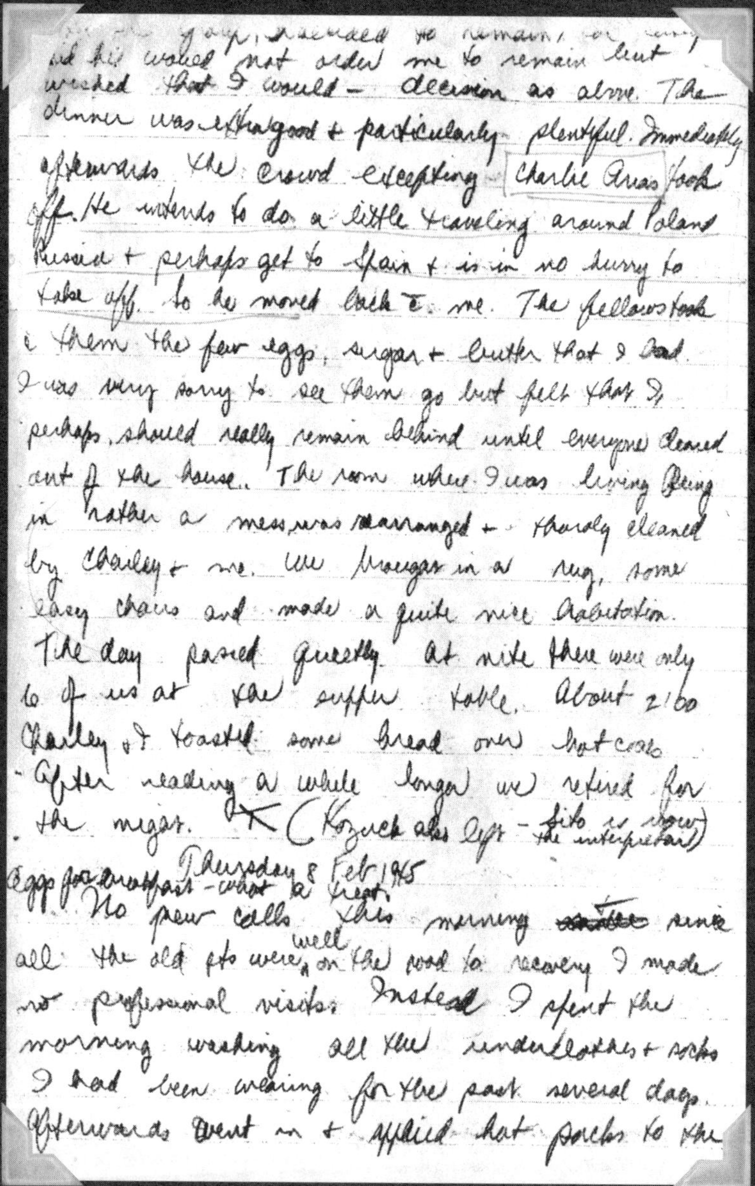

... gap, I decided to remain, or rather
as he would not order me to remain but
wished that I would — decision as above. The
dinner was extra good & particularly plentiful. Immediately
afterwards the crowd excepting Charlie Arias took
off. He intends to do a little traveling around Poland
Russia & perhaps get to Spain & is in no hurry to
take off. So he moved back c̄ me. The fellows took
c̄ them the few eggs, sugar & butter that I had.
I was very sorry to see them go but felt that I
perhaps should really remain behind until everyone cleared
out of the house. The room where I was living being
in rather a mess, was rearranged & thoroly cleaned
by Charley & me. We brought in a rug, some
easy chairs and made a quite nice habitation.
The day passed quietly. At nite there were only
6 of us at the supper table. About 2:00
Charley & I toasted some bread over hot coals
After reading a while longer we retired for
the night. X (Kozuch also left — Fito is now the interpreter)

Thursday 8 Feb 1945
Eggs for breakfast — what a treat.
No new calls this morning ~~[illegible]~~ since
all the old pts were well on the road to recovery I made
no professional visits. Instead I spent the
morning washing all the underclothes & socks
I had been wearing for the past several days.
Afterwards went in & applied hot packs to the

Dr. Parker's journal entry, from early 1945

Pound Ridge

12-1-89

I feel like a snoop, digging up all this stuff on a man who retreated from all exposure. I'm really no better than the Army inquisitor who tried to find out why he was captured three times. Well, right or wrong, I've started my snooping. Motives? To get closer to him? To understand him? Lesson(s) to learn? Find meaning in what happened? Yes, and peace of mind.

12-15-89

Reading more Primo Levi, his account of last days in Auschwitz. He mentions dates like Jan. 27, 1945, and all I can think about is what my dad must have been doing that day a few hundred miles to the north.

2-2-90

Finished Dr. Parker interview today in Pound Ridge. Snow outside, lakeside view, tranquil. Served sandwiches. Parker seemed so sane, so professional.

He called Daddy Charley. Only knew him as Charley, never Armando. Said he was "happy-go-lucky—on an adventure."

Parker wrote in notebook every night about their escape from the march out of the camp and across Poland. Journal was for his wife.

Said he was seven years older than Daddy. Was surprised "Charley" was so young. Seemed older.

"Maybe Charley was too controlled, and that's what did him in. Later, that is."

Was sad to know Daddy's world came apart after Korea.

Dr. Parker met me at the door of his "weekend" home in Pound Ridge, New York, not far from my home in Stamford, Connecticut. It was the first time we spoke face to face, and I think we were both pleased we could finally visit the past in a comfortable setting without the distractions of our workaday worlds. He was away from the concerns of patients and colleagues, and I was free from the requests of editors and fact-checkers.

A cordial, compact man, Dr. Parker led me into the dining room, where I sat at a long sunlit table with a postcard view of a lake bordered by snow and gray, leafless trees. He had offered me a snack and now said, "Make yourself at home. I'll get the sandwiches and coffee."

It had taken me months to find him. Whenever I had free time between assignments, I'd go to the midtown New York Public Library and work through telephone directories, medical association lists, and other sources, jotting down numbers and names of doctors, clinics, hospitals, nursing homes, and medical schools. George Herr, the former POW I had met in San Diego, told me he thought Parker lived in Tennessee, so I began there and worked my way east on the map. Finally, as I was calling a number on one of my lists, ready to line-out the name—this time calling the Bronxville number of a **Parker, Julius G., MD, gastroenterology—** a female voice answered and confirmed at least one fact. I said I was looking for a particular Dr. Parker who may have worked in Tennessee and would be about seventy years old. There was a pause, then the voice said, "Yeah, he's up around there, but I don't know about Tennessee."

"May I talk to him?"

"He's busy with patients. I'll give him the message."

"Thanks. Oh, the doctor I'm looking for was once a prisoner of war in Poland."

"Got it."

Moments later, when the phone rang and a male voice said, "This is Dr. Parker," I knew I had hit the target. Pay dirt.

That was weeks ago and now here I was, about to share sandwiches and drink coffee with the man who had traveled through wartime Poland and Russia with my father. Dr. Parker returned from the kitchen with our snack. He wanted to know about my work at the magazine, so at first I did most of the talking. I kept thinking our time would run out and I would lose my chance to hear about "Charley." Dr. Parker's alert, inquisitive eyes kept me going, and for a while I obliged.

After we had finished the tuna salad sandwiches, he rose from the table, went into another room, and moments later emerged with some papers and a notebook. "I kept a journal," he said. "I'll read you the section where I'm with your father. But remember, he called himself Charley."

"Why the alias?" I asked.

Dr. Parker shrugged. "A nickname?"

I said I'd never heard him called that, but then his brothers had nicknames for him that I'd also never heard, names like Rata and Hank.

"Well, here goes," he said, lowering his gaze to a bookmarked page in the notebook.

January 21, 1945.
We started off in a column. Within 30 minutes no semblance of order remained. Some men began dropping back. Others speeded up, so that the different platoons were hopelessly intermingled. The guards were careless and seemed nervous. On leaving for the gate we were again counted and Oberst Schneider was there to see the departure. Get-up of various men: sleds, poles, pieces of tin to slide over the frozen surface of the road, mattress covers, wooden suitcases, slings of various sorts, Red Cross boxes tied with string. . .

On that morning of January 21, 1945, Dr. Parker and almost 1,500 other POWs trudged out of Oflag 64. They left behind 86 men who were considered too sick or weak to make the 345-mile trek westward to a new camp in Germany. Russian troops were advancing quickly from the east, liberating towns and cities from German control, and a mood of expectation, apprehension, and fear had spread among prisoners and guards alike.

Temperatures during the first day's 13-mile march from Schubin to Exin were below freezing, food was scarce, and everyone shouldered the possessions they had accumulated during their months or years of captivity. The prisoners also had to share the frozen road with bedraggled crowds of civilian refugees, some pulling wagons, carts, and sleds piled with belongings, pushing wheelbarrows and carrying or dragging more bundles. Dr. Parker, who like his eventual companion "Charley" had been a prisoner for only four months, had not yet accumulated many goods.

Unburdened by such loads, he carried mostly scrounged food and a small stash of medical supplies.

At Exin, the prisoners were supposed to board a train to transport them to Germany, but no arrangements had been made. They would stay the night in cow barns or in whatever shelters they could find in the icy, barren countryside.

It seemed we would sleep on the ground. This was a low point. After a few minutes, I ate a can of strawberry jam and one cracker. It was bitter cold. After an hour, we were told to go into a barn. A great struggle ensued as three men attempted to get thru the door at one time. The cattle were there in full force. A beautiful cow smell pervaded the barn. George and I secured a small place to sit. No order was present.

Later that night Dr. Parker and three others found a way up to the second-floor hayloft and immediately dug a six-foot hole in the huge mound of straw so that they could hide from the guards. The plan was to stay hidden for about twelve hours until it was probably safe to come out. Before long, many of the other men had the same idea—to hide and then escape eastward toward Russia. In this way, by hiding or slipping away from fearful and inattentive guards, about four hundred American officers succeeded in breaking free. Over the next month or so, most of them would find their way south to the Black Sea and the port of Odessa. From there, Allied ships would take them to Cairo, Naples, England, and on to the United States.

Dr. Parker would not actually link up with my father as a traveling buddy until February 2. They were still hiding out in barns, sheds, estates, or abandoned houses, waiting for the Russians to appear, resting, waiting for news, and staving off hunger with watery soups and pieces of stale bread.

We were to leave immediately and proceed to a farm about two miles away. Charley had been there earlier today in a successful quest for bread. It was 1730 when we left. The warmer weather was continuing, with the result that most of the ice had melted and much of the ground was a quagmire.

That night the small group of American officers reached a walled estate, once the home of a baron and still impressive in its size and furnishings. They were offered lodging and meals at the nearby home of a town superintendent, and for the first time in months they ate fully and well. Supper consisted of bread with "delicious butter, milk, cold roasted pork, cakes, and cookies similar to doughnuts." Their hosts were the Polish "superintendent," estate servants, and other local citizens, some of whom spoke German. Dr. Parker, who had grown up with a good knowledge of Yiddish and some basic German, could take part in the dinner conversation, while Charley and the other Americans had to rely on a Polish interpreter who had joined the group.

Saturday, February 3, 1945.
Arising about 0800 I felt well rested and more at peace with the world in some several days. Today makes two weeks since we had received orders to move out of Schubin. Breakfast was hot milk and bread with goose grease spread over it. After breakfast several of us went over to the large house and began rummaging. It is a beautiful, three-floor house with a large basement. Several rooms have oil paintings. A very lovely piano is in the music room. Children's toys are much in prominence. Furniture that must be very costly is strewn about. Everything

is in the wildest confusion. Straw in great amounts is present in several rooms. Beautiful rare wallpaper, valuable and extensive library containing much Hitler lore. These people were evidently ardent Nazis. The Russians spent some little time here. Riding crop, top hat, personal stationery, real china dishes and all sorts of little things one would expect to find in such a house. It was to be an endless source of amusement to rummage thru the house.

The Poles in the area of the estate were especially generous with their gifts of food and attention to the Americans, especially to Dr. Parker. This was due to his freely offered services as a doctor. Daily he would set out through the village, sometimes accompanied by Charley, on his rounds among the sick and injured, lancing boils, applying hot packs, dispensing pills, tending to fevers, chills, diarrhea, and other common ailments. His "little country practice" was growing. He was also seeing to problems among some of his fellow G.I.s who had escaped from the main body of POWs headed west. Some of these men were still in Exin or in the Schubin camp. Others were passing through or staying at the estate. One particular colonel had a badly infected foot that required that frequent hot packs be applied to it.

Charley, meanwhile, would forage for food, scout around the countryside for information about train runs and troop movements, wash clothes, and clean and arrange the rooms in the guest house where they slept and lived. Confirming what others reported later, Dr. Parker heard Charley say he planned to leave and go off on his own: "He intends to do a little traveling around Poland, Russia, and perhaps get to Spain and is in no hurry to take off."

My father must have relished this chance to be useful in a place and time where instinct and common-sense resourcefulness were the keys to day-to-day survival. Russian troops and artillery and supply trucks were beginning to pass through in pursuit of the retreating Germans, locals were looting unguarded shops, homes and farms, and small-arms fire could be heard in sporadic bursts. Danger, risk, surprise—these were the real-life constants in a new kind of classroom for the eighteen-year-old high school dropout. To confront this world, he said he was best off going it alone, not with a large group.

In this regard, he and Dr. Parker appeared to be on the same track. Both sensed, for different reasons, that salvation most likely would come by traveling alone. Dr. Parker had relatives in Warsaw and other parts of eastern Poland, and though he didn't believe they had survived "the general mass murder" by the Nazis and by cooperative anti-Semitic Poles, he thought he might check for himself. At this very time, such death camps in Poland as Maidanek and Auschwitz were being liberated and the accounts of atrocities were quickly spreading everywhere, mostly by word of mouth and by radio.

For Charley, the urge to strike out on his own probably stemmed from the "happy-go-lucky" spirit of adventure that Dr. Parker noticed in him. Even though my father said he wanted to head south to the Balkans, an area of intense allied intelligence and partisan activity, it seems doubtful that he had any kind of specific mission. Manley Dotson, who worked for Colonel Thomas Drake, the senior American officer in Oflag 64, might have known. Through his wife, he told me my father was a spy, but unfortunately because of his stroke, Dotson was unable to tell me what kind of spy. In Oflag 64, there were various kinds of secret espionage and spylike activities. Certain men sent messages in code written in the text of personal letters home. After German censors read them, the letters would then enter the postal stream, arriving in the United States and routed first to military decoders, then to the addressee. The coded messages requested everything from disassembled radios sent piecemeal to the camp in sealed Red Cross food cans to actual weapons sent in parts by other means. There were also men detailed to slip out of the camp to scavenge for needed items such as rope and electrical wire, and of course gather information about the surrounding terrain. My father may have participated in some of these tasks, but more likely his label as a spy stemmed from Dotson's and perhaps Col. Drake's knowledge that Lieutenant Arias had gathered intelligence behind enemy lines in France.

Once while they were waiting to move eastward, Dr. Parker and Charley briefly transcended their situation with an exquisite gastronomic interlude. For a moment the war and their concerns would retreat.

Charley and I decided to take a short walk around the estate. It is even larger than we had anticipated. The nicest spot seen was inaccessible—a small isle in the center of the lake on the grounds. The isle is covered with weeping willows. Heaven on earth must exist here in summer time. It required nearly an hour for a leisurely trip around the place. On the way back our path led us by the large manor house. Suddenly, as if led by our guardian angel, I spied two jars on the sill of a small window in the basement. Upon investigation we discovered they were two, half-gallon jars of cherries, one red and one white. With no hesitation we hastily removed the jars and took them with us to our room. After a brief taste—and were they ever delicious—we returned to the manor house, attempting to find the room where we imagined all sorts of jams, cherries and other preserves to be. We found the room but it contained nothing but some seedy tomato juice. Thus our loot was only the cherries. But this is just what we needed to make our meals complete, a good dessert. Yes, we were quite elated over this. After supper, we had white and red cherries and they were ever so delicious. Now we are eating better than at any time since I came to Europe.

Finally, on February 12, they left the estate area and walked the dozen or so miles to Exin. From there, over the next several days, they hopped rides on trains, once on an open flat car crowded with civilians. It was on this flat car that an infant was smothered and killed during the rainy, chilly night. In the morning the mother wept and no one would console her.

When this train stopped after an hour of waiting, part of the group—about eight men and women—began to walk the ten miles or so to the next town. The march was led by Charley, and periodic rest breaks were called out by Dr. Parker. At the town they were given rooms and food by locals, and the Americans—joined by a Russian officer—spent part of the evening eating, drinking a potent home-brew, singing, and dancing. About this time a Pole named Alex became interpreter for the two G.I.s.

On February 17, the Americans, Alex, and a Russian hitched a ride on a truck for another twenty miles. They were let off at a junction where they met a "very happy crowd" of Russian elite guard troops. All had been at the front and were returning on leave to Russia. They "informally adopted" Charley and Dr. Parker, who would now travel under their auspices. Being elite guard troops, they had no trouble securing rides on passing trucks. In the town where they first stayed with the Russians, Dr. Parker treated a local woman who was sick with the flu, and afterward the ten or so guests were given food and drinks.

The next day they hitched more rides, the Russians singing and even teaching Charley one of their songs. After spending another night as guests of local civilians, on Sunday, February 18 the group reached the city of Kutno, where Alex said he wanted to go look for his wife in a nearby town. The Americans decided to stay a few days in Kutno, so they parted company with the Russians and were soon offered a place to stay at the home of an acquaintance of Alex.

In fact, two people argued about where we should go. The winning man had two girls along, one a plump, not very attractive, fairly well dressed girl, about 22, and the other a 13 or 14-year-

old, very attractive, moderately shy girl. After a short walk we arrived at their villa, a very nice house surrounded by a high fence. The family's name was Sienkiewicz. Their house during the German occupation was occupied by the brother of the German agent who ran the eastern part of Poland. His name was Geisler. He had evacuated the house in such a hurry when the Russians advanced that he had even forgotten his dog. The house had very good furniture and as yet there were no lights and all water had to be hand pumped.

Mr. and Mrs. Sienkiewicz provided the Americans with a filling meal of meat, potatoes, cabbage, and wine. Another daughter, the middle one, and a brother-in-law of the family patriarch also joined them. The conversation was mostly in German, and Dr. Parker learned that the brother-in-law, who had hidden in a barn during the occupation years, was head of the local militia and charged with "farming out" captive resident Germans for work in Kutno. The Americans also learned that their refined hosts were related to one of Poland's greatest writers, Henryk Sienkiewicz, a 1905 literature Nobelist and author of the historical novel *Quo Vadis?*, his best known work and, coincidentally, my mother's favorite.

Before playing a card game with the girls after dinner, my father listened with rapt attention to the translated talk of politics, war, history, and Polish culture. Given his limited education, he must have felt unprepared and unable to participate. As I listened to Dr. Parker read aloud from his journal, I remembered the handwriting, spelling, and vocabulary lessons my mother would give him. I also thought of the mediocre grades on the transcripts I found in the Chorro Grande box of his effects. Until then I believed he'd been a brilliant student, especially in math. Yet he received many Cs, Bs, and incompletes in finishing high school through tests and correspondence courses. He was not much better in completing two years of college while in the army.

But what he lacked in formal preparation, he tried to make up with his stiffly formal speech and quiet, dignified demeanor. My father may not have joined the bookish, refined conversation at the table, but he was always up for exploring real-life places around him. In this he found a kindred spirit in Dr. Parker, the two frequently going off to check conditions and meet people in surrounding areas. So when the two youngest daughters suggested they walk around Kutno, the Americans enthusiastically agreed. And when they heard about a nearby atrocity site in Radogoszcz, Charley and Dr. Parker immediately decided to go and see this for themselves. The next morning the two younger sisters took the Americans to Radogoszcz by streetcar.

Saw burned bodies, femurs, skulls, scorched flesh. Fifteen hundred to two thousand people had perished thus by fire. The building there had been saturated with gasoline and set afire. Anyone jumping from the building was shot. It was a very horrible site. Many people were there looking at this. Suddenly we heard an anguished cry and saw this woman weeping wildly. She couldn't stand the sight of it all.

Curious about what they would see, the Americans and the two younger Sienkiewicz sisters in the afternoon boarded a crowded passenger train for the short trip to Lodz. Until now they had traveled almost always in boxcars, so even though their cubicle was crammed with families, the accommodation was a homey and welcome change. They stayed the night in the home of a friend, and the next morning they met a Mr. Weinberg. He had somehow survived the ghetto in Lodz where, they were told, out of an estimated 250,000 Jews, only 900 remained. Dr. Masur, a local physician who had also survived, as well as another man named Friedman, who owned an electric company, explained that the

Jews had been brought from all parts of Europe. Friedman said he hoped to write a book about what happened to the Lodz Jews.

Years of torture, cruelty and sadism were related to us. Dr. Mazur had been in the ghetto the entire time. Finally, when only one thousand or so remained, they were put in a concentration camp near Lodz. Dr. Mazur hid in the cellar of a building for six days prior to the Russians' arrival and was actually saved from being killed by the Germans. He was very enthusiastic about the Russians. Later, Mr. Friedman told us that at least two to three million Jews had been killed throughout Europe. He then described Maidanek where one million Poles and Jews had been gassed and cremated. Also talked with a Polish Jew who had been at Oswiecim, or Auschwitz, where he had been forced to lead people to the gas chamber and then remove the bodies to the crematory. Told us stories of seeing children thrown against the walls, and a bet between two Gestapo agents. They called a young Jew in and had him sit with hands together under his chin, everything symmetrical. Then one agent took an axe and won the bet by successfully splitting this man in half.

Dr. Parker paused, probably as shocked as he was when he and my father first heard this account forty-five years ago. Then he continued reciting what the Polish Jew finished describing—the "three warehouses full of shoes, hair, gold, bone, everything systematically utilized. Very thorough."

Dr. Parker stopped reading and said his journal ended at this point, because from then on, after leaving their hospitable new friends in Kutno, they moved eastward quickly. He never managed to find his relatives in Warsaw, and his young companion never went "knocking about the Balkans and Spain." What happened is that they fell in with a group of Russian air force officers, one of whom happened to be Jewish and spoke Yiddish. Soon the two Americans crossed into the Soviet Union and eventually were flown south to Odessa, courtesy of the Soviet air force. There they spent two "miserable, rainy weeks" waiting for a ship to take them home.

When I asked Dr. Parker for anything else he might tell me about my father during such an impressionable period for an eighteen-year-old, he answered that the journey had been so long ago that much of what he read to me struck him as something he had experienced in another life. "It was difficult to see and hear those things," he said, "so it's natural to want to suppress them. Your dad may have felt the same way." I thought of the little Dachau pamphlet I found in the box of his things and the faded *Time* magazine clipping about Auschwitz. I could see the connection but I was sorry he never shared or could never bring himself to share any of his memories with me, harsh as they were.

Then, as I was leaving, Dr. Parker seemed to take in my relatively short height and asked me how tall my father was. I told him about six feet, though I reminded him I was a stepson and therefore not much like him physically. Then from his squint and the tilt of his head, I realized that that wasn't why he had asked the question. Apparently, he was matching my answer with his image of Charley. He wanted to make sure Charley and Armando were the same.

A year later, Dr. Parker sent me a small brownish photograph he had found packed away in a box of old pictures. It shows him and Charley in winter uniforms, standing with Mr. Friedman between them, arm-in-arm and all wearing gloves. Dr. Parker wrote that he believed the picture, taken against a blank wall, was snapped in Lublin, where Friedman had accompanied them. At a glance, I recognized Daddy's familiar stance, his left foot forward and turned outward. Of the three men, he's the only one not wearing a cap or hat. His curly black hair is neatly combed back, and the serious, wrinkle-free face has yet to grow a mustache.

El Paso

My grandmother's old dairy was now a mini shopping center. My bedroom was a small shoe store, the kitchen a taco takeout place, and Mama's bedroom a barber shop. The thick adobe walls were plastered over and painted, and the little picket fence in front was gone, replaced by asphalt pavement with white diagonal lines marking a row of parking spaces. Around the back, the chicken coop, the goat pen, the cement water tank, the outhouse, and the cowsheds—all were gone. And the big barn this side of the irrigation canal was being used as a warehouse.

I poked my head into the shoe store, hoping I'd see something familiar from my childhood, some decoration, some light fixture or piece of furniture. I scanned the room for anything that might bring me closer to those delicious afternoons when I would nap, falling asleep to a warm radio voice singing the *Ave Maria*. Past the display tables and stacks of shoeboxes, I imagined my bed against the wall, and over by the window, the metal washstand and its green enameled basin.

Then I noticed a bald man seated in a corner. He looked up from a small TV set. "¿Sí?"

"Uh—nada," I said, gesturing with my hand that I wanted nothing. Then I backed out of the doorway, got back into my rented car and drove toward the center of town. I cruised by my old grammar school, Ascarate, then visited Evergreen Cemetery, where

Mama's father, husband, and two of her sisters are buried. Next I drove down along the border over to the few remaining structures of what had been the Fort Bliss quarters of the mounted cavalry. I had come to El Paso for one day only in order to interview a man who had shared the same prison camp room in Korea with my father. Since I had about an hour's time until the interview, I thought I'd at least look at where my father had started his military career.

I turned off the road onto a gravel parking lot belonging to a Mexican restaurant. I left the car and walked over to a squarish two-story concrete building that looked like a former barracks but was now used for offices. I went around the side and looked around back, expecting to find some remnant of stables or an old corral. But I found nothing that hinted at the cavalry's former presence. As with my visit to the old family dairy, I could see no reminders of a particular time long since past.

Yet it was here my father would have learned to ride and care for horses. Sometime in the fall of 1940, as a fourteen-year-old private reporting for duty, for the first time he would have worn the First Cavalry shoulder patch—the black profile of a horse's head above a black diagonal stripe, all on a golden yellow background. He would not meet my mother for another three or four years, but it would be in El Paso where he would court the lively, pretty Emma Estrada, mother of two small boys and about to be divorced. If I were to understand him, I would have to define my young mother.

I have a photo album of her growing-up years from 1920, the year of her birth, to 1937, the year she left El Paso for Los Angeles. The album contains snapshots of her as a baby, of her as a toddler with Mama, of her as a seven-year-old with her younger brother Chalo—my Uncle Tuy—and her as a teenager with Mama, with her girlfriends, with students at a vocational school in Fabens, Texas, and with cousins in Chihuahua. In many of the photos her expression is glum or passive; the smiles and half-smiles look forced, camera-ready. She poses next to a black thirties-style sedan, vamps on a dune in White Sands, wears the props of Mexican serape and sombrero in Juárez, or wraps an arm around the waist of a girlfriend in front of a garden in 1935. Both girls wear shin-length dresses, and a spit curl decorates the left side of my mother's forehead. Every picture is identified with names, dates, and places, all in my mother's neat and graceful handwriting.

I have only one other personal relic of her early El Paso days. It's a cooking notebook for Miss Leda Blazek's home economics class at Ysleta High School in the year 1933. The pages are filled with recipes and nutritional advice on meats, vegetables, grains, fruits, vitamins, and minerals. There's also a section of notes under the title "The Modern Handbook for Young Girls." When I read her words today, I can easily see her fourteen-year-old mind accepting it all as gospel truth.

We think it right to control other feelings—anger, fear, for instance. Why not then, the impulse to fondle—that is, until such time we know it is due to true love and is the right time to let it have its way? We want to keep tokens of affection for the really suitable occasion, true love and marriage, just as we keep our party dress for the right occasion and not wearing it to school or work. Otherwise these tokens—and a kiss is one—are going to fall short of expressing love for those of us who have given them away for less. If you treat your favors as valuable, they will be prized as jewels, if you treat them as 5 and 10 cent store baubles, they will be accepted so.

The part on dating and love ends with the following counsel:

Finally, if, still in your "teens," you find or fancy yourself truly in love, perhaps hopelessly so, or with marriage possible only in the distant future—yet you can think of nothing and nobody else—do not let it get the better of you. It may be only an infatuation. It may be, after all, the most real experience you have ever had, the most wonderful and hardest to bear. Turn to some creative work and throw yourself into that, heart and soul.

As to jealousy, never show any, and cure yourself as fast as you can of feeling any. It shows you feel yourself neglected and inferior, a feeling no girl of any spirit need ever have.

Unfortunately, in 1937, three and a half years after she wrote these words, my mother ran off to Los Angeles and married for reasons other than love. Maybe this was because she had been raised without a father, or because her mother, austere and overly practical, sent her away to a boarding school in Las Cruces. Whatever the causes, it's clear Mommy did not have a cheerful, loving childhood. As Tuy explains in a letter to me:

Emma was bored, restless and didn't care for El Paso at all. I remember when she left because I went with her to the place where the rides left from. In those days you could travel to L.A. by train, bus, or private cars that were advertised for passengers to help owners defray the costs. Emma went in one of these cars. I took her to assure myself that the people involved were trustworthy, etc. Luckily, the car owners happened to be a married couple with one child.

My mother knew people in L.A. One such person was Adelita Loya, who happened to be Frank's aunt—they lived in Lincoln Heights and knew us quite well, since we had stayed at their house several times while we vacationed in California. Adelita sort of took care of Frank and his three brothers. At any rate, this is where Emma went to and that's where she met Frank.

Frank had an eye on her right away, but Emma was not interested in marriage; however, after a certain length of time of looking for work (which was very difficult to find in those days), she agreed to marry Frank. My mother was not in favor of the marriage, since she knew that Frank didn't have a "glowing background." But she couldn't prevent it and Emma married Frank in 1937. It was a church wedding with all the trimmings but without true love. Instead of having to return to El Paso, which she detested, she decided marrying Frank was more convenient. She stayed married to Frank until some time in 1944 or 1945. I remember this because I was still in Germany and she wrote to me in October with the news that she planned to marry Armando later that year.

They had met, maybe for the first time, at a party in El Paso when my mother was visiting from Los Angeles. She had driven her own car and was about to return to Los Angeles when the uniformed army lieutenant, fresh from the war, volunteered to help her drive back. Mama insisted that her fifteen-year-old daughter, Helen, accompany them as a kind of chaperone.

Anyway, it was agreed and they drove back to L.A. It must have been during this time that Armando proposed, and Emma really cared and loved the guy. So she agreed and they were married sometime after they arrived at the house where she and her sons lived.

My mother had bought the house. In fact, since her marriage to Frank, she showed a natural bent for working, saving, and dealing with bankers, lawyers, and real estate brokers. Her series of jobs—cocktail waitressing, riveting bombers during the war, color-tinting photographs, even doing stints as a Hollywood film extra—allowed her to save enough money for a down payment on the little two-bedroom place on Knox Avenue that my uncle refers to in his letter.

The Knox house in Lincoln Heights is also the first memory I have of a home, though most of my third and fourth years were spent with baby-sitters while my mother was working. Luckily, these women were tremendously caring and affectionate. But I have no memory then of Frank, who I later learned was away in the navy. Bobby, however, does remember the uniformed Seabee who visited him on leave. Frank had paid for Bobby's first year at Black Fox Military Academy, and over the years Bobby would secretly savor that generosity, plus a few things Frank had taught him, like how to wriggle his ears or roll his corn in butter. After Daddy came into the picture with his array of suspicions and punishments, Bobby would sometimes ache for the kind of playful, understanding touch he remembered from his moments with Frank. As my brother tells me now:

> *We were always coming up with little schemes for making money, and I wanted to have a car race. I was all excited. So I went to the butcher store and got some big butcher paper, and I drew my sign announcing a grand race was going to take place in our back yard on Coolidge Avenue. I made little roads and all. I didn't know what I was doing, but I must have been about nine. All I remem-*

ber was that he belittled everything I said about it, about the car race. And I was real confused. He tore down my sign and punished me for something. I didn't think I did anything. I didn't damage anything. But he lectured me that I couldn't do that. The next day I didn't feel like going to school because I was embarrassed. So the whole day I just—I walked to school but I didn't go to school. I stayed up on a hill and I just looked at the cars all day long, watching how people shifted and stopped and everything, and when school was over I walked home. I don't think he ever knew. I guess I was always competing with him. There was an implied threat there with Mommy. I don't know.

"Did she ever defend you?"

I guess she did. She must have. I remember a couple of times when I must have been really bad. I remember telling him, when he would spank me, "You're not my father, you're not my father!" He seemed closer to you than he did to me, but then I was older. You were only three or four. I don't know what it was about me, but he had very little confidence in my ability to ever amount to anything. I think part of what I've been striving to accomplish is to somehow prove him wrong.

On this occasion when I interviewed my brother about Daddy and our family, I felt Bobby wasn't expressing any bitterness or regret about the past, only a kind of ongoing befuddlement by our father's actions. So stern with us on the one hand, yet on the other hand so concerned in the practical matter of surviving the dangers around us. For him, deceit and treachery, greed, and selfishness, were as basic to human nature as thirst and hunger. Just as he advised me not to enlist in the army during the Vietnam War, he reminded Bobby of a few golden rules just before my brother went off to army boot camp.

He told me to always carry more than enough ammunition. He said, "Always depend on yourself. Take care of number one. You can count on one person only and that's yourself. You never know what the other person's going to do. They'll chicken out on you, or they'll go away.

That was the Daddy who came into our lives in 1945, just after his experience in war and in a prison camp, just after he had seen the results of Nazi atrocities, of what humans are capable of doing to each other. After my parents married, Daddy formally adopted Bobby and me. We moved into our house on Coolidge and for the next four roller-coaster years he tried to make a living as a civilian. He had a string of taxing, long-hour jobs, from roofer to baker to short-order cook, while Mommy added to the family income by color-tinting photographs.

It was during this time that the letter from France, relayed to him by his parents, arrived with the news that he was the father of a child born to a woman in the farming family that hid him after one of his escapes. As far as I know, he never denied or confirmed paternity, but the suspicion, hurt, and jealousy my mother felt were enough to drive her to an emotional collapse. "Sort of a nervous breakdown," my uncle calls it.

It was devastating, because she always wanted to have a family with him and she couldn't because Frankie had kicked her or something and she was unable to give birth. She had had two miscarriages already. And now here he was fathering a child by another woman. But he tried to be a good provider and, in his own way, tried to be a good father to you boys.

Max Medema, the Arizona friend who coincidentally had been in the same German prison camp with my father, mostly remembers the boisterous parties my parents used to give at the Coolidge Avenue house:

> *Great big wild affairs. Your mom at the piano and we'd laugh and sing and just whoop it up. About thirty or forty people would be there. Sometimes I was about the only Anglo there and you'd hear a lot of Spanish. He'd call me Maximiliano and he and your*

mom would get the biggest kick out of my accent in Spanish. We got so close in those days. I'd just drop by and visit with them. I can remember you guys running around, and they just seemed so together. They were perfect, those two. Armando and your mom, they had something special between them. So how sad that they had their problems later.

Somehow, despite my father's roving eye, my mother remained deeply in love with her "Daddy." They limped along financially, later remembering this period as their happiest time together. Then my mother came into some money from Mama's sale of a part of her El Paso property. With this money and against the advice of a financial advisor, they bought a burger-and-fries malt shop. For about a year, in 1947 and 1948, they ran it themselves with hired help, my father cooking and my mother serving customers behind the counter. But the business never did well and nearly put them into bankruptcy. Then the final drain of their assets occurred just after they closed and sold the malt shop.

My father was driving their year-old cream-colored Nash in the city, when he stopped to pick up a young male hitchhiker. Not long afterwards, another car ran a red light and smashed into the Nash, sending my father unconscious to the hospital and the rattled hitchhiker to an attorney. The hitchhiker's attorney accused my uninsured father of recklessness, and a judge agreed, resulting in the plaintiff's getting thousands of dollars in damages for his minor injuries and emotional distress. All the family assets were tapped and even Mama loaned my parents money to help pay legal costs and the damage award. To further increase my parents' debt, they also had to pay off a big bill for my father's hospital stay, during which surgeons replaced a chunk of his skull with a metal plate.

After his recovery, he took a chef's job at the Ambassador Hotel on Wilshire Boulevard. Medema recalls:

It wasn't long before he was back on track. I think he always saw himself on the upbeat, improving himself, optimistic. But the clue to what happened later on may have begun right about then. It was his disillusionment after the Second World War of not being able to move into the mainstream of American life, as he saw it, without the stereotype of a Mexican who will take a cook's job or this or that physical-labor job. I know he thought about it because he talked to me about it. Hell of a thing, he said. He could walk in and want to manage a restaurant and they'd talk about the cook's job. And he had proven, demonstrated leadership ability. Yet that was the only kind of job he could get. That's when he decided to go back into the Army, into the reserves. And that changed his whole life. It may have started right there. He never got back to that other life. He stayed in the Army until he retired.

One morning in late 1948, not long after he began reporting to his reserve unit at Fort MacArthur in San Pedro, my beaming mother walked in through the front door carrying what looked like a bundled pet of some kind in her arms. Daddy followed behind her, also all smiles. The bundle was our new baby brother, Armand, Jr. Mommy sat down by a window, and I remember we all gathered around and goo-gooed over the little guy, sharing the glow that came through the gauzy curtain. Junior's arrival seemed to ignite a happy spark in our lives. None of us could really keep our hands off him. My father especially liked to hold and caress his Cabezoncito, his Little Big Head.

At the time it never occurred to me that my mother was never large and pregnant. I was seven years old and perhaps should have known enough to at least think about asking the obvious, but apparently I swallowed her matter-of-fact explanation that "I just brought my new baby home from the hospital." I suppose I thought that was how babies were born. You just went to the hospital and got them.

Of course, it never mattered to me that Armand was adopted. In fact, I never really thought about it until my mother brought it up a few years before she died. It happened when she was so desperate that she went to see Frank to ask him for money. She had asked me along so I could drive her from Oceanside to Los Angeles. On the way up she made a passing remark about Junior's adoption, then moved on and said nothing else about it. No details, no specifics. And as usual I had been so conditioned not to question or probe my parents about their past, I could only listen. When I was at Berkeley, I used to wish I had a troubled family like Eugene O'Neill's, hoping this would inspire me to write magnificently dark and tragic plays. With my mother that day, as I heard another tribal secret pop out, I was wondering what O'Neill would have made of my family.

What was never clear—and I heard a number of contradictory accounts—was whether or not Daddy was Armand's biological father. Given his romantic reputation, it was certainly possible, though our parents and others on certain private matters would never explain the bald truth to us. Regardless of what that was, I'll always believe it was hurtful, wrong, and unfair to Armand *not* to tell him the facts of his adoption, especially after my parents' marriage had fallen apart. They had nothing to lose or gain by continued silence on the matter.

I don't believe my mother ever gave up her dreams. She never stopped trying to live up to the idealized world she once described in her notes on "The Modern Handbook for Young Girls." The ninth-grade notebook is filled with admonitions about proper clothing, proper diet, proper exercise, proper posture, proper dating, proper table service. The notes seem to say that if you behave properly, you're guaranteed perfection if not happiness. But nowhere are there tips on correcting an imperfect world. What if you have no father as a child? What if your mother sends you away to boarding school? What if you don't love your first husband and he sometimes hits you? What can you do? There are no instructions for the young girl, certainly none for the middle-aged wife and mother. I've searched my mother's little ninth-grade notebook cover-to-cover, and I cannot find a word about truth or honesty or just talking things out frankly and openly.

So my mother invented her way through improper times, invariably draping ugliness in euphemisms and distortions, deceiving herself and her children with convenient lies and omissions. Maybe this response to an imperfect life was the only way she could cope. For his part, Daddy, who was no stranger to deception and secrecy, went along—as did others in my family. I once asked my Aunt Helen about Armand's birth parents, and she wrote me a typical truth-avoidance answer: "I remember only too well all the skeletons in our family's closet. But Ronnie, enough on that subject."

Is any human action ever too deep, too dark to tell? Or do we hide truth because we're afraid of the consequences? If so, I would never know what Mommy feared in telling the truth.

I was now driving along Mesa to the north side of El Paso, feeling the dry afternoon heat and wondering why my mother had invented so much about her past in this city. Though she was born in 1920, she changed her infant picture dates in the photo albums to 1922. And after her second marriage, she had Daddy *add* five years to his age, so that they would appear to be the same age. In truth, she was seven years older than he was. Vanity, I suppose. But why should she gloss over her entire childhood, never telling us about all her trips to visit relatives in Mexico, her run-ins with the nuns at the boarding school, her adventures with all the barnyard animals at the dairy? Why didn't she share any of this with her sons?

As Tuy writes, she was bored and restless in El Paso, a place she "detested." But at least my uncle, who was two years younger than my mother, relished his years growing up in the city in the twenties and thirties and having Juárez just a stone's skip across the river.

Juárez was a great place to go shopping for whatever you wanted—jewelry, foodstuffs, liquor, etc., and it was safe, no danger of any sort. I enjoyed the bullfights! People just had a wonderful time. Another thing—El Paso was still segregated. Restrooms had "For Whites Only" and streetcars had signs "For Colored" in the rear. But I never experienced any discrimination against Mexican Americans in E.P. Our dairy also provided a beautiful setting too! I really enjoyed watching the workers milking the 100 or so cows by hand, and I loved drinking fresh milk all day long.

My uncle's rosy view notwithstanding, by the time I arrived at the home of Vince Cobalis I was slicked with sweat, dust pooling in dark lines on my forearms, hands, and face. I parked next to the curb in front, picked up my tape recorder, notebook, and pen, and walked to the front door. I wiped my brow with a shirttail, then tucked it back into my pants before ringing the doorbell. I was thinking: Mommy, at least you got it right about the heat and the dust.

Circa 1952
in Camp 2,
Pyoktong,
N. Korea

In North Korea, prisoner of war camp 1950–53
Armando Arias, 3rd from right

Washington, D.C.

Vincent Cobalis, on his captivity in Camp 2, Pin Chong Ni, North Korea:

> *There were about ten of us in a room just big enough to where ten guys could all stretch out on the floor, some on this side and some on that side, on a straw mat, no covers, just in our quilted outfits. At this time they took all of us officers who were not Caucasians, so-called minorities, and put us in one room. I'm Filipino and there was another Filipino officer, then two Puerto Ricans, five or six Negroes, and Armando. . . . Your dad was a quiet, thoughtful person, had a lot of sympathy for people, a gentleman. He was closest to the Puerto Ricans. I don't recall speaking much Spanish with them. . . . You'd have fights break out among the other men, and we or the Chinese would break them up. Most of the prisoners tended to stay pretty isolated. I was a no-make-waves man. I'd stay off by myself, didn't associate much. I went through the whole ordeal in a detached manner, just sort of built up this defense. Others were more gregarious. They'd form little cliques with ringleaders, and everyone would go along. Our group had no ringleader. . . . People dying? Oh, yes. We had one guy who just refused to eat. You'd get this bowl of millet or rice and there would be maggots all over, and you would just clean off the maggots and eat the rice. He would talk about steaks and stuff and as a result he couldn't eat any of this rice*

and he died of malnutrition. . . . We all lost weight. What I craved most was food, but if you thought a lot about food, you'd go off the deep end. A couple of times I thought I would die I was so sick. Almost all of us had diarrhea. We had two American doctors and a British doctor. They'd try to get whatever they could from the Chinese. I was sick for almost a month. They hadn't expected me to live. A lot of guys died of diarrhea and pneumonia. I guess the Chinese just took them away. No burials. You just stayed there when you got sick. When I got sick they all moved out except one fellow, and he nursed me back to health. He'd force me to eat. . . . The Chinese made us write a lot. They'd call you in and try to indoctrinate you, basically, into their type of thinking. They'd call me out and they would come up with, "Well, what do you think?" And I'd come up with my standard answer, "I guess your system is okay, but I prefer ours." One time when I didn't write enough for them, they took me outside and made my kneel down and put a gun to my head. . . . They had other ways of controlling us, like the hole. It was just a little confined space in the ground that you got into where you really sort of had to sit cramped up so you couldn't stretch out or anything else. They put a corrugated metal cover on top of The Hole, and you stayed for whatever length of time they decreed. I heard it was much worse in Camp 5 the first winter. I wasn't there, but your dad was.

Cobalis, who had been a chief warrant officer when he was captured, couldn't give me much more on my father. No conversations, no anecdotes, only adjectives and summaries. I might have pried more, but he seemed uneasy remembering so many dreary, painful images. He and his wife were comfortably retired and I wanted to leave them as undisturbed as possible by the memory of such a grim time.

I returned from El Paso to New York to resume my work at the magazine. It was the summer of 1990 and so far in this particular year my assignments were as unpredictable as ever. Sometimes I might spend two months commuting from Connecticut to my office in order to write ten or twelve stories from reporters' files. Then suddenly I'd be shot out into the news world in pursuit of another story about someone who was living on the dramatic edge of life. As a precaution for those occasions, I kept a backpack in my office with a change of clothes, a valid passport, and a laptop that had replaced my old portable Olivetti. I never knew for certain what was coming my way.

Earlier in the year, for example, I'd been plucked from my relatively tame office routine and dispatched to the Canadian far north to write about an "ice trucker," or someone who drives a forty-ton rig across frozen lakes to supply gold miners working near the Arctic Circle. Excited and eager for a change, I caught the first train home, packed my cold-weather gear, kissed Joan goodbye, and headed for the airport by cab. From there, a photographer and I flew to Yellowknife, changing planes in Toronto and Edmonton. Admittedly, such trips were quick-hit reporting and writing jobs, but I always got a tremendous rush from the newness and drama of it all. I'd parachute into a stranger's life, sample the walk on the tightrope, then hurry back to my sedate, office-bound world in New York. Invariably, I'd learn something about survival, often in the most mundane, simplest forms of advice. "If you don't see the crack in time, in the drink you go, truck and all," my driver said, as we moved slowly into the whirling, falling snow. Then he added, "Always drive scared—and dress warm."

It was a tip my father might have offered. So I wore my fleece-lined boots, thickly insulated gloves, and layers of covering under my North Face parka. Yet even as protected as I was, I still whined about the bone-deep chill throughout my body and about the pain in my fingers and toes. Outside, on the ice during stops, I shivered and wondered how my father could have survived the subzero winter of 1950 and 1951 in North Korea. Not only were those months unusually frigid, but he and the other POWs had to live in drafty, lice-infested, dirt-floor hovels, eating little more than watery rice and sorghum. At least my ice-trucker host could offer me hot coffee, ham sandwiches, taped music, a heater, and hundreds of miles of an awesome white vastness of trees, tundra, and the occasional caribou herd.

Long before I interviewed Vince Cobalis, I had begun reading the available books on the Korean War and the POWs captured by

North Korean and Chinese troops. I had also corresponded with some of the survivors of the prison camps just south of the Yalu River along the border between China and North Korea. One of these men, Dr. William R. Shadish of Redding, California, was especially helpful in providing me with a strong description of camp conditions and the often horrific treatment of prisoners. I had informed him that my father, a first lieutenant leading a combat patrol of the First Cavalry's Eighth Regiment, was captured by Chinese troops near Unsan, North Korea, on November 5, 1950. From there he and the several survivors of his platoon were marched north in freezing weather toward the northern border camps.

Dr. Shadish was one of several captured military physicians who treated officers and enlisted men from mid-1950 until the repatriation of surviving POWs in 1953. This was during a period that saw an alarmingly high rate of death among the 7,140 captured Americans, conservatively estimated at 38 percent, though Dr. Shadish believes it may have reached 60 percent or more, given all the unreported dead on what came to be called the "death march" north. By comparison, the death rate among American POWs in Europe during the Second World War was only two percent, while in Vietnam it was 14 percent, even though many prisoners spent much more time in captivity there than captured Americans did in Korea.

Dr. Shadish, who did not specifically remember my father, sent me copies of two presentations he made at two ex-POW conventions. In both papers he makes a convincing plea for more government attention to the many former prisoners' health problems that can be traced to the harsh and grossly neglectful treatment they received in the camps, particularly during the first months. I was particularly interested in several passages of the paper he prepared for the 1990 national convention of American ex-POWs in Seattle. The first passage concerns the general reluctance of ex-POWs to speak out about their ordeals during and after the "forgotten war." After stating that he believes it's impossible to fully understand the POW experience without having gone through similar emotional and physical trials in captivity, Dr. Shadish seems to come eerily close to how I imagined my father's behavior.

As a prisoner of war one learned to accept his situation in order to live, to survive from day to day. One learned to form a hard shell to crawl into for self-protection from his captors. One learned also that it didn t do any good or help his situation to complain. So the POW made the best of what he had, and this was learned over the months and years as a way of life. Having done so then, isn t it fair to see that this is something not easily unlearned, even with freedom returned? Consequently, when you were asked on release from prison camp, Are you all right? Do you have any problems? i n the opinion of men receiving long-awaited freedom and with this way of coping so deeply ingrained, it seemed that most denied any problems and they said, No problems. Yes, I am all right. I just want to go home. As the years went on and problems did worsen the joint aches, back pains, even early on, the chronic G.I. complaints, did you ask someone about it? No. *To a man most ex-POWs did not and would not.* Their first reaction was to withdraw into oneself. If you believe this is not true, just ask your wives and families how it was.

My father fit the picture. After Korea he withdrew into frequent stretches of solitude, sitting alone in his recliner for hours, listening to his grand symphonies and concertos, or slipping behind a stoic, sphinxlike veneer when confronted with the tangles of marriage or sons he thought had stepped out of line. And there were years of contending with nightmares. He would never mention such uncontrollable nocturnal attacks himself. I would hear about it from my mother, who told me of his shivering cold sweats in bed when he would cry out in his sleep.

Dr. Shadish mentions the nightmares, insomnia, and excessive moodiness of former war prisoners, but what most drew my attention was his description of the most common scourges among the men while they were prisoners of war, especially during the first winter in the notorious Camp 5, one of the two main officer camps.

As far as I am concerned anyone who has been in a prison camp, as I was in Korea and you were in Korea, Japan, Vietnam and some of the European camps, has suffered from every one of the diseases and difficulties that they could relate to their current problems. You name them: hepatitis, dysentery (dysentery to the point where you never had a solid bowel movement for years), malaria, malnutrition and starvation, with all kinds of syndromes associated with the deprivation of nutrients and vitamins (beriberi, pellagra, neuritis, osteoporosis, scabies, dermatitis, gingivitis and tooth decay).

The food was barely enough to live on and everyone lost an extreme amount of weight. In our camp about 50 percent of total body weight was lost early on in captivity. The men looked like living skeletons, similar to the ones shown us in photographs from Buchenwald and Auschwitz. In our camp the bodies of those who died were stacked up like cords of wood by the enemy the first winter, in a similar fashion to those shown from the German extermination camps. At the primitive hospital and on daily rounds I saw them die each day, by the dozens and dozens. The deprivations by the enemy I have mentioned were inflicted to sink the prisoners into such a state of degradation that they would perhaps accept what the enemy wanted and submit to indoctrination attempts. Yet I saw these honorable men, Americans and Allies alike, resist and not accept—except under the most extreme torture.

My father never complained about his premature loss of teeth, but I was reminded of his dental problems whenever he would click his dentures with a little saliva-sucking sound, or rub them with his tongue, moving it around behind his lips.

One other passage in the presentation adds to what Vincent Cobalis told me of the infamous punishment hole, which my father on more than one occasion had to endure in a constant fight against death.

In Korea, the weather was with the enemy. It was 30 and 40 below zero in the camps in winter. The Communists could and did take all heat, blankets and clothing; put one in a "hole" (solitary confinement) and let you freeze to death or develop pneumonia, which was almost always fatal without antibiotics. I saw to these men who were sick and dying; they didn't die easy. Some were tortured and beaten to death, but most died of slow starvation, exposure and sicknesses that were allowed to go untreated or were related to purposeful deprivations.

We had practically no medications to give. As a physician in the camp I remember seeing the men dying and feeling that if only I had some antibiotics, some food, some vitamins, how many of these young, previously healthy, wonderful American soldiers could have lived! Instead, they were caged without food, left to melt away.

Not long after I read these paragraphs, my favorite editor again sent me to retrieve another story about some poor soul teetering on the edge. This time my target was a twenty-seven-year-old American, a gold mining supervisor who had been kidnapped by Colombian guerrillas along the Colombian-Ecuadorean border. With a photographer, I flew to Quito, Ecuador. Then we boarded another, smaller airplane to fly to an oil drilling town in the country's eastern slice of the Amazon basin. From there, soldiers escorted us north by truck to the San Miguel River on the border with Colombia. Finally, we climbed into a fiberglass skiff with an outboard engine and chugged upriver through clammy, warm air between banks of dense jungle on both sides, the north side being the sanctuary of the guerrillas.

Our three escorts were heavily armed, dressed in jungle camo, and appeared quite professional in an alert, snap-to kind of way. As we plowed through the dark-brown water toward the kidnap site, I talked with the escort leader, a young major, about the hardships endured by guerrilla prisoners or hostages. This wasn't the first time Colombians had crossed the border to snatch a few foreign workers they believed would produce ransom money. As a matter of expediency, the major had become a student of hostage taking. I asked what it was like being held prisoner as a hostage.

"They're scared and desperate," the major said. "But, you know, as a rule they are not beaten, tortured, or starved. It could be worse."

I brought up my dad's experience as a prisoner of war, and the major's eyes perked up. I gave him the brief version of what I knew, then he asked if my father had survived "intact, here," and he pointed the muzzle of his semi-automatic rifle to his forehead.

"Apenas," I said. Barely.

That was the first time I admitted to myself that my father had certainly had moments of occasional derangement, fueled mainly by the POW experience. Until now I had concluded only my mother had serious psychological wounds—in her case, from bad marriages and maybe other hurts I knew nothing about. It wasn't that I thought my parents were both wacko. Most of the time they behaved sanely, working, shopping, going to church, paying taxes. But during emotional crises they sometimes crossed the limits of normal behavior. My father tortured Junior with the bugs, or he hacked up and denuded a tree he intended only to trim. And my mother regularly exploded in plate-throwing frenzies whenever she had "had it up to here," or she dropped all pretense of sweetness, a la Jeykll and Hyde, and instantly changed to a lioness in search of her ex and some of his money. Through the family grapevine I learned that my mother also had a nervous breakdown after learning of my father's affair with the young French woman. So she had suffered from bouts of mental or emotional instability. No, these didn't seem like the actions of normal folks. But were their troubles enough to force them completely over the edge? Could Daddy have been driven to murder? Or Mommy to suicide?

I didn't mention any of this to the young officer, a pleasant man with an easy smile. Instead, we chatted about his family, his training, and his present mission in guerrilla areas. I took notes and asked questions. The photographer, Chris Little, took pictures. Later, I realized what had happened. Underneath and around the patter, unavoidably and once again, I was enthralled by a figure in fatigues who reminded me of that other soldier in uniform, the one sitting in my brain, enigmatic and forever brooding.

After my assignment in Ecuador—which concluded after a ransom was paid and the hostage released—I went to Washington, D.C., to attend another reunion of ex-POWs, this time Korean War vets. The gathering was held at the Georgetown University Conference Center, and the event appeared to be a repeat of the Oflag 64 reunion in San Diego. I registered along with thirty or so old-timers and some of their wives. There was a hospitality bar for cocktails and a dinner to continue the gabfest among friends brought together once again by a war a half-century old.

Mostly I hung out with William "Moose" McClain and Bernard Radoszewski, the two men I had corresponded with the most and who had known my father. McClain, a burly, affable man in his seventies, had been my father's E Company commander in North Korea when they were both captured. They knew each other as fellow prisoners for the next thirty-four months. As for Radoszewski, he first saw my father when the officers in Camp 5, which was run by the more merciless North Koreans, were moved in October of 1951 to Camp 2, operated by the more benevolent Chinese captors. "When they came into our camp," he said, "it was like a repatriation for them. They were in a very, very poor condition."

Radoszewski said at first the newcomers stayed among themselves, then gradually they joined the others in games and work projects. I listened to both men's brief descriptions of the camps, heard about the so-called "brainwashing" interrogations, the various escape attempts, and my father's single-handed triumph in rebuilding the camp's dayroom, or rec center. "Our home away from home," McClain said. McClain also recalled the revered Father Emil Kapaun, the Catholic chaplain from Kansas whose many humanitarian acts helped pull so many men through the deadly first winter, only to die himself at thirty-five, sick and emaciated, in May of 1951.

I then mentioned the army's attempt to "eliminate" my father from the service after he returned from Korea in 1955. The two men said they both had testified on his behalf and that whatever they said then, since it was so soon after their prison camp ordeal, would be much more accurate and complete than what they could tell me now. Their memories were fading. They agreed that the key to my understanding what really occurred to my father would be found in the transcript of the elimination board hearing.

"Your dad was a fine, patriotic soldier," McClain said, explaining that unfortunately another prisoner was apparently jealous of my father's friendship with an unpopular camp eccentric. After his release, the jealous man accused my father of collaborating with the enemy. "It was all bunk," McClain said, "but the army decided to investigate all the allegations."

Radoszewski added: "The written record will be your answer to your dad's position during the trial. Get that transcription and don't stop chipping away. There's always more."

Not long after I returned from Washington, I received a letter from William McClain. He wanted to tell me a few more things, and I was glad he did.

. . . As I mentioned to you, your Dad was a fine gentleman and fine officer. He was quiet and I never saw him get excited about anything. It is really unfortunate that you and your brothers, for whatever reasons, never had the opportunity to really get to know him. When I knew him he was a devoted family man who loved his family very much. We spent many hours together talking about our families and what we were going to do when we got out of the Prison Camp. I was somewhat surprised when you told me that you boys never got to know him and he never discussed his experiences with you. I have been thinking a lot since talking with you and I m unable to reach any conclusion as to what happened. Perhaps we will meet again sometime and discuss it further. Always remember, though, your Dad was a fine man and loyal to his country and fellow man.

Hope this finds you. Good luck and keep the faith.

Stamford 1

When the package arrived at the house, I was paddling my boat out to a particular buoy anchored about two miles offshore. I would usually set myself a goal, somewhere to head toward, and just ease my stroke into a regular rhythm, hardly straining, senses alert, mind relaxed. Eventually, I'd reach the buoy, loop around it, and return home.

If only my journey, or quest, for answers to my father's behavior had such a simple course. I kept losing sight of a goal or destination. With my father's story, the target was always moving. New places, new jobs, new friends, new routines, new compromises. He wasn't a snapshot; he was a movie, an entire life, dynamic, changing with age, birth to death. Every *Eureka!* discovery I made seemed to dissolve into more questions, and I could never conclude anything. Prematurely, I also kept trying to write my family's story, trying to bring it all together in a tidy narrative. Nothing worked; I was lost.

Then, thanks to the Freedom of Information Act, I finally received a transcript of my father's elimination hearing. After I read the 215 pages, at last I felt as if I had spotted the ultimate buoy in my quest for truth. Filled with allegations, witness statements, and testimonies the written record of his behavior in Korea gave me direction. On the important points, there were almost no ambiguities, omissions, conjectures, blank spots, or rumors. For at least those three years on the periphery of survival, I had him revealed, his character naked, stationary, easily examined. For once my target was not moving.

When my father appeared before the elimination board officers in October of 1955, he and his military counsel had to disprove all the many allegations of collaboration with the enemy and traitorous acts against his fellow prisoners of war. He was then stationed at Fort Carson, Colorado, which was where the hearing took place. Some of the accusations may seem tame today, but they were made in the aftermath of Senator Joe McCarthy's hunt for un-American activities. Any hint of sympathy toward communism still created instant alarm.

In a letter to my father, the army's adjutant general, by order of the secretary of the army, states:

1. Action is hereby initiated pursuant to Section V, SR 600-220-1, dated 18 June 1954, to require you to show cause why you should be retained in the Army. Information has been received by the Department of the Army which furnishes reason to believe that your retention in the Army Establishment is not clearly consistent with the interests of national security. This information is to the effect that while a prisoner of the Chinese Communist Forces:

a. You informed your captors of the conversations and activities of fellow prisoners of war, contrary to the established customs of the service.
b. You cultivated the friendship of your captors.
c. You frequently reported to and visited with camp officials, day and night, by invitation and voluntarily.
d. You assisted the Chinese Communist Forces propaganda program, as evidenced by the following: 1) You were a study group monitor, in which capacity you led discussions, kept discussions in progress while the Chinese were not present, and prepared

and read articles under the supervision of the Chinese instructors. 2) You were a member of the "Peace Committee" and participated in the "Peace Rally," spoke in favor of the peace appeals, and influenced others to sign peace petitions. 3) You contributed subversive articles to the prisoner of war camp newspapers, "Truth and Peace," "The Spark," and "The Standard." 4) You competed in a contest to see who could write the most derogatory article about the United States Government. 5) You volunteered to and did make recordings to your family containing propaganda for broadcast over the Chinese radio.

To help refute the charges, my father asked his former prison mates, the ones who knew him and his activities best, to provide the board with statements on his behalf. Forty-three responded. All affirmed his innocence, depicting a quiet, courteous, unobtrusive, patriotic man who many times acted selflessly to help others, much to the detriment of his own health and safety. To a man, they all swore they would gladly serve with him in combat or anywhere. That is, they would trust him with their lives. Lieutenant Colonel John J. Dunn expresses a common opinion:

It is impossible to live within the close confines of a prison camp with a man without gaining an accurate estimation of his character, his ideals and what he believes in. I saw Lt. ARIAS almost every day for a year and spent many hours talking with him. In my opinion, without any mental reservation, I believe that Lt. ARIAS is completely loyal and trustworthy and that he never willingly made any statement or committed any act against the interests of the United States.

As background for camp conditions as a whole, Lieutenant Colonel Dunn also explains:

. . . The period from the time of our capture until the beginning of the Armistice Talks in July 1951 was characterized by every form of harassment and abuse that the enemy could devise. It was a period of cold, starvation, beatings, killings and never-ending propaganda pressure. It was during this period that ninety-five percent of all the propaganda activities involving prisoners and the outward appearance of cooperation with the enemy occurred.

When providing specifics, the statements of support dwell mostly on two aspects of my father's time as a prisoner: his two escape attempts and subsequent captures and punishments, and his creation of a recreation or dayroom. The matter of his friendship with an unpopular camp eccentric as well as the jealous author of the allegations is taken up by the three people who appeared at the hearing to answer questions under oath—Lieutenant Colonel Dunn, Captain McClain, and my father.

About his escapes and captures, the following are typical comments in the statements submitted as evidence for the defense:

On 25 December, Lt. Arias and four other POWs escaped from our camp known as "The Valley." All of them were recaptured about four days later and brought back to camp. . . . Instead of being punished, they were appointed by the enemy as squad leaders and monitors. After being threatened by our captors and after being out in the woods for four days in sub-zero weather, hungry and sick, there was no alternative for them but to accept, and this was the way Lt. Arias became a monitor. As a monitor, Lt. Arias read articles and kept discussions going, but only in the presence of a Chinese instructor. If the instructor would leave, Lt. Arias would change the subject and talk about his family, home or some other topic.

In April or May 1951, Lt. Arias escaped again, this time from Camp 5. As before, he was captured shortly with the prisoners that had gone with him. The four of them received punishment this time. I recall having seen Lt. Arias with his arms and hands tied behind his back and being pushed around by the enemy, then put in solitary confinement.

The Chinese kept him bound in a hole for a few days. Later he was marched to a formation before the entire compound and made to say that he had done wrong and would not try to escape again. His appearance at this time showed very rough treatment; his eyes were sunken and he appeared too weak to stand from hunger.

He participated in an escape party, of which I was a member. Upon recapture, I saw him brutally bound and physically abused. He was confined for about ten days with me and with a Japanese civilian named Yoshio Taniyama. He underwent considerable harassment from the enemy during this period, to include being paraded on a leash like a dog through the village of Pyoktong, North Korea, with me. He subsequently served two weeks at hard labor for his escape.

Reading these recollections of the abuse and punishment inflicted on my father, I began to see him as a victim cut off from all the easy retreats and comforts of a civilized society. He had nowhere to run, no one to help him, no sanctuary for restoring his body and mind. I saw him hanging by the wrists from a single rope tied to an overhead beam. He had been captured many hours before in the snow-swept hills south of the Yalu River. The gaunt faces and tall thin figures of the escaped Americans had been easily spotted by local farmers as non-Koreans. Weak, hungry, and poorly dressed, the unarmed escapees had tried in vain to elude the soldiers who came after them. The North Korean troops forced them to surrender, gruffly tied their hands together, kicked them while they were on their knees, then hauled them to their feet and shoved them forward with more kicks and occasional rifle-butt blows to the body.

From the testimonies and published accounts of escape and capture from the notoriously brutal Camp 5, it was clear that the soldiers pulling the prisoners through villages were indifferent to their sufferings. To the enraged villagers, the bleeding and bedraggled captives were a kind of gift they could punch, kick, strike, and pelt with whatever weapon was handy—fists, sticks, shovels, hoe handles, rocks, metal pipes, anything they could use in a free-for-all explosion of jeering men, women, and children. Near starvation themselves, they too had suffered from the bombings by enemy planes. Or they had lost men to the war. Now they could vent their wrath on the evildoers paraded before them.

In Pyoktong, the town adjacent to the camp, the locals were well practiced in beating escapees. Thus, just prior to being hung with his toes only just brushing the frozen ground, my father had stumbled through a final gauntlet of crunching blows to his head and body. It was in this condition that I envisioned him. He was nearly senseless but struggling to will himself to an awareness, however dim, of conscious thought. The pain in his wrists and arms, which were yanked back and unnaturally upward, had surpassed all other hurts. His shoulder sockets screamed for relief, yet movement to another position was impossible. His only focus now was enduring this specific blazing pain.

When I was a kid, just after he came back from Korea, he taught me to run for endurance. I learned to focus on a certain way of breathing. He said it was like self-hypnosis and that the goal was to enter a trancelike state in which only blank thought and the regular rhythm of your breathing exist. I would like to think he had shed the pain this way, but the hanging position would not have allowed him to breathe easily or well. Given his beaten, starving, exhausted state, he was surely suffering almost beyond a human's ability to cry and moan. *I saw him brutally bound and physically abused . . . paraded on a leash like a dog*, one witness said. *His appearance at this time showed very rough treatment*, another testified. *His eyes were sunken and he appeared too weak from hunger to stand.*

By the time he was dragged away and shoved into The Hole, he might have been unconscious, but at least one witness reported, *Lt. Arias had survived the punishment, but could not walk.* The torture in below-freezing weather, the once-daily watery food ration, the excrement gathering at his feet, the bruises and open wounds—all encouraged a dire sense of a helpless, hopeless future. As he once did tell me, only his visions of us, his family, kept him from complete despair.

And so it would be until his third and last year of imprisonment. By then, with Camp 2 under the less brutal control of Chinese captors, my father had concluded that escape back to the UN lines hundreds of miles to the south through hostile mountainous terrain was impossible. So he decided to make himself useful and perhaps lighten the dreary, despairing mood still gripping most of the surviving prisoners. Fueled by a sense of mission and wishing to make himself useful, he volunteered to repair a dilapidated room that was attached to the crude classrooms of a school that now served as the prison camp. He rebuilt this recreational area, the dayroom, virtually by himself, and later the prisoners, in their testimonies, overwhelmingly praised his inspired, generally thankless efforts.

From January 1953 until repatriation, Lieutenant Arias took charge of a room that was set aside for recreation, and it is my opinion that he contributed tremendously in making the life of prisoners of war in Camp number 2 comfortable and healthy. This room contributed toward the health and welfare of the entire camp and proved to be our main source of relaxation and recreation throughout the latter part of captivity.

I know he spent many hours in negotiations with the Chinese to get equipment facilities in there so we could have something to occupy our minds. And I know that he spent many hours of hard work gathering up sawdust and mixing mud with it to fix the cracks. He'd done this himself, and he'd done it for the reason to help all the other prisoners in the camp, and they all benefited by his work. Naturally he had to come in contact with the Chinese because he was getting this equipment. Eventually they gave us cards to play with and chairs, and it was only through his work and effort that we ever got those things.

Lt. Arias did not receive preferential treatment from our captors. He ate, slept and lived like the rest of us. The only special job that Lt. Arias occupied, other than being a monitor, was that of being put in charge of fixing the day room for the camp. He thought it would be possible to obtain playing cards, chess sets, ping-pong tables, etc., from the Chinese. He took it upon himself and worked in the winterizing and preparation of the day room It is true that the day room was occasionally used by our captors as a class room and meeting place, but it was mainly used for recreational purposes. In the winter of 1951 and 1952, it was used to its capacity and it can be said that it was through Lt. Arias' effort in fixing this room that many of the prisoners did not get sick or think much of home. The room was the closest thing to home that we had in the camp, all due to Lt. Arias' efforts.

Such a project to lift the spirits of the other captives was also reflected in his acts to help them in other ways.

Lt. Arias also took care of wounded and sick prisoners during the march north and while in camp. He used to get up early in sub-zero weather to cut wood and boil water for bedridden POWs in our compound. He took special care of Father Kapaun, the Army chaplain who died in prison camp, and many times pulled details and work for other prisoners who were sick. He would do this consistently during winter and summer. He was also a cook in our kitchen and in many instances gave his rations to sick prisoners. Later on, when things improved, Lt. Arias organized a softball team in camp and he taught Spanish to English-speaking prisoners.

I first met 1st Lt. Armando Arias about 22 November 1950 when recently captured officers were herded into a small Korean house in the Valley Camp about 5 miles south of Pyoktong, North Korea, which was on the Yalu River. The weather was bitterly cold that winter, the ice on the lake being about 3 feet thick. POWs had mostly summer clothing. The North Koreans commenced a program to starve the POWs in order to force participation in propaganda activities. We lived in filth and squalor, freezing cold, living on a small portion of cracked corn mush twice daily. Prisoners began to die of pneumonia and dysentery. Later, beriberi and jaundice attacked us.

On 24 December 1950 Lt. Arias escaped with a small party of officers led by Capt. McClain, including Lt. Dowe, Lt. Nardella, and Lt. Smith. They used my knife and compass. The attempt was unsuccessful because of the snow and intense cold, and all were recaptured.

Lt. Dowe became ill with a strange fever (probably typhus, since we were all crawling with lice). He was quarantined in my room, the coldest in the house. I was extremely ill myself. Anyway, Lt. Arias came and brought food to Lt. Dowe and nursed him back to health. I was a witness to this.

As I heard at the ex-POW reunion in Washington, D.C., the many allegations against my father were made by one man, an army lieutenant who had been a friend of my father's before and in the early months of captivity. Two years after the war, in 1955 when the elimination hearing was about to take place, the army tried unsuccessfully to locate this man, who for privacy's sake I will call "Lieutenant W." The report from my father's legal defense counsel indicates that Lieutenant W was an embittered West Point dropout who was "ridiculed in captivity to some extent" because he had been captured alone and away from the rest of his unit. Also, Lieutenant W's wife reportedly was "untrue" to him while he was a prisoner. After his repatriation, he left the army and the United States for a life of exile in Europe, possibly Italy. I too, tried to find him in order to ask him myself why he wanted to ruin my father's career, but all my leads and trails came to dead ends.

Captain McClain, in his Q and A session with the three board members (one lieutenant colonel and two majors), testifies, among other matters, that the camp rumor mill may have fueled Lieutenant W's jealous behavior over my father's friendship with the odd but brainy Captain D.

Q: How do you account for rumors beginning or continuing?

A: Well, that's a difficult question to answer. Rumors start in a place like that for various reasons. I remember cases where people would start rumors just to see how long it took to get back to them. Because an individual didn't like another individual, he'd say something about him. By the time the rumor got around to five, ten, or twenty men, it would be a so-called fact, and that's the way I took it when these rumors would come out to me. That is the way I accepted them, and it happened in several cases. But the people, the personality clashes—because a guy didn't like the way another guy looked, or said something derogatory about him—would start a rumor and three or four days later it would be a fact.

Q: Did you believe that Lt. Arias had many, not enemies, but people that disliked him?
A: That he had many people that disliked him?
Q: That is right.
A: To my knowledge, there was only one man that disliked him.
Q: Who was that?
A: Lt. W.
Q: W?
A: Yes, Sir.
Q: Were these two officers extremely close when they were first captured?
<u>DEFENSE COUNSEL</u>: They were both members of your company?
<u>WITNESS</u>: Yes, Sir.
A: Lt. W was a member of my company, one of my platoon leaders, and they were very, very close. . . .
Q: Did Lt. W ever come to you and talk to you about Lt. Arias?
A: No, Sir. If they were close in the beginning, to the best of your knowledge, what would cause enmity between them?
A: Lt. Arias' association with Capt. D, I think, was the reason for that.
Q: Would Lt. Arias' association with D cause others, other than Lt. W, to have doubts about Lt. Arias?
A: I don't know, it's quite possible that it would in some cases.
Q: Rephrasing that, would it be possible in the life that you were living in the couple of camps for individuals to attribute rumors as factual information to Lt. Arias when they might have been aimed at D or someone else?
A: Yes, Sir, very possible.
Q: Do you know of any camps where a thing like that happened?
A: I can't recall any, not offhand. I do know that D was very much disliked in camp.

Q: How popular was Lt. Arias?
A: Oh, he was as popular probably as the average person, probably as popular as I was.
Q: Were you popular?
A: No, Sir.
Q: Other members?
A: This Captain D.
Q: What was his general attitude toward communism?
A: I don't know. D was, I don't know—I'd say he was an opportunist. He made a statement one time that he was going to find out all he could about communism while he was there, and he also made a statement that the only way you can comment on anything is if you know all the answers about it. But he had this funny personality.
Q: Did he attempt at any time to influence any of the prisoners as far as spreading communistic propaganda?
A: Not to my knowledge. . . .
Q: Earlier, why did you say you were surprised that Lt. Arias was selected for a hearing?
A: I think the thing that surprised me was that he was one of my platoon leaders. It might be that they picked him because of his personality. He was one of the few that wasn't boisterous or made any derogatory statements against anyone. As I've said, he's a very quiet individual. He doesn't have a lot to say. During my 34 months with him, I never heard him get mad at his fellow prisoners or the Chinese or anyone. I have never heard the man utter a curse word. He acted as a gentleman and talked to people—he'd answer them briefly, if they asked him a question.
Q: In other words, he wasn't very verbose and running off at the mouth?
A: That's correct.
Q: Do you believe Lt. Arias' basic personality and mannerisms of not being loud, of not using profanity

and such, led, in dealing with the Chinese, to rumors of his being a pushover for them?

A: I don't think so. No, Sir. I go back in this to Capt. D. I don't know what the reason was that Lt. Arias associated with him. I don't care. That was his business. But D was teaching Arias mathematics and music, and I know that Lt. Arias spent many hours on this study. They were things he was picking up from D, who I believe had a doctorate in chemistry. I know they got up to high mathematics and, as I said before, I think the reason these allegations have been brought about on Lt. Arias is this association.

Q: Then, you believe that Lt. Arias was naive enough not to feel what repercussions could come from the association and was using this brilliant, if unpopular, individual to pass away the time and improve his own knowledge and such?

A: I think that was one of the reasons and I think that—I mean, this is my opinion—that Lt. Arias was trying to help this D because he was unpopular. And from past experience I know that he helped several PWs by actually taking care of them like a mother would when they were first captured, and one or two of these people turned against him later on. I remember that Arias got a hold of a blanket one time, and he kept these people warm at night and naturally he took care of them when they were sick. He certainly had a lot more patience than I would have or did have with anyone.

Q: Do you know of any cases where Lt. Arias gave the camp officials or guards a hard time?

A: Just when he escaped. . . .

<u>DEFENSE</u>: One other question. Did you put Lt. Arias in for any award after you were repatriated?

A: Yes, Sir.

<u>DEFENSE</u>: What?

A: Silver Star.

DEFENSE: Do you know what happened to that?

A: Returned for no action.

DEFENSE: Was that because of this, until this was cleared up?

A: Yes, Sir.

DEFENSE: Thank you. I have no further questions.

Lieutenant Colonel Dunn, who was a major when captured, likewise portrays my father as an officer of decent character and reserved manner, a man who believed strongly in American ideals. "One time he indicated to me he would be willing to stay in prison if the United States would inflict a military defeat on the enemy," the colonel says. "That was his attitude."

Of Captain D, he testifies that none of the top officers in camp viewed him as dangerous or pro-communist. "He was never taken seriously," Lieutenant Colonel Dunn explains. "He was rather naive—just out of the country, so to speak—and easily pushed around." Like Captain McClain, the colonel also expresses his "mild surprise" that my father was selected for an elimination hearing. In explaining why he is surprised, he also describes camp hardships, my father's plight, and how the prisoners coped with Chinese indoctrination.

Unless a person was there to experience the first winter, they will never be able to understand it. The first winter the prisoners were broken down, to an almost sub-animal status. They were starved, beaten, kicked around, frozen. No person can stand cold. They can stand starvation and beating, but not cold. That winter broke these people down to where nothing seemed important but staying alive. And I don't believe there was one prisoner in camp that anyone back home would take seriously when he wrote or said things he normally wouldn't. When the enemy were putting so much pressure on prisoners to sign these things and join these peace movements and so forth, the men just didn't have, in my mind, the courage left to resist them, and figured no one would take it serious anyway.

I don't know how Arias got mixed up in this stuff. It was that they would simply grab someone and say, "You are it." And another method was they'd have phony elections and the prisoners would elect the committee themselves, and everyone was trying to get it off his back. They would vote for a person as a head of that peace committee or monitor of a squad or any other group in camp, then they'd criticize him for having a job. So in my opinion, I think that's where it all started.

When I joined this camp in 1951, Camp Number 2, they were still conducting these forced indoctrination classes. They'd herd us all in a room with the guards around the room, and you'd have to go back and write what they called an "appreciation," or what the squad thought of the lesson. And each squad had to appoint what they called a monitor to conduct this. Arias was a monitor of a squad. Monitors would say, "You are a good writer, you go ahead and handle it. Just put a guard at the door and watch for the Korean guards and play cards during that period." The field-grade officers would tell them, and they'd go back and write up something that meant nothing. It was just a lot of rubbish, there was no meaning in it. The duties of these so-called monitors were usually pointed out because they could write. In some squads, if they couldn't find someone who was pretty good at it, they would rotate it around. Well, they kept that up and the Chinese were making so little progress with the officers that in February of 1952 they dropped the classes completely.

We never had any propaganda after that except the time when the bug warfare charges started coming in and no one listened to them. They forced everybody to go through the exhibits. They had phony rat skins and things of that nature. They claimed we were dropping disease, but from February 1952 until we were released, there was no more propaganda in the camp and no more classes or anything. They got discouraged and dropped it.

I think the way this thing got started was statements made by people on the activities of prisoners during the first winter. But I wouldn't hold anything against a man during that first winter unless he informed on a prisoner. . . .

PRES: I don't know as we need you again. You are excused. If we do, we know where to get you.

DEFENSE: Thank you very much, Colonel.

[The respondent's witness upon being excused withdrew from the room.]

DEFENSE: It is my intention to call the only other witness in this case for the defense, and that is Lt. Arias. Is it all right to proceed?

PRES: Yes. Proceed.

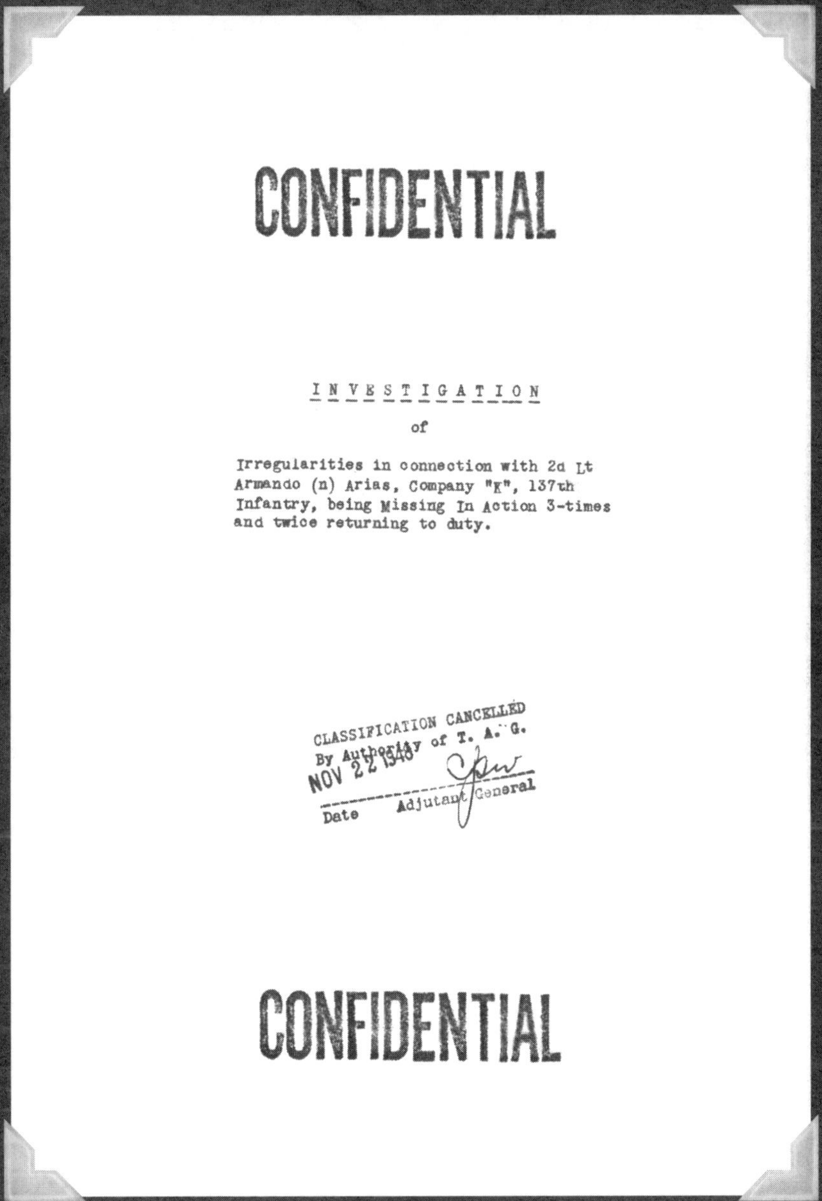

CONFIDENTIAL

INVESTIGATION

of

Irregularities in connection with 2d Lt Armando (n) Arias, Company "K", 137th Infantry, being Missing In Action 3-times and twice returning to duty.

CLASSIFICATION CANCELLED
By Authority of T. A. G.
NOV 22 1948
Date
Adjutant General

CONFIDENTIAL

Cover of declassified army document regarding investigation of his World War II service.

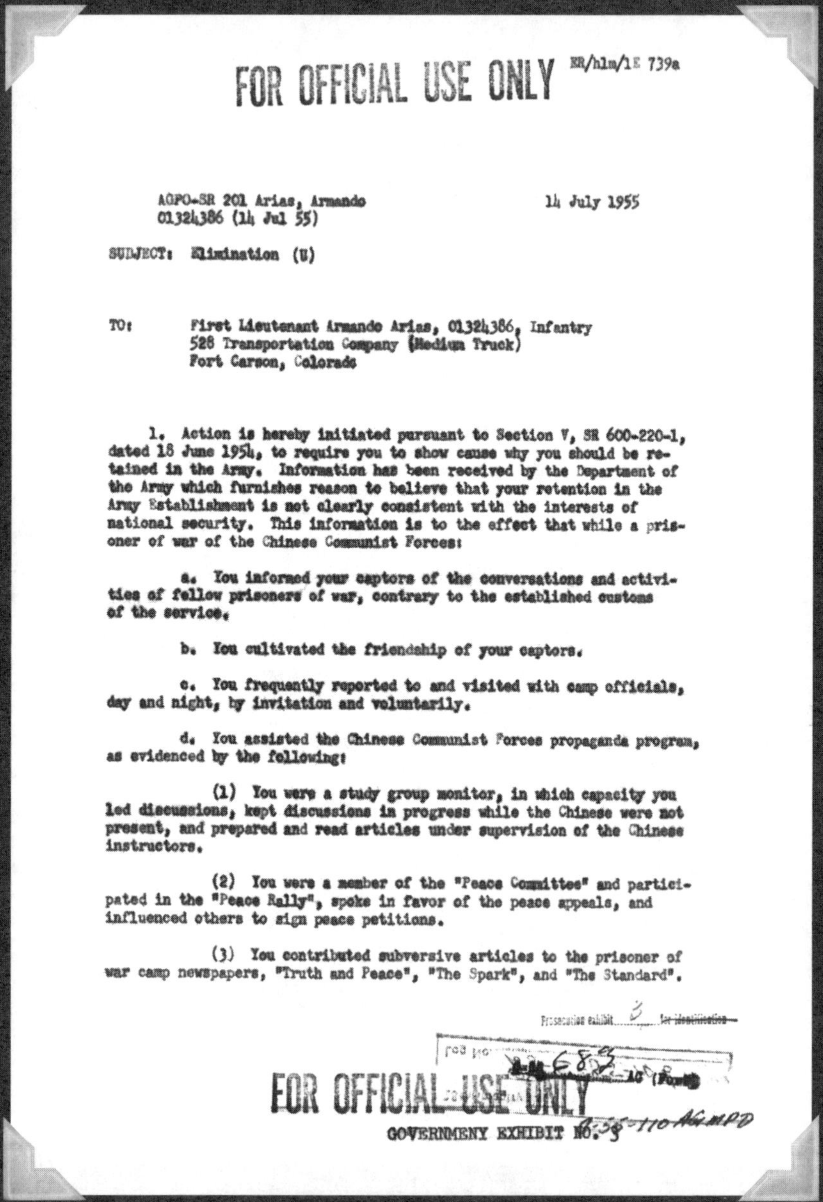

FOR OFFICIAL USE ONLY ER/hlm/1E 739a

AGPO-SR 201 Arias, Armando 01324386 (14 Jul 55)

14 July 1955

SUBJECT: Elimination (U)

TO: First Lieutenant Armando Arias, 01324386, Infantry
528 Transportation Company (Medium Truck)
Fort Carson, Colorado

1. Action is hereby initiated pursuant to Section V, SR 600-220-1, dated 18 June 1954, to require you to show cause why you should be retained in the Army. Information has been received by the Department of the Army which furnishes reason to believe that your retention in the Army Establishment is not clearly consistent with the interests of national security. This information is to the effect that while a prisoner of war of the Chinese Communist Forces:

a. You informed your captors of the conversations and activities of fellow prisoners of war, contrary to the established customs of the service.

b. You cultivated the friendship of your captors.

c. You frequently reported to and visited with camp officials, day and night, by invitation and voluntarily.

d. You assisted the Chinese Communist Forces propaganda program, as evidenced by the following:

(1) You were a study group monitor, in which capacity you led discussions, kept discussions in progress while the Chinese were not present, and prepared and read articles under supervision of the Chinese instructors.

(2) You were a member of the "Peace Committee" and participated in the "Peace Rally", spoke in favor of the peace appeals, and influenced others to sign peace petitions.

(3) You contributed subversive articles to the prisoner of war camp newspapers, "Truth and Peace", "The Spark", and "The Standard".

Prosecution exhibit 3 ~~for identification~~

683

FOR OFFICIAL USE ONLY

GOVERNMENY EXHIBIT NO. 3

Charges against my dad in declassified transcript of the army's "elimination" hearing, Colorado Springs, Colo., 1955.

Stamford 2

<u>DEFENSE</u>: The defense would like to have the respondent sworn and take the stand as a witness in his own behalf.

[The respondent, 1st Lt. Armando Arias, took the stand and was duly sworn.]

Q: Now, Lt. Arias, I want to go back a little bit to the background, not to elaborate, but enough to give the Board the benefit of your background. When did you first enter the army?

A: I first enlisted in the Army in October 1940.

Q: How?

A: I enlisted in Phoenix, Arizona, and was assigned to the First Cavalry Division at Fort Bliss, Texas at that time, Sir.

Q: I take it you were an enlisted man during that time?

A: Yes, Sir.

Q: How did you obtain your commission?

A: Attended Officers Candidate School at Fort Benning, Georgia.

Q: After you successfully completed your OCS training, where were you assigned?

A: For a short period thereafter I was assigned as an intelligence agent at Fort Sam Houston, Texas, at that time working as an agent along the Mexican border. Shortly thereafter, or six months thereafter, I was assigned to the 86th Infantry Regiment at Camp Livingstone, Louisiana, working as the Battalion intelligence officer.

Q: Did you go overseas in World War II?

A: Yes, Sir.

Q: What outfit were you connected with at that time?

A: I joined the 35th Infantry Division in Europe, Sir, in Normandy.

Q: Were you a prisoner of war, made a prisoner of war, during World War II?

A: Yes, Sir.

Q: Did you ever escape while you were a prisoner?

A: Yes, Sir, I did.

Q: How many times did you escape?

A: There were four escapes, Sir. Two are a matter of record.

Q: All right. In all, how long were you a prisoner of the Germans?

A: Approximately six months, Sir.

Q: What happened to you after the war?

A: I came back to the States and was separated from the service. I was out of the service for approximately three years and subsequently reenlisted in an enlisted status.

Q: You came back in 1948 as an enlisted man?

A: Yes, Sir.

Q: When did you go to Korea?

A: I was called to Korea in August of 1950.

Q: Where were you assigned?

A: I was assigned to I and R platoon of the 8th Regiment Cavalry.

Q: Who was your CO?

A: Captain McClain, Sir.

Q: Were you captured on or about this time of the year?

A: Yes, Sir, I was captured on the fifth of November 1950.

Q: All right, let's not be too elaborate, but briefly would you tell the Board how it came about that you were captured and the circumstances?

A: On the last day of October 1950, the enemy hit us. During the course of the fire, which lasted approximately five or six hours, the enemy managed to make a penetration through our lines. I had been placed in charge of the extreme right sector. At the time I was inspecting the line and when I came back from my inspections of the extreme right, my platoon sergeant met me and immediately informed me of the circumstances which had taken place in my short absence—that was, that the Chinese had broken through the adjoining platoon and they were pouring through the gap which they had breeched, thereby cutting us off completely from the parent organization. I had lost contact with the company and battalion, so our main concern was that the enemy was pouring in and swerving around behind the unit. We could observe them and we could see Captain McClain had withdrawn the rest of the unit back to the next higher ground, so we couldn't get back to him, due to the gap that was filled with the Chinese coming through. I took my men up to higher ground until daylight would come and we could get another situation and attempt to get back to the lines.

Q: How long did you and your men hold out before you were captured?

A: Five days, Sir.

Q: Did you have anything to eat during that five days?

A: No, Sir.

Q: Were you ever able to get back and join the rest of your company or battalion?

A: No, Sir, we were not.

Q: Then it was five days before you and your men surrendered, is that correct?

A: That is correct, Sir.

Q: Tell the Board some of the circumstances at the end of the five days as to what happened?

A: During this five-day period, we were attempting to get back to our organization and station, to our own lines, and during the course of our wanderings we encountered two or three groups that we had to fight our way through. Finally, on the fifth day we came across a rather strong element which we were able to fight through, but they trailed us. By this time we were a bit spent and fatigued and then it was during the night that we were able to get away from them. We took them up to high ground and set up a perimeter defense there and the next morning they were right behind us and concentrated an attack on our position.

Q: Did they surround you?

A: Yes, Sir. While we held the perimeter of defense, we could see all around us and there were Korean villages all about us, and a great amount of activity—soldiers coming out of the huts, etc. In other words, I could see that we were surrounded. At any rate, there was a skirmish put up and finally two of our men were wounded and another two killed. I gave the order to raise the white flag.

Q: Did you feel that it was necessary to surrender yourself and your group at that time to save the lives of your soldiers?

A: I could see no way out, Sir. We could have possibly continued at the cost of the entire complement, but I could see no way out of it.

Q: Did you feel your men were in a position to fight further?

A: No, Sir, not physically or materially. Our supplies were almost nonexistent.

Q: What happened after you surrendered?

A: We were taken to one of the Korean villages where I tried to negotiate with the captors to get the dog tags of the individuals who had been killed. I met with no success. They kept telling me they were all right, that they had been buried, and the dog tags were being sent to our lines. In other words, it was to no avail. They wouldn't let me have the dog tags.

Q: When did you encounter other American officers after you were captured?

A: Two days later.

Q: Were any of your fellow officers of Easy Company out of that group?

A: No, Sir. When I finally came across members of my unit it was possibly five days after capture. They marched us back to what you might call a POW collecting point approximately ten miles from Pyoktong, and there we were kept for approximately three months, because in February of 1951 we were taken from the Valley Camp to Pyoktong, which later became Camp No. 5. In the fall we were moved to Camp 2. . . .

Q: About this day room, was this your idea?

A: Yes, sir, it was.

Q: What did you do?

A: I started out with what was available there in camp, like rags, to plug up the cracks in the walls. The place was like a big, wide-open barn, extremely drafty and deteriorated. I took sawdust and flour and cooked them together to make a compound to fill the cracks. But all this material was not available in camp, so I had to cultivate the friendship of our captors.

Q: Did you ever, in obtaining these supplies, did you ever rat or welsh on any other prisoner to get the favor of the Chinese to get you materials?

A: I have said it once or twice before. I never by word, action or deed implicated anybody in anything with our captors. . . .

Q: It is alleged here that you volunteered to and did make personal recordings to your family. Did you do that?
A: Yes, Sir, I did.
Q: The recordings contained propaganda for broadcast over the Chinese radio. Would you explain about these recordings?
A: The recordings were to the effect that I was in good health, I was being given food, shelter and medication, and that I was studying mathematics and a couple of other subjects.
Q: Why did you tell your family you were in good health and that you were getting along all right, or led them to believe that?
A: I had not received any mail from my family at that time. I had been a prisoner during the Second World War and my wife had a nervous breakdown just after that period. In Korea, I anticipated what she was undergoing and not having heard from her, I was ready to do anything to reach her and through this medium I did. I told her I was in good health, being treated well, had food, shelter, medication, and I was studying. I didn't want her to worry.
Q: In these recordings did you ever say anything derogatory about the government of the United States?
A: No, Sir, I did not.
Q: While it is fresh in our minds, I'd like to interrupt our line of questioning to try to clarify this animosity between yourself and at least one other officer. I think the record will show this is not a general thing around the camp—these remarks that were made about you. What was your relationship with this Lt. W?
A: Lt. W and I were in the same organization prior to capture, and we were both captured approximately the same time and we met once again as prisoners.

We were on rather intimate terms, close relations with each other up until sometime in late winter, 1953.

Q: Did you remain friendly?

A: No, Sir, we did not.

Q: Explain to the Board what happened.

A: I was studying under this Captain D, studying mathematics, algebra, trigonometry, physics, chemistry, English grammar, and music. Lt. W approached me and requested that I discontinue my association with him, and Lt. W went ahead to say that Captain D was under suspicion and that he was an opportunist and a progressive, etcetera. I asked Lt. W if he could give me any specific information to that effect. I repeated my request at least three times during the course of our discussion. I kept asking him to give me something concrete to base my actions on, something I could base my break with Captain D on. Lt. W was not able to give me anything concrete, or did not want to, I don't know which.

Q: You did get the impression that he disliked Captain D, that he was bitter toward Captain D?

A: Yes, Sir, extremely so. One day he approached me and stated that due to my association with Captain D that he would have to break off our friendship. I informed him that if that was how he felt about it, if that was how much he valued our friendship, then it was his doing entirely. . . .

Q: How many people were in the squad in which you were a monitor?

A: Approximately 12, Sir.

Q: How many were Negroes?

A: Five or six.

Q: How many in your squad were of Spanish origin?

A: Two of us, myself and another.

Q: Were there any other minority groups in your squad?

A: There were two or three Filipinos, Sir.

Q: How many white, or Caucasians, were in your squad?

A: In Camp No. 2, Sir, there were none. It was entirely composed of minorities, so-called minorities. However, in Camp 5, there was no segregation at all.

Q: Do you believe that any of your treatment, good or bad, at the hands of your captors was based on your being a member of the minority group?

A: Yes, Sir.

Q: Do you believe your being a monitor or your being able to get material to fix up the day room was based on your being in a minority group?

A: They made it appear that way. Yes, Sir. . . .

PRES: Did you ever know of a fellow prisoner that thought he caught you eavesdropping on other prisoners?

RESPONDENT: No, Sir, that is erroneous, and if I might have overheard, inadvertently, anything that was said, it wasn't intentional eavesdropping. And if I did learn of it, it did not go beyond me, especially to the captors. I venture to say, Sir, that I knew of derogatory information or activities concerning some of the people who may have accused me, and the Chinese never learned of it—not through me.

PRES: Did you believe you were unpopular?

RESPONDENT: I was resented, Sir. I don't want to give the impression that I am going to build myself up at the expense of others. That is what makes it so difficult for me. As has been brought out by Captain McClain and Colonel Dunn, and possibly some of the statements on my behalf, I always carried myself as an officer and a gentleman. I addressed all my superiors in a respectful manner. I always considered myself their junior and addressed them as such, which was not the habit in camp. I never cursed. I never grabbed about for food to eat or tobacco to smoke. Rather than doing that, I quit smoking, which was not the case with many others. It is felt that my conduct—

DEFENSE: You've got to speak up regardless of your hesitancy to speak ill will of other people.

PRES: This is your show.

DEFENSE: I have found you reluctant to speak ill of anybody and you have got to do it if it's the truth, and now is the time to do it.

RESPONDENT: Sir, throughout my captivity at all times I tried to set a code that I had learned as an officer. Throughout my captivity there was no time or incident when I was not carrying myself as an officer of the United States Army and representing them to the best of my ability, which was not the case with many PWs. This was resented, I know. By the same token I did not participate in tirades against the communists behind their backs. If I had something to say to them, I'd say it.

PRES: Did you ever have anything stolen from you?

RESPONDENT: Yes, Sir.

PRES: Tell us about it.

RESPONDENT: Another one of my close friends during captivity, Captain Ortiz from Puerto Rico, and I started receiving sugar rations sometime in the latter part of the second year of captivity. Captain Ortiz never ate his sugar, never used it. We had put our sugar together and I had not used too much, so that eventually we had built up a tremendous bag of sugar. In addition, we had some softball games played, and we would wager a half-cup or a quarter of a cup or a cup of sugar on a particular game. We had been fortunate to have saved through two or three wagers a reserve of sugar. But this sugar was lost, stolen.

PRES: Who stole it?

RESPONDENT: Sir, I would not be able to answer that on a factual basis. If I gave a name it would be—

DEFENSE: Arias, you are here because people assume things by hearsay and rumor, and by what they thought. I know you are hesitant because your own example, it's been set against you. But if you have an idea, if you think somebody, even without it being based on anything, if you believe a certain person stole it, then you should answer the Colonel's questions—because the man you suspect probably knows you suspected him.

PRES: Let me help you like this. Are you reasonably sure in your own mind you found out who stole it and when did you find that out, what did you do with that information?

RESPONDENT: I went to see one of the senior officers with the information, Sir. He investigated it and advised that the matter be dropped, that the officer connected was very unpopular in camp. So I followed the suggestion and dismissed it from my mind.

PRES: O.K. Continue on.

DEFENSE: Since then, in your own heart, have you forgiven the man for stealing your sugar since? I mean, have you become—you and he—fairly friendly afterwards?

RESPONDENT: We are on speaking terms, yes, Sir. I never blame anyone for stealing food over there. But it was one thing stealing from our captors, and it was another thing stealing from fellow prisoners.

PRES: Fine. Now, tell us about Captain D.

RESPONDENT: Father Kapaun—Emille Kapaun, you may have known of him, now deceased—approached me and asked me to have a talk with Captain D because he was acting in a way which was alienating him from the rest of the POWs. I asked Father Kapaun, why me? Why not approach him himself? Father Kapaun, as some of you may know by now, was a great humanitarian, one of the greatest heroes that was ever in a prison camp. He said he didn't want to approach D himself because he was a Catholic chaplain and D might take an adverse view of that, since he was Protestant. He might think that a Catholic might want to convert him or something like that. So I approached Captain D.

PRES: Was this your first contact with him?

RESPONDENT: No, Sir. I had known D for approximately five months. I never had too much to do with Captain D up until that time. So I approached Captain D and told him that his actions were putting him apart from the other PWs and before very much longer he would find himself an outcast if he continued. Captain D did start mending his ways from that time forward, to the extent that at Camp No. 2 he organized all the study classes, conducted them as has been brought out. He was quite an intellectual. He had all those subjects right at the tips of his fingers, not of memory alone. He drew up texts on the studies, drew up songs, hymns, music lessons, everything—physics, chemistry, geometry.

At any rate, Captain D broke away from the Chinese completely in Camp 2, and he had this study program. But his personality and some of his actions had already alienated him from a good number of POWs.

PRES: Actions such as what?

RESPONDENT: Earlier, at Camp No. 5, Captain D didn't know what he was doing. That is the impression he gave me. He was naive. For example, sometimes he would do typing work for the Chinese, and he would come back from these typing sessions and brag about having made a glutton of himself while he was with the Chinese. And he would fail to bring any food back for the other men.

PRES: In other words, if the others were hungry and they saw him come back and then brag that he had sated himself, you feel that that was the cause of their hate?

RESPONDENT: That was a good cause.

PRES: Back to Camp 2, what happened regarding Lt. W and Capt. D?

RESPONDENT: I was asked along with some others to give up my association with Captain D. I told this individual who asked me—his name has already been brought out—I told Lt. W that I did not go along with what he and a few others were trying to do. First of all, I asked for concrete facts on which I could base a break. Secondly, I informed them that I wasn't in the habit of being told who to associate with.

Thirdly, I told him I did not go along with this business at all because of what we had witnessed back in Camp No. 5. Those people who did not belong to a clique, who were sick, died because no one would bring them a glass of water because no one liked them. Lt. J is a vivid example of that. Lt. J was an arrogant individual, God rest his soul. Everyone in camp hated him because he was selfish and he didn't hesitate to tell anybody off, including the enemy. But when he got sick, he died without a friend.

Having witnessed a couple of those incidents, I told W that I did not think it was right, that that is exactly what the enemy was trying to do—break us and separate us—that as Americans no matter what our origin, we should stick together. And that was my philosophy throughout.

PRES: Did you believe then or now that Captain D was pro-communist?

RESPONDENT: No, Sir, I did not then and I do not now.

PRES: What color is Captain D?

RESPONDENT: Caucasian, Sir.

PRES: Those are all the questions I have at present [to the respondent, still on the stand], unless there is something else you would like to say that you think pertinent in questioning.

RESPONDENT: My only request, Sir, is that I would welcome, I would welcome any questions or as many questions as any member of this Board would pose to me. I feel that, as I mentioned before, I do feel there is too much being left out. I don't want to recount and rehash this needlessly, but I do wish that more questions would be asked of any phase, because my purpose was to come up here and start from the beginning and go through the whole thing to the very end, and I thought I could cover it. But it hasn't been that way. We have been, more or less, jumping back and forth, and I feel there has been too much missed.

PRES: Lt. Arias, for your information, one of the more important reasons why you have been investigated is that some of your interrogators and persons evaluating your reports and investigations felt that you are not giving all of the information you possess. I can't elaborate on it because I don't know any more than that. For your information, I say that there are persons evaluating your case who have made that statement.

RESPONDENT: I can appreciate that, Sir, due to the fact that I have never been given to much conversation. It's not that I'm deliberately attempting to withhold anything. When I was interrogated after my release I thought I would lay everything out before my people, which I thought I had done. I told them I was a monitor, a squad leader. I thought I had told them everything. If there are points I missed, I think I would attribute that to my state of anxiety or nervous condition at the time. My intention has never been to withhold anything from anyone, and I stand on this statement, Sir.

Each and every one of those men I have contacted or written to I have expressly requested that it is not only favorable information I seek. I want it down—to put it down in black and white—anything that they can remember about me, whether favorable or otherwise. I explained I wasn't looking for a favorable side. I wanted to get everything before the Board. Sir, I know I am not much of a talker and when I had this interview after my release, I may not have brought all this out. But my purpose was not to withhold anything, Sir. It never has been—it is not the purpose, it never will be the purpose. As I say, there is nothing in my life I hesitate to bring out.

DEFENSE: I believe that is enough.

RESPONDENT: It was rumored that I had a brother who was a member of the communist party in California, and alleged that I had a relative who was a leader in Panama. In reference to this, I'd like to read a paragraph from—

PRES: It's not necessary, we are familiar with it.

DEFENSE: I don't think that is necessary.

RESPONDENT: I did not state that President Arnulfo Arias, former president of Panama, was my cousin. My statement was: The root of our family was in Spain, and that our family branched out all over the world from Spain, and possibly he might be a distant cousin of my father's. But I did not know and to the present I do not know. I never asked my father.

DEFENSE: Gentlemen, do you have any further questions you want to ask him?

PRES: We have no more questions. You may go back to your seat, Lt. Arias.

[The respondent upon being excused resumed his seat at the defense table.]

DEFENSE: I think we can put these sworn affidavits before you and we can take a break then. I think the reporter is getting tired.

RECORDER: That is correct, Sir.

DEFENSE: Before you adjourn, Sir, I respectfully ask that I might be able to make this very brief statement in Lt. Arias' behalf.

PRES: Your closing statement?

DEFENSE: Yes, Sir. That is all I have left.

PRES: All right.

DEFENSE: I have very little to say to you because of two reasons. I don't feel that anything that I could say would sway you one way or the other—maybe before a jury, yes—but I have enough faith in mature, American Army officers to know what they are doing and realize that they are not going to be changed by the evidence or by the testimony that you have heard.

I would only like to say that I think we are playing right into the hands of the Chinese when we take a young American officer like this, force him through the disgrace to come up here and try to defend himself against rumors and hearsays that happened in a prison camp. I have never been a prisoner of war, but in my life I have talked to wardens of penitentiaries in this country, and they tell one of the things that they have to worry about most is small cliques. When men are shut up as these men were through three winters, I can understand it. I honestly can.

I am proud of this officer. He has an unusual personality, in my opinion. You can see the difference in personalities. You saw Captain McClain, strictly Irish, lantern jawed—he is the kind of guy who would tell the other prisoners of war to go to hell if he heard such rumors, probably tell the Chinese the same thing. But Lt. Arias is different—just as good an American as McClain, maybe better in some respects, but because of his training prior to entering the Army, he is a polite man. He is a quiet man. He is a reserved man. He is a type of officer I would be proud of. Now, the fact that he didn't go around through that prison camp over there moaning and cussing his captors—that's no reason to kick him out of the Army.

I won't go through the hardships. That is an old story to us. We are a peculiar race. Take, for instance, the broadcasts. We all knew they weren't getting medical treatment. Who'd they fool? We had pictures in Korea of people who were killed with their hands tied behind them. Our people knew how those prisoners were treated. But that shows you what Lt. Arias has to come up here and answer to.

An American officer senior to him tells him he can send a message home by radio. It's in one of the statements presented as evidence. And yet we force Lt. Arias to come up here and answer to that kind of allegation.

I don't believe this man would take an oath before God and tell you a lie, and I don't think you believe it either.

I thought at first I'd comment on all these things. Now I don't think it's necessary. I will comment on the remark made by the representative of the Red Cross who spoke with the men upon their release. You know everybody got in the act on this thing. The psychiatrists—and I verified this with a lot of POWs—they treated them like guinea pigs. They probed their minds, but they weren't in any mental or physical condition to give a damn whether the psychiatrist thought they were nuts or not. They just wanted to get home. But the psychiatrists and others—and I don't mean to be disrespectful—had to report something back. They had to fix something, and many people suffered for it.

Now, I know that we had Americans who were a disgrace. I have been told that not by Arias, because I can't get him to speak harm of anyone. But I talked to McClain and others. They saw high-ranking officers humble themselves for a cigarette, for a bag of rice. But that is no reason to make every good American officer suffer. And this man's conduct throughout three winters he was a POW was not such that you gentlemen should not recommend that he be retained on active duty.

He doesn't make the best witness in the world, before you, but maybe he is under too much strain. At times he hesitated. You know why? It wasn't because he was trying to fool you in any way. This man hesitated because he was so sincere and so afraid he might tell you something that wasn't true. He's that conscientious. And even if he answered, he wanted to be sure he was right.

I don't know what else I can say to you men. I probably will worry later that maybe I should have said something else. But you have heard it all. There are 43 people who have given you sworn affidavits and statements, and there is every kind of descendent in the world—Russian, Polish, you name it—Ivanushka, Peppe, Coxe, Cordero, Anderson, Van Orman—it's a cross-section of American life. I don't believe these Americans are going to cause this member of a minority group to be broken, because that is just exactly what the Chinese would want us to do.

If Lt. Arias hasn't convinced you, if he hasn't touched you, if he hasn't proved to you that he is a loyal, American officer, regardless of the fact that his father came from Spain or any other reason, then I don't feel that any words of mine can do more than he has done. I know how I feel, and we can let the matter rest with you. This completes our case. Thank you.

PRES: Lt. Arias, do you have anything further to say?

RESPONDENT: No, Sir, I have not.

PRES: Then the Government has completed its case.

Three weeks after the conclusion of the elimination hearing, on November 4, 1955, the board sent my father the following conclusions and recommendation in his case:

CONCLUSIONS:

1. This Board of Inquiry finds insufficient evidence to substantiate the allegations, other than the ones on propaganda pertaining to signing a peace petition and making the recording.
2. Lt. Arias did contribute to the Communist propaganda program by making his personal recording and signing the peace appeal. The Board feels it has attached appropriate significance to these acts.
3. The quality of the evidence and information concerning the other allegations is such that this Board feels that it fails to uphold the case

against Lt. Arias. Also, the statements presented in behalf of Lt. Arias outweigh the sum and substance of the material available to support the allegations.

4. This Board in drawing its conclusions encountered indecision due to Lt. Arias' unique and peculiar personal code of ethics and conduct. This code can readily be misunderstood and apparently was during his tenure as a prisoner of war.

Nevertheless, this Board believes that Lt. Arias had while a prisoner of war and has now a personal code of conduct sufficiently high to perform his duties as a commissioned officer in the Army.

RECOMMENDATION:
That 1st Lt. Armando Arias, [serial number], Infantry, be retained on regular active duty without change of station.

Dated this 4th day of November, 1955, at Fort Carson, Colorado.

Sarajevo

Three years after I read how the army tried to "eliminate" my father, I was in Sarajevo thinking I wasn't far from elimination myself—not by panel of military judges nor by a sniper's bullet, but by a roomful of farting firemen. We were all sacked out in a dark, unventilated room on the second floor of the city's main firehouse, and for hours I had squirmed around in my zipped-up sleeping bag, listening to them snore and cut loose. I was suffocating. The stink from the basso profundo bombs was killing me.

Gasping, I unzipped my bag, sat up, and surveyed the darkness. Slivers of light from the kerosene heater in the center of the room cast ghostly, flickering shadows on the prone shapes around me. How could they sleep? I was gagging and they were relaxed, at peace in a paradise of unbridled flatulence. Bean soup and rice, the staple meal of the fire station, must have changed their sense of smell. My hosts had become so infused with the odor of beans and bean gas that they could no longer tell the difference between the good stuff and the bad. Beans in any form—it didn't matter. They had become one with the beans.

Nauseous, I raised myself up to a crouch and groped my way to the door. No one stirred, lost as they were in a dreamland of gassy release. I opened the door and stepped into the icy hallway. The sudden chill cut right through my layers of sweatshirts, jeans, and long johns. After taking two restorative breaths, I crossed the concrete floor for a look out the window. Through the blackness I could see a few glowing spots, probably from basement windows of either apartments or underground cafes, still serving a city that felt safer, less visible in darkness. Once a jewel of the Balkans, at night Sarajevo could at least pretend there were no ruins and only occasional random sniper shots. In candlelit basements below ground even the thundering blasts of exploding mortar rounds seemed distant and not so deadly.

My father wanted to reach the Balkans after he slipped away from his German guards in Poland. Why the Balkans? I never found out, although one former Oflag 64 prisoner suggested it might have been because that was where partisans supporting the Allies were strongest. And since my father had been helped in France by the Free French underground, he may have figured he'd do best by traveling south to Yugoslavia. But then he joined up with Dr. Parker and together they headed east to Russia.

By the time I arrived in Sarajevo in November of 1993, I had all but abandoned research on my father's life. Most of the big questions had been answered. I had pieced together enough of his and my mother's story so that I could reduce them to normal human size in my mind. I could explain causes and effects. I knew why my mother was desperate to leave dull and boring El Paso. I knew why he had fled Nogales, knew what he did in the wars, knew how he could lose it, babbling before a dumbstruck group of American legionnaires who'd come to hear all about his prison camp experience in the Korean War. I knew these and a thousand other facts about my parents, yet I felt no satisfaction, no relief.

I had read and reread my collection of facts: my notebooks, my mother's journals, interview transcripts, military papers, letters, newspaper clippings, articles, books, and all kinds of documents, such as death certificates, police reports, tax forms, medical receipts, and school report cards. I kept them all in a wooden orange-crate box. My Puzzle Box, my Death Box, sometimes my Writing-Project-From-Hell Box. The truth was that I still couldn't envision how I should tell the story. What was the structure? What was I after? What was the point, the purpose? My box of revelations had no shape.

Yet, unprovoked, I could still talk excitedly about the many *parts* of the story—my dad's escapes in France and Poland, in Korea the beatings leading to The Hole, the army's attempt to boot him out, suspicions about my mother's death, his suicide attempt, his disappearance, the Indians at Chorro Grande. I knew the details by heart, could give you the short version or long, could spout dialogue, summarize a scene in one sentence, remember moments: butchering the tree in Oceanside, my mother's crying as she listened to her Mexican rancheras, Junior standing under the lightbulb in Junction City, Kansas.

At the same time, with each recitation, I felt like a puppet, my dead parents either pulling the strings or watching me stumble about trying to fill in the gaps, trying to make meaning out of the tiniest bits of reality. In frustration, I stored my box of facts in the attic of my Connecticut home, hoping I might get over my need to pursue the tale any further, thinking that by keeping it out of sight, it might fade in importance.

At the magazine, the Death-Disaster-and-Destruction beat still beckoned, so I seldom lacked heartfelt distractions. Sometimes the reporting experience was so emotional that my quick-trip hits to the edge seemed to blend in with my parents' story. In an odd, boomerang kind of way, my adventures on the road intensified the connection to them. I was longing to get them back so I could tell them what was happening to me. The deeper the experience, whether tragic or whimsical, the more I wanted them back. Maybe I could make them cry or laugh, maybe I could bring them together again. Of course, that was impossible. Whatever sense of sorrow and futility I felt about how they lived and ended their lives had meaning only for me. Alone, I might talk to them, wanting them to live my day. I spoke to Joan every few days by phone, but my monologue to my parents was so private that I felt like a child again.

Once, the year before I went to Sarajevo, I was hitchhiking in the wastelands of western Australia on my way to a desert town to interview an aboriginal couple whose two grown sons—one a local soccer hero—had died while in police custody. The cops said the young men had hanged themselves, but everyone, especially the parents, knew differently.

Maybe my raw notes of that day in April 1992 were directed as much to my parents as my mother's "chatterlogs" were to me. Didn't Mommy herself start me on this habit? Shouldn't a family share it all? As usual, I had the aching need to save images and emotions in words, crude and quick as they were.

Young miner (actually a heavy-equipment operator) picked me up on the highway north to Meekathara. He offered me a lift at a gas station. Car full of all his belongings. Recently divorced. TV, clothes, books, curtain rods, shoes, boots, all of it a jumble in back seat. Hugh, friendly enough, drove a dusty old Chevy with a Roo-bar in front as a bumper. We outraced a storm of magnificent, sweeping, backlit clouds [here a drawing]. Went thru flooded patches of the highway. Stopped at the "world's largest emu farm." Met the keeper of 45,000 birds. I hugged one. Later, had to relieve myself, so Hugh pulled over and I went off into the brush. I pissed on what I thought was a moundish, long rock, maybe 6 feet end to end. The rock moved. I froze, absolutely terrified. Then I backed away. It was a giant monitor lizard called a goanna. I told Hugh of the Arctic ice-truckers. Like them, Hugh worked in chunks of time—6 wks on, 6 wks off. I described the world's biggest open-pit gold mine in Brazil. Then we discussed Aborigines. He grew up with them. He was in-between on the subject. There were good and bad. Unfortunate they couldn't get jobs. I mentioned my Meekathara story. The 2 sons, hangings, etc. Hugh silent.

I suppose what I wanted the most as I wrote these words in a fly-ridden motel that night was to hear both my parents laugh when I told them about pissing on the dragon. They would ask me details about the emus. People rode them like ostriches. Almost as big. Then I would describe the thunderstorm and how we raced its edge until later when it caught up with us and threw down hail the size of my fists. Finally, I wanted to tell them I heard a father's story of losing his two sons. Poor man. Hardened, handsome face locking in whatever numbing misery he might have felt inside. The man didn't express this pain any more than I had to my father about the death of my own son Jonathan. My father was still alive then, but he wasn't around. If he had been, maybe we would have spoken and certainly we would have embraced each other.

Another time, later that year, I was twice sent to Somalia, arriving at remote desert towns by military cargo plane. In Belet Huen, where I stayed a week, photographer Donna Ferrato and I trailed a young public health nurse from Los Angeles. She worked among thousands of starving victims of prolonged drought and famine, dispensing medicines and food, separating the dying from those who might have a chance, literally deciding who would live and who would die. In such a place, death and suffering were commonplace, yet Mary, our gentle, compassionate story subject, never lost her composure, her sense of mission, her perspective. "If I gave in to my emotions," Mary said, "I'd be useless."

As Mary spoke, I thought of my father and his attentions to the starving, dying men in Camp No. 5 that first winter in North Korea. My father would have understood Mary's altruism perfectly, as would my mother. Mary was a sacrificing missionary nun without the religion.

Before volunteering for Red Cross duty, Mary had worked in San Francisco as a hospice nurse for AIDS and cancer patients. Helping the dying was her calling, she explained. What about burnout, I asked. Not yet, she said, adding some inadvertent advice for anyone still alive: "The most common last thing people say before they die is 'I wish I had done this' or 'I should have done that.' " Years from now Mary didn't want to say that she *should have* gone to Somalia.

11/6/92, 5:30 a.m.

Sitting on roof terrace of the ICRC house in Belet Huen. Middle of Somalia 50 ks from Ethiopia near the banks of the Shebele R. Flies, a breeze, sounds of a rural, provincial capital: goats, cows, doves, roosters, people—all blending, floating over the brown and white maze of flat roofs. Puffy clouds to the north, pink from the rising sun.

Listened to short-wave news. More on Clinton victory. Looking for item on Somalia but could find none.

A paranoid, fearful place, if you listen to the local NGO people. They're a young, savvy bunch. Swiss, French, Irish, American, even one pony-tailed, blond, harmonica-blues-playing surfer from Namibia. Tonight, they're giving Donna and me a party. Meaning wine and good food.

Odd to think that this morning's peaceful scene is surrounded by displaced, starving people living in thornbush shelters, and that squads of "crazy technicals" roam the town in Mad Max-like pickup trucks and other dusty off-road vehicles modified for war. The rule of anarchy and guns controls everyday life. Just below me on the narrow, walled-in road, men and women—mostly dressed in thin desert robes and head-gear—pass by on their way to gather wood, buy food, take their livestock to the river, pray at the nearby mosque. Donkeys, kids, men holding hands, an occasional car bumping by—something wherever I look. Now a baby cries, a donkey brays. Not much different, really, than Peru, than my old street in Sicuani—rock and adobe structures, glass bits cemented along the wall tops for security. But then you'd hear gunshots. Maybe serious, maybe somebody firing a few rounds for the hell of it or to check out a weapon.

Today we follow Mary again. She should be our protection. But, as we were reminded, you never know. An argument, an outburst at the slightest provocation. It doesn't take much to light the fuse.

11/7, 8 p.m.

Sitting in my room, waiting for dinner and listening to a French imitation of Bob Dylan with a rock beat. Too loud— but, ah, someone's lowered it. Now, Italian booms out. Pavarotti.

This afternoon we were actually surrounded and had to face down some hot-headed "technicals" all wired on Qat, the local chewing narcotic. They hopped off their Mad Max contraption and one guy pointed a loaded grenade-launcher at me, then shifted his aim to Donna as soon as she raised her Leica. Two other crazy-eyed guys cocked their weapons and also pointed. We'd been backed up against a wall, and I shouted with obscene emphasis for Donna to put the camera away. I was certain they had nothing to lose by shooting us.

After she lowered the camera, our translator, who'd been hanging back, caught up with us. He talked to the technicals, and suddenly they retreated and left. Apparently, they were operating without permission of their clan leader, and our translator threatened to call the leader if they didn't leave immediately.

Inevitably, on that occasion in Somalia, I compared myself to my father. I wasn't calm or collected in shouting at Donna, but the shouting or the shriek of panic in my voice did get the road warriors to relax their fingers on the triggers. Also, earlier, as Mary went from one feeding station to another, taking stock of the clusters of skeletal desert refugees, I imagined my father caring for my fragile, underfed mother, much like his guiding water into the pitiful bodies of emaciated fellow prisoners, holding a hand or covering a body. As Julio told me in explaining his younger brother's failures in romance:

Maybe he just found himself doing those things. He was able to give of himself with his fellow prisoners, whereas when it came to a lasting, intimate relationship with a woman, it was more difficult to give of himself. In prison camp the deed was its own reward. With your mother, there was no reward—unless it was to overcome any feelings of guilt he might have had. Guilt about what, I don't know. Maybe relations with other women.

After my Somalia assignments, I had a run of five more war-related trips: one to interview hostages in Baghdad and Kuwaiti refugees in Jordan, two to Saudi Arabia for Operation Desert Storm, one to Croatia for a medical relief piece, and one to Bosnia for a story on a former marine, now a Rhode Island fireman teaching locals how to fight fires under fire. Big John, as I was calling him, was one of those snoring the loudest in the fart-filled room I had just left. Ken Regan, the photographer on the assignment, was also asleep in the room. I had worked other rough parachute gigs with Ken, so I knew he had a higher tolerance for abuse than I did. He could also sleep through just about anything. I figured he'd eventually wake up, sniff the foul air, shrug, and maybe go back to sleep for a while longer.

Like so many journalists who scramble after what we can capture of war, Ken liked to ride in the front seat of the roller coaster. But he wasn't a hardcore war junkie like some who can do nothing else, who only feel truly alive when they're pointing cameras into gun muzzles. I was always along for the safer excitement, always seeking cover, never really feeling the fear of the overpowered victim. I knew I could always leave, whether it was Nicaragua or Somalia—it didn't matter. My safety net was always a plane out, a safe city, and money to spend on a good hotel and good food. I was confident only because I knew I wasn't trapped. But some of the other pencils and shooters—which is what the officers called us at pre-Gulf War briefings—seemed to be trapped by their own obsessions. As I wrote in a journal from Saudi Arabia:

Hanging around all the shooters and pencils gives you perspective. Listening to the photographers discuss the next big story (maybe Moscow), I was reminded how ephemeral all stories are—even war stories. These veteran journalists, running from one crisis spot to another, appear to be a detached lot. They have a great-story meter all their own. They do get excited at times, but I think the longer they work stories, no matter how momentous and world-center-stagey they are, it takes increasing levels of emotion, weirdness or adrenaline rushes to get them excited. Like drug addicts, they—and maybe I should include myself here—need bigger and bigger doses of the narcotic for it to have a strong effect.

Another journal entry has me revving up my enthusiasm for military hardware and possibly for the war itself.

Last night while I was talking to Joan by phone I started sounding like a Bush defender, saying Saddam doesn't have a chance—Iraq will be flattened, he'll be responsible for the death of his people. My blustering was probably caused by having driven seven hours into the desert yesterday and having seen the massive war party the military has prepared for the Iraqis. Everywhere, we saw compounds, camps and weapons. Tanks behind every dune, rows and rows of personnel carriers, missiles poking up from the sand, all pointing north toward Kuwait. Hour after hour you could look away from the highway and usually see herds of camels in the distance, along with clusters of camouflaged tents, vehicles, sandbagged bunkers, stacks of supplies, and maybe some choppers poised on the edges of the camp like fat scorpions. And the asphalt highway was filled with convoys of flatbed trucks loaded with tanks and troop carriers, lines of Humvees and tractor-trailers stacked with food crates, giant water bladders, shell casings, and big guns all folded and tied down. Most every vehicle going north was loaded, most going south were empty.

It all looked very threatening in a grand, awesome, inevitable way. Desert D-Day approaching. . . . No wonder I sounded like a militarist.

I suppose I was caught up in the grand *mechanics* of war—the hardware, the logistics, the precision and order of it all. I was a kid again playing with my plastic soldier figures, buzzing the enemy with my Spitfire, rolling over them with my Sherman tank. Kid stuff then, but now?

We hung with the Marines. We slept on cots in tents with them, ate their chow, rode on their M-60 tanks, flew in a cargo helicopter called a Sea Stallion, and skimmed over Persian Gulf waters in a nifty rubber-bottomed patrol boat. I reported and wrote; Ken shot. The war had yet to start, so we sent the magazine relatively tame human-interest stories. One was about the lives of a tank crew, another about a chopper pilot, and a third about an Ohio reservist grandmother who operated a 50-caliber machine gun mounted on the patrol boat.

As the pre-invasion preparations stretched from a few weeks to a few months, I became increasingly frustrated and impatient with our military minders. All our requests had to go through channels, and we spent many days waiting in Dhahran for approvals. Joan was also missing me as well, anxious about the idea of my following troops into combat. She needn't have worried—it was obvious it wouldn't be that kind of war. In early January of 1991, I asked the magazine to replace me and I flew back to New York. At the time I was feeling a lot like the old-timer I describe in my journal before leaving Saudi Arabia.

1/2/93

At the briefing this morning the Newsweek guy was grumping about how different it was in Nam. No military flaks hounding and roadblocking your every move. You just went outside and hitched up with some troops, and you got your story. No permission this, permission that. "Not like in Nam," he was saying. "No fucking officer telling you what you can and can't do. You just went out and did it. You might get your ass shot, or you might get your story."

Ken stayed on, went north into Kuwait, saw some awful sights of enemy corpses, and eventually returned to less grim duties in the United States.

Now here we were in Bosnia, several years older and just as fascinated by the military trappings and arrangements of warfare: the U.S. air force flight from Ancona, Italy, the dicey landing under low clouds, the sniper fire, the jog across the tarmac to the terminal bunkers, our helmets and flak jackets jangling, the weapons everyone seemed to carry, the uniforms, the language of salutes, commands, and clipped responses, and for me, all the familiar yes-sirs and no-sirs. However, as I would soon find out, all my flirting with the military world would not prepare me for that moment when I was convinced a sniper was about to blow away my head.

I was shivering in the hallway, thinking about re-entering the stinky sleeping quarters of my firefighting hosts, when the clanging of the metal triangle began echoing throughout the old brick firehouse. In minutes everybody was heading for their suits, boots, and the trucks downstairs. Big John said he would drive his own Ford pickup truck to the fire, following behind the station's two pumpers. Outside a cold drizzle fell on the walled-in yard where the pickup was parked. Among the shadows cast by flashlights, I could see figures yanking on boots, hitching up overall suits and slipping into yellow coats like so many cumbersome moths molting in reverse.

I draped a plastic poncho over my flak vest and parka, then climbed in the back with Ken. His main camera bag was in the cab with John. As soon as his two American volunteers, Rick and Heidi, arrived and scooted in next to John, off we went after the pumpers. By the time we arrived at the burning two-story structure, the firemen had already begun shooting streams of water into the flames bursting from the broken windows. Moving up the street toward the fire, the bulky former marine handed me a pistol and asked me to keep it dry under my poncho. As a neutral, UN-sanctioned relief worker, he wasn't supposed to carry a firearm, but John wasn't taking any chances. "They love to pop firemen," he had told me earlier. "I know they'd love to get me at close range. That way they could be sure they got The Beard. That's what they call me."

In the twenty months since Big John had been equipping and training firemen in Sarajevo, sniper rounds and rocket-launched grenades had killed twelve firemen and wounded another forty. "Fortunately," he told me, as he started toward a door he intended to bash down with his fists—which he did—"snipers don't like to work in the rain."

At odd free moments, I had pulled out of him the basic facts of his life in Rhode Island: his female companion, his friends, his volunteer firefighting work, his efforts to generate funds and equipment donations, including used fire trucks. All this I dutifully jotted down. Yet there was something deeper, hidden in vagueness, that he kept from me. It had to do with his marine past, his abrupt exit from the corps, and an allusion to having done special operations or mercenary work in global hot spots he wouldn't name. I pleaded for clarity, saying my editors would be all over me about these omissions. But John was as tight-lipped and enigmatic as my father used to be. In the end, all he would say was, "I've done enough of the negative. Now I want to do something positive."

I left it at that, concluding Big John was entitled to secrets he may have sworn to keep. Still I wondered if he was on a mission of atonement. In this regard he reminded me of my father. Was it atonement when he went on caring for my mother after she found him one night with another woman? After Mommy died, did he have reason to atone for anything else? Why the attempted suicide? And why, after his rehabilitation, had he gone to Denver to see Father Prohens, his long-ago confessor and friend? Only recently had I located the old Spanish priest. Now in his eighties, he said he wanted to see me in person, and I promised I would try to get to Denver sometime soon.

As I watched Big John in Sarajevo, knowing the little he had told me of his past, I sensed a kind of penitence in action. I also began to see the similarities and connection to my father. What had he told Father Prohens? What was his confession? What did Daddy say about the day Mommy died? A priest cannot divulge what someone confesses, but there are many ways to say something. I would take anything, no matter how disguised it was.

In his way, the big ex-marine helped me renew my hunt for family truth. In my journal I vowed to get back on track.

Meanwhile, in Sarajevo, when Ken and I weren't with John, we tagged along with CNN's Christiane Amanpour for a second on-the-job portrait story. Classy, smart, and driven, she was definitely among the true war hounds. But unlike so many, she had the edge of anger and she believed her reports just might make a difference, just might stop some of the killing and destruction.

"Other correspondents before me had World War II or Vietnam," she said. "Well, this is my Vietnam." Then, gazing at one of the shell-blasted walls of the Holiday Inn, she added, "Winter is coming and a lot of people are going to die. I'm just here to report it. Let's see if others will do something about it."

I believed her, but I couldn't share her commitment. After a week of hearing sporadic sniper fire and the loud, crushing thumps of shells exploding sometimes only a block or two away, I was ripe to leave. I had seen desperate, fearful, hungry faces before—I could cope with that. Nor was I overly bothered by all the wounded at a hospital where war surgery never stopped. What finally got to me was my own fear.

Fortunately, Big John appeared to have no fear. In fact, he seemed to challenge death every day, openly baiting the Serbian snipers. He claimed they were yokels who scored hits only by accident. He offered to drive us to the city's airport, which unfortunately could only be reached by a dash along what everyone called Sniper Alley, a wide boulevard splattered with bits of concrete and with very little building cover. For a half-mile's distance, the passage offered observers from the heights above a clear shot at anything that moved. About the only vehicles shuttling people and goods between the city's center and the airport were UN armored carriers or John's white 1988 pickup. "It doesn't have armor, but it's faster than the carriers," he explained as Ken and I tossed our luggage in the rear, then climbed into the cab.

Entering Sniper Alley, John began to accelerate, turning the steering wheel one way, then another, zigzagging, swerving around concrete chunks in the way. Our three bodies leaned in unison. As usual, John wore a baseball cap instead of a helmet. At one point, he gestured to our helmets and laughed. "Won't do you no good," he said, "not even in an armored carrier. The caliber bullet they use is big enough to go through two inches of steel, *then* take your head off—with or without the friggin' helmet."

By the time we reached the end of Sniper Alley, I had willed my naked self into the tiniest of creatures, hearing the pings of ricocheting bullets, wanting to shrink even more, imagining bullets ripping into the pickup, hoping they would miss me, the shriveled speck who was frozen with fright. When we arrived at the sandbagged parking area of the airport, we unloaded and thanked John for duty above and beyond. "You deserve a medal," I said.

"No way, what would I do with a medal? I need money to finish the new station."

We checked our luggage, ran across to our plane, boarded, and found our seats. After takeoff, I began to think of my father's medals. He never got his Silver Star, that official army blessing a notch or two below the Medal of Honor. This was probably because he didn't display "gallantry in action." His heroics in the camps were about sacrifice and discrete kindnesses done to keep men alive. Later, after repatriation and the hearing, he never reminded anyone about his commanding officer's Silver Star recommendation, and the moment passed.

Instead of symbolic praise, the army tried to disgrace him. This was part of its effort to finger a few scapegoats or those POWs who were perceived to have violated the military's code of conduct for prisoners. He cleared his name, but in reading his hearing transcript I can tell he's desperate and uncharacteristically wordy. For a while even his defense counsel can't shut up the normally taciturn man who pleads his innocence of all charges. Ironically, he embodies the very qualities the army most values in its ideal gentleman-officer. Yet these same qualities are misread, which is what almost cooked his goose.

By the time we landed back in Ancona, I had a monster craving for pasta and an antipasto or fresh salad of anything handy but beans. We had gotten our stories and I had survived my nights in the firehouse. More importantly, my Sarajevo stay had awakened a renewed sense of purpose in my pursuit of the facts of my family. I started thinking that I wanted to erase doubts about who my father really was; I wanted to bring some measure of redemption to his checkered life. To do this, I would have to take another look at my mother's death and at the intervening years leading to my father's death at the age of fifty-three.

Bridgeport

After Sarajevo the magazine sent me on my all-time dream assignment. I was to take my kayak to paddle off the southern coast of Kauai with Paul Theroux. He had just published *Happy Isles of Oceania* and my editors thought readers might want to tag along for a vicarious paddle with the famously irascible author. Checking my folding boat on the plane as luggage, I flew to Oahu, met Theroux, then we caught a local, smaller plane to Kauai.

Having read some of his travel books, I had envisioned meeting a curmudgeon. Fortunately, he turned out to be quite charming, endlessly curious, and a thoroughly pleasant, easy-going companion on the water. We got along just fine. We even had the same kind of rubber-and-canvas take-apart boat.

On our first full day we launched from a small cove just east of Poipu. We paddled through light surf, then headed south about two or three miles offshore. We were cruising along side by side, watching a school of spinner dolphins leap into the air, when we sighted three or four humpback whales approaching. At first they kept their distance, then one of the massive, crusty creatures surfaced about twenty feet away from our boats, which were comparatively tiny and completely vulnerable next to sixty tons of curiosity. The whale eyeballed us for a while, perhaps getting its fill of something strange and apparently harmless. Our giant visitor then left us, easing forward below the water's surface with hardly a quiver of its fluke. Mostly, we were silent during and after this entrancing interlude, actually a gentle communion with a being so sentient that for a moment size didn't seem to matter, only mutual respect.

Around noon we pointed our bows toward a palm-shaded cove where we could get out, stretch, and eat lunch. About halfway to the beach, I felt the clutch of heartburn in my upper chest. "Hey, Paul!" I shouted, setting down my paddle on the deck. "Can you toss me another soda?"

"Diet Coke or Seven-Up?"

"Seven-Up."

"Right. Here goes—catch!"

Theroux, who had the soda pop stashed in a cooler bag between his legs, threw the can right on target into my hands. "I think I had too many chips," I said, opening the can. Earlier, before we'd seen the whales, we had finished off a bag of tortilla chips. Now, as I swallowed the cold, fizzy liquid, I was hoping it would quickly do its work and bring up some big-time belches. I finished the can and burped some, but the heartburn continued all the way to a smooth landing on the beach. After we carried our boats up onto dry sand, I drank some water and lay down. A while later, I was feeling hungry and fine again.

A few weeks later, after my story about Theroux and the humpbacks appeared, we spoke by phone. He said I had him "smelling like roses." I answered that it was easy to do. In paradise everyone smells like roses.

In early February of 1994, however, flowers of any kind were the last thing on my mind. A nasty storm had dropped a big layer of snow on the northeast states, and one evening when I got home from New York I realized I would have to clear the driveway to get my car into the garage. Joan was in Colombia on a business trip for IBM, my neighbors on both sides were also out of town, and the snowdrift in front of the garage was about four feet high and growing. The street had just been plowed, so I left the car at the bottom of the driveway incline, trudged up to the front door, entered and came back out with a wide-bladed aluminum shovel. About an hour later, exhausted, I heaved away the last shovelful of snow from the asphalt, then drove the car into the garage.

I boiled spinach spaghetti and heated some basil and garlic sauce for dinner, watched the eleven o'clock news from bed, then clicked off the TV and lights before the late-night shows began. About two-thirty in the morning, I was awakened by the same heartburn sensation that had hit me in Kauai. I took a bottle of Maalox from the bathroom medicine cabinet and chugged three or four swallows of the stuff. Maybe too much garlic, I thought—not the red wine, but the extra clove I chopped and added to the sauce. The antacid brought up a few good burps, but the heartburn remained.

I lay in bed in the dark, waiting for it to subside, eventually falling asleep again. Then about half an hour later, I sat up, this time feeling the same burn, along with a tightness in my throat and a pain along my left arm, shooting from armpit to fingertips. That's when it occurred to me I might be having a heart problem. I swung out of bed and crossed the floor to the bookstand, where I yanked out the medical dictionary. I read the heart attack description and realized I had the classic symptoms of a coronary blockage. I thought of calling for help, but decided against a 911 call because the snow had covered up the address number on the fence outside. I didn't want to wait for the paramedics to find me already about to croak, collapsed and in extremis by the front door.

Instead, as calmly as I could, I got dressed, then stuffed a change of clothes, a toothbrush, my electric razor, and a few books into a sports bag. Downstairs in the garage, I backed out the car down to the street, glad I had shoveled it clear—although the exertion was probably what had provoked my most immediate problem.

It took me about sixteen minutes of maneuvering icy, snow-rutted streets to reach St. Joe's. The chest burn, throat tightness, arm pain, and gaspy breathing kept me company all the way to the curtained-off emergency-room gurney. In short order a young doctor listened to my heartbeat with a stethoscope, a nurse drew blood to test for the presence of certain cardiac-arrest enzymes, and an orderly hooked me up to an electrocardiogram, or EKG, monitor. People came and went, then I believe someone injected me with a blood thinner. The pain and tightness subsided. So far,

I had avoided the classic, elephant-sitting-on-your-chest whammy that a massive myocardial infarction usually causes.

Stretched out, face up, listening to the bleep-bleep of the heart-rate monitor, I was blithely relieved to know the cause of my so-called heartburn. No more nagging mystery, no more ineffectual gulps of Maalox.

After a while, the doctor appeared and told me I had had an acute, unstable angina attack.

"What's that?" I asked.

"You're lucky. Probably no damage was done to your heart."

"But what happened?"

"It looks like you had everything but a complete blockage of one or more of your coronary arteries. We won't know until we do an angiogram. As I said, you're lucky."

Two days later, Joan, who had dashed back from Colombia, accompanied me in the ambulance for the trip up 95 to St. John's in Bridgeport. My angiogram "procedure" was scheduled for the next morning, so my admission was calm and routine. On the heart patient floor, I was given a room to myself and told to wear paper slippers and a flimsy, knee-length gown that flapped open in the back. For the next five days, this comfortable but charmless room with a view of Bridgeport's industrial plants and warehouses would be my introduction to the land of cardiac cripples. I would have my arteries threaded with tubes tipped by tiny inflatable balloons that would push back the plaque in my clogged coronaries. I was told I had "lumpy, bumpy" arteries all around my heart. They would open up the most occluded of these, but the doctor cautioned that about forty percent of the angioplasties they did at St. John's failed within five or six months. If I lasted that long without angina symptoms, I would probably be cleared to resume a normal life.

I took medical leave from work and moped at home, feeling depressed and useless. Then the symptoms returned and I went back to Bridgeport for another reaming of the coronaries. All told, including the previous unclogged spots, I now had six blockages that had been given the balloon treatment. Two years later, another four "pipes," as the doctor called them, would be opened up. In the future, he said, if I had any more serious angina attacks, "we'll have to split you open for an open-heart job."

Little did I suspect at the time that all my funk over my heart setbacks would lead me into the world of cardiothoracic surgery and its "end-stage" patients—to use the common but ominous label for people with the sickest hearts, often transplant candidates kept alive by artificial pumps. I would spend months researching, interviewing, and witnessing many open-heart surgeries in order to write a book about heart disease and "complementary"—or alternative—medical therapies. I got into yoga, massage, meditation, acupuncture, herbalism, energy healing; I dabbled and practiced; I changed my diet a half-dozen times. I went from a non-oil, lowest-fat-possible regimen—Joan called it my cardboard diet—to one with a balanced dose of vegetables, carbohydrates, and some low-fat meats such as poultry and fish. I toted around jars and other containers filled with capsules and tablets of vitamins, minerals, fish oils, herbs and a cholesterol-lowering drug generically called a statin.

When I had my first attack, probably paddling in paradise with Theroux, my cholesterol level had risen dangerously above 400. Normal is 180 to 200. For years I knew I had elevated numbers and I was also a binge smoker—that is, I only smoked when I faced the anxiety of having to write. Then once I wrote a story without a cigarette and realized I could throw away my crutches for good, which I did just after my fiftieth birthday. At the time I thought exercise and a moderately vegetarian diet would keep heart disease in check.

After my problems started in earnest, I discovered that my liver produces cholesterol amounts determined mainly by the genes I inherited. Of course, diet, exercise, and other lifestyle factors also affect cholesterol and the other blood fats coursing through the body. My cardiologist told me I had a "closet type-A" personality, which meant that I was easy going on the outside, but inside—as a psychotherapist put it—I was a ball of angers and anxieties.

The therapist specialized in treating "cardiac blues," a common problem among recovering heart patients. I saw him six times, the sixth visit ending when he fell asleep listening to me run out of things to tell him. I rose from my recliner and tiptoed out of the room, leaving him a note to mail me the bill. I figured either my patter bored him or I had learned to relax and "let go" of the anger, anxiety, and fear. The message, I concluded on my own, was to grow up and stop bellyaching over bogus slights and slams against me by authority figures, especially my late father. Once I had reduced him to human proportions, once I understood his failings as a husband and father, the weight in my chest gradually lightened until it became a phantom stone easily tossed away.

Head trips aside, my body was now my biggest survival project. Again I set aside my work on family research. For the next three years I narrowly focused on regaining my health. To do this would require patience and an attitude makeover. After spending years observing others walking the edge, I was now the target of attention, the person testing life's limits. I felt like my own version of Kafka's beetle Gregor Samsa, on my back, emotionally fragile, poked, probed, and helpless. Prior to this period, I had reported dozens of stories in which compassion came easily to me because there was so much to pity and feel compassion for. But in my new reversed situation, *I* was the one drawing dreary, poor-guy looks. *I* was the one with the cardiac cripple sign around my neck. Anytime my pulse raced and my heart began thumping away as if it were trying to escape from my chest, *I* was the one with the anxiety attack. People now made allowances for *me*, the invalid with all the physical and dietary restrictions.

Yet through it all, throughout the initial rehabbing and therapeutic flurries, all I really wanted—sometimes with desperate impatience—was to be whole and normal again.

My moping, whining, and lashings of self-pity would finally end when I took on a book project for a cardiothoracic surgeon at New York's Columbia-Presbyterian Medical Center. Dr. Mehmet Oz needed a storytelling journalist to write a book about him, his patients, and his journey into alternative approaches to healing. I agreed to do the work, thinking I'd learn more about improving my own condition as well as boosting my own sagging ego. I also needed to show everyone I could work again.

I did learn a lot, but more importantly I began to shed my feelings of inadequacy as I got to know patients with truly sick hearts. I saw some of the actual physical hearts, and in one case even held the lifeless, purplish organ in my hands after it was removed for a transplant replacement. When it came to physical damage, compared to these pathetic hearts, mine was an Olympic marathoner. And as a recovering heart-disease patient, I felt like an imposter, a voyeur in the wards of the doomed or very doubtful.

Reading my journal entries from this period, I see that I used my heart disease as an excuse to live like a victim—wounded, insecure, and paranoid. However, once I began the Oz book, trailing after him on rounds, watching the inner workings of bodies in the OR, I gradually demystified the human heart in my mind. I could visualize it because I had touched it. I had poked my fingers into the ventricles, felt the dishrag-thin, blood-starved parts of the muscle. I could now conjure up my own tactile heart. It was no longer a metaphor for everything from illness to love and courage, but a twitching, throbbing, rhythmic reality. Arterial plaque was the brittle bit of white stuff that I rolled between my fingertips; a bypass was a vein from a lady's calf used to detour blood around a blocked vessel. Beating hearts were now tactile pumps to me, a matter of mechanics, while emotions and moods were matters of the mind. Of course, heart and mind affect each other instantly and continually, but at least I could now distinguish physical from mental. Anger and anxiety were mental; cholesterol and coronaries were physical.

I used to say that when your heart fails you, it's like having the wind taken out of your sails. Today, using another but more accurate cliché, I would say it's like a car engine running on fumes. I've always jogged and played intense physical sports. But when my coronaries clogged up, it was as if the fuel for my engine was being dispensed from an eyedropper. At first, I couldn't climb one flight of stairs without resting every ten steps. After rehabilitation, I was jogging four and five miles a day.

Samples of what I wrote, from the days just before my first "episode" to the time in early 1998 when I began to write *Moving Target*, trace the progress I've made in healing both heart and mind:

8-30-93

Starting Daddy project again. Have to do this, now that there's more distance.

1-7-94

Been told I'm in a slump, not to worry—it happens to the best of writers. Compared me to baseball slugger Don Mattingly, who suddenly, inexplicably, can't see the ball. Then one day it starts appearing big as a pumpkin. He can't miss.

So . . . are my stories like baseballs? Or am I losing desire? Is there another kind of writing I should be doing to get back the enthusiasm, the satisfaction, the joy of getting it just right?

Don't know. I've been told over a polite, softening-up lunch with two editors, to write up my notes in files whenever I can prior to writing the actual story. Outlines, too, as if I don't already. But, of course, maybe my first drafts and all the fiddling and fixing I cause the editors all up the line make it seem as if I really do write without an outline. Maybe they're right. Certainly won't hurt, and it's one way to make writing stories less fitful and worrisome.

Am I losing interest in writing at work? Don't know, but something's definitely going on in the brain. Is it my age? 52. Beginning a slow unwinding toward senility, or at least enfeeblement? It's bad enough starting to worry about decreasing sexual appetite and "performance." Now I must contend with a recovery campaign in my livelihood.

12-13-94

Started writing description of what I saw around me. Nurses, pregnant women, then wrote my tiny stories as my mother asked me to. Now, 40-some years later I'm back in a hospital writing my thoughts as I wait for my pre-procedure sedative—since I must be conscious while the good doctors work their magic with the catheters.

I'm thinking of Mommy, long gone from heart problems too.

2-30-94

Back home, staring out the window like a Hopper mannequin. I wish I were normal. I wish I could get out and run. I wish I could eat a burger or just fries, for chrissakes. I wish I were off all these pills I carry around. I wish I'd never heard of a heart-rate monitor.

4-20-94

Went into the office for visit and felt like Jimmy Stewart at the end of It's a Wonderful Life. Was completely open, friendly, glad to be healthy and strong again. Physical and mental therapy have got me back and more. No more feeling wounded and picked on. Talked to everyone without fear. Great relief to have my parents off my back at last. Their eyes and judgments were all in my head. Maybe rehabbing's working.

7-8-94

Been off for 5 mos. following the heart problem. Now back— 1st day at work in the office. Feel well and strong physically and emotionally. For the time being I've bagged the writing efforts on my father.

7/15/94, Fri.

3:30 pm, home early from work bec of summer-hours work schedule. The sky was overcast, uniformly gray wherever I looked. Hardly a breeze either, so the surface was flat with just a little lift to my boat from the mini swells coming from the Sound.

I live on the shore of an estuary called Holly Pond. It's about a 1/2 mile across at its widest and a mile long, from the old dam on the Sound side to the creek that feeds the "pond" at the other end. Once I paddled out to the middle, which I heard was the deepest. With the handle of a leaf rake I measured the depth at about 5 ft at low tide. A full-moon high tide would raise the water another five or six feet. So HP, my bit of ocean in front of my house, is shallow enough that even storm waves never reach the scary heights of waves on the Sound.

8/10/94

Late afternoon, out on chair on front lawn. Beautiful blue sky with a few puffy clouds catching the lowering sun. Waiting for Joan to come home. Also waiting for tomorrow's procedure, my second angioplasty.

8 swans drifting by. Usual joggers, bikers, walkers, bladers and after-work traffic.

I'm a bit anxious about going back to the hospital. Even when angios are done, people die. No guarantees. But I have to trust all will turn out OK. Put on a game face, as Mommy would say.

I can also say it's been great living. Not many complaints really. I've had more than my share of luck, successes and ego pats. I have Joan, my son Michael, and lots of friends. I've traveled, I've usually had money to spend. What's to regret? I'll never get youth back, but I still enjoy a physical life—if my heart permits. Hope it all continues. . . .

8-13-94

Bk again. Heart patched and at home watching Missing Link and realizing in person and on the screen how thin the margin is between life and nothing. Nothing for me, that is.

Primitive man, hunting and hunted. And me, preyed upon by my own genes and appetites—both clogging the coronaries.

Consider pain. What is it? Besides a hurt that is felt, pain is also a focus. The greater the pain, the more intense we focus on it. I can think of many kinds of pain—some I've felt and some I haven't. An ache in the knee joint, my chin cut by a razor while shaving, a sinus headache, a woman's strain in childbirth, a twisted ankle, a throbbing, infected molar. Then there's the chest pain during an angioplasty. It's really a mini-heart attack that occurs when the little balloon expands and shuts off the flow of blood to a part of the heart muscle. For maybe 15 or 20 seconds, it's as if a sumo wrestler were sitting on my chest.

8-15-94

The angioplasties have to work this time. I don't want to return to the hospital. 2 unpleasant experiences. First, I get a stubby-fingered klutz to draw my blood prior to the angio. This short, tree-trunk of a woman plunges the needle into a part of the vein that made the crook of my arm feel as if she had jabbed me with a red-hot poker, then twisted it around some. "It's coming so slow," she said. I said nothing, almost cried.

Then, later, the nurse stuck me in the left cheek muscle with an industrial-size needle filled with a relaxant. "Nembutal is thick," the nurse said, as she massaged the goo into the muscle. I immediately started trembling—an allergic reaction, I was told later.

As I lay on the gurney between the elevator banks of the 6th floor cardiology unit, I was suddenly seeing everything through a Felliniesque, fisheye lens. Big garish faces, clear, loud, distinct voices (Joan repeating, "Breathe deep! Breathe deep!" and even the doctor calmly saying, "Well, well, what's this?"). All the time I'm staring up, chilled, trembling, jerking in spasms, wondering, too, what was happening to me.

Then they shot me with more downers and all I remember after that was the distinct pressure-pain of the actual balloonings—not as real-time occurrences but as part of some fuzzy dream where a giant would step on my chest or some monster would clamp a vise on my chest, then the pressure would be released just as I was about to burst. (The real clamp came later when the Dr. squeezed off my femoral artery in my thigh to keep the puncture for the catheter from bleeding.)

9-8-94

Supposed to keep my anger down, but how to suppress or talk away anger at my body, my heart, my liver?

At Hawaiian Shirt Day party at the office today, Nancy and I exchanged our medical stories—she with cancer and me with my bum heart. So serious, so sensitive, the two of us, members of a club, right-of-passage initiates. We've crossed a line.

I was subpar today, tired, a bit of jaw tightness. I'm not free yet.

9-19-94

I don't know if I'll ever heal myself, but I'm trying. Every time I did anything physical I waited for the pressure in the chest, the tightness around my neck and jaw, the trouble catching a deep breath. This time none of these things have happened. I jog, I take stairs two at a time, I paddle my kayak for an hour or more into the Sound, I use my bike for 6-mile errands, and I walk a lot. All of this and I haven't been brought down yet.

9-22 Thrs.

Good news. Dr. B announced with pleased surprise that my cholesterol tested at 183. Lipids great.

9-30-94

I worked hard for the past three weeks, but for the moment I'm done. I had to report and write a very tight, affecting story about a family of 5 who died last month in a US Air crash near Pittsburgh. I spent 5 days interviewing about 50 people, then another work week transcribing my taped interviews, and finally, this week, I wrote the piece.

The obvious theme is grief, so that's what I stressed in the reactions I observed and heard from people. Now, how does my usual work on the death beat affect my heart? Does emoting and empathizing and occasionally letting slip a tear worsen my heart condition? Does the memory of Jonathan dying on a gurney—with me helpless beside him—does that image prompt the release of a surge of adrenaline and cholesterol into my blood stream? Does that sympathetic, choked-up feeling I get when hearing or seeing agony in a face—does that feeling close up the arteries feeding my heart? Or cause these tiny vessels to go into spasms?

That time with Taro in Nicaragua with the kids, did it shorten my life? We were given 20 minutes to photograph and talk to a children's ward full of new amputees from grenade and landmine explosions. No painkillers available, not even aspirin. Most of the kids were screaming, crying, one little girl, her two pink leg stumps in the air for us to see.

I don't know. But I do know I'm more in touch with my own humanity when I get this close to raw sensation.

3/26/95

I have to stop blaming my parents for all my problems.

10/25/95

All right. Tough time breathing trying to make the 6:07. I can do it from my office to Grand Central, at a fast walk, in about 11 mins. But this time I had about 9 minutes. So I did some jogging, alternating with stretches of walking. I slipped into the last car with about 20 seconds to spare.

But I was feeling the pressure in the throat and beneath my jaw. What's happening? I was doing fine for the last few months. Jogging, playing two sets of tennis full out, biking—sometimes getting my heart rate up to 150–160 with hardly any pressure. Feeling OK and out of the woods.

Is this the start of something ominous and long lasting? Or is it just a reaction to last week's particularly stressful duties. Too many details, too many tasks, too little time. I'm overloaded. Or is it the colder weather?

10-29-95

I'm sitting in my hospital bed tethered to an IV tube that's dripping blood thinner into my body. This is my third trip back to the hospital to have my coronaries cleared. The first time I was just past 52, almost the age Daddy died. Now, nearly two years later, I'm frustrated and wondering how much longer I have to live.

The cheerful cardiologist who just walked into my room tells me, "You just never know." He says this quickly as a matter of fact. Just a doctor doing his rounds. He must see the whole range of patients waiting for more life. (This is not a cancer ward, so I'm assuming all of us are thinking positively.) It's a doctor's standard, easy line and he's just being realistic. Like the doctor who said it was too bad I didn't get to choose my parents because they gave me a lousy liver, one that excels in producing cholesterol.

Nurse Lisa comes in and tells me the doctors will be doing ten patients today. But until they have their morning coffee they won't know who's going in first, second or last. "Ask them if I can go third," I say, "after they warm up." Nurse Lisa pats my arm as she checks the IV bag. "Whatever you say," she answers, barely reacting to my lame attempt at humor.

11/4/95

Back home. Hope it takes this time.

6/6/96 a.m. train to NY

A great beginning for a day. Went for a 2-hr. paddle. Vigorous, steady. Then took home-cholesterol test before brkfast. Result was astounding. The reading on the scale, which I read over and over, thinking there might be a mistake, was 126! Incredible. I've never been able to drop it lower than 180 or so. But Gould's diet of much more protein and a lot less sugar and carbos, plus 3 gms daily of niacin—whoa! Doesn't get better than this.

6/10/96

Tested myself again this morning after a 32-mile bike ride, a light dinner and a night's sleep. The scale barely hit 14, which put my cholesterol level somewhere just under 120. Fantastic, of course, but is it too low? I'll inform Dr. B today.

7/5/96

Now on the Dr trail, gathering stuff for a heart book. Physically cruising. Strength is there most of the time, except when I'm very active 2 or 3 days in a row. Get the blahs and exhaustion comes. Then I nap to recuperate. Did so yesterday, Sun., and Sat. Full energy back. Symptoms rarely in my consciousness.

8-14-97

Bk to the Father Book. I wrote the Oz book at a sprint, and I believe I'm past the worst of my heart problems. Back to work fulltime as a NY correspondent. Lighter, more mechanical duties. Need only reporting skills.

9-3-97

Health my life project of the moment, although I'm finally emerging from this body-centered version of navel gazing. My lab #'s are good, pump strong, pipes stable. Dr. B says they should stay well for another 30 or 40 years! Optimist, or else didn't he check my age on the charts. Looking to 60 now.

Hope the magazine can move us back to L.A. next year, which will be good for the heart and the head. Then I can push ahead on the memoir.

10-16-2000

Finished the 26th chapter of Moving Target. Finally coming into the home stretch.

CERTIFICATE OF DEATH
STATE OF CALIFORNIA

5600 — 1711

STATE FILE NUMBER — LOCAL REGISTRATION DISTRICT AND CERTIFICATE NUMBER

DECEDENT PERSONAL DATA

1A. Name of decedent—first	ARMANDO
1B. Middle	-
1C. Last	ARIAS
2A. Date of death (month, day, year)	July 28, 1980
2B. Hour	0300
3. Sex	Male
4. Race	White
5. Ethnicity	-
6. Date of birth	February 2, 1925
7. Age	55 years
8. Birthplace of decedent (state or foreign country)	AZ
9. Name and birthplace of father	Julio Arias - Spain
10. Birth name and birthplace of mother	Maria Lopez - MX
11. Citizen of what country	USA
12. Social Security number	527-16-1573
13. Marital status	Widowed
14. Name of surviving spouse (if wife, enter birth name)	-
15. Primary occupation	Major
16. Number of years this occupation	adult life
17. Employer (if self-employed, so state)	U.S. Government
18. Kind of industry or business	Army

USUAL RESIDENCE

19A. Usual residence—street address (street and number or location)	4530 Hendrickson Road
19B.	
19C. City or town	Ojai
19D. County	Ventura
19E. State	CA
20. Name and address of informant—relationship	Self Before Demise

PLACE OF DEATH

21A. Place of death	At Residence
21B. County	Ventura
21C. Street address (street and number or location)	4530 Hendrickson Road
21D. City or town	Ojai

CAUSE OF DEATH

22. Death was caused by: (enter only one cause per line for A, B, and C)

	Cause	Approximate interval between onset and death
Immediate cause (A)	Respiratory Failure	Hours
Due to, or as a consequence of (B)	Squamous Cell CA of Lung	Mos.
Due to, or as a consequence of (C)		

Conditions, if any, which gave rise to the immediate cause, stating the underlying cause last.

24. Was death reported to coroner? NO
25. Was biopsy performed? YES
26. Was autopsy performed? NO

23. Other conditions contributing but not related to the immediate cause of death:

27. Was operation performed for any condition in items 22 or 23? Type of operation: NO — Date:

PHYSICIAN'S CERTIFICATION

28A. I certify that death occurred at the hour, date and place stated from the causes stated. I attended decedent since (enter mo, da, yr): 6-25-80. I last saw decedent alive (enter mo, da, yr): 7-22-80

28B. Physician—signature and degree or title: R. Gordinier MD

28C. Date signed: 7/28/80

28D. Physician's license number: G7890

28E. Type physician's name and address: Dr Gordinier, M.D., 204 Pirie Road, Ojai, Calif.

INJURY INFORMATION

29. Specify accident, suicide, etc. — 30. Place of injury — 31. Injury at work — 32A. Date of injury—month, day, year — 32B. Hour

33. Location (street and number or location and city or town) — 34. Describe how injury occurred (events which resulted in injury)

CORONER'S USE ONLY

35A. I certify that death occurred at the hour, date and place stated from the causes stated. As required by law I have held an (inquest-investigation) — 35B. Coroner—signature and degree or title — 35C. Date signed

36. Disposition	Cremation
37. Date—month, day, year	7-30-80
38. Name and address of cemetery or crematory	Grand View Crematory, Glendale, CA
39. Embalmer's license number and signature	Not Embalmed
40. Name of funeral director (or person acting as such)	McDermott-Crockett Mortuary
41. Local registrar—signature	Sarah L. Miller, M.D.
42. Date accepted by local registrar	JUL 29 1980

STATE REGISTRAR: A. B. C. D. E. F.

VS-11 (10-78)

CALIFORNIA DRIVER LICENSE

MUST BE CARRIED WHEN OPERATING A MOTOR VEHICLE AND WHEN APPLYING FOR RENEWAL

EXPIRES ON BIRTHDAY IN **1982**

N0796950
ARMANDO ARIAS
PO BX 672
OJAI, CA 93023

SEX	HAIR	EYES	HEIGHT	WEIGHT	PRE LIC EXP
M	BLK	HZL	6-00	165	78

DATE OF BIRTH
02-11-25

OTHER ADDRESS: WILBERS RANCH HWY 33

Armando Arias

DO NOT LAMINATE

Death certificate with my dad's correct birth date.

Oceanside

The same fog blew in off the Pacific, sweeping over rooftops and skinny palm trees, up the hill five or six blocks, silently rushing on through streets and alleyways, pasting wetness on windows, rising, cresting at the top where the house she died in still stands. I drove by the front and noticed a new fence in back and what looked like a new deck extending out from the dining room. The wooden siding was still yellow, and I recognized the tree that Daddy almost reduced to a stump. It was now huge and bushy with leaves.

How many families had lived in the house since we left in 1969? I was tempted to knock on the door to see if the present occupants would let me look around, but decided not to bother them. Better to keep the house as I last remembered it, although I would just as soon forget how I felt toward my mother the last time I saw her alive. She was in a fog of drugs, depression, and hurt, and all I could do was pity her and try to get away.

Five years before she died, when I had just returned from Peace Corps duty in Peru, she gave me a birthday card, which I keep and occasionally read as a reminder of her inability to change the inevitable.

30 November 1964

Twenty-three years ago I welcomed you and as I heard your first cry I fell asleep—to wake up, looking into your tiny face, weaving dreams for you of the future to be.

And now, you have come from across the seas to keep me from the grave. I will not extinguish your faith in me, my Beloved son, and tho I live a hundred years, I could never repay your patience, kindness and understanding. I thank God for a son such as you and am Always proud of having been chosen to be

—Your Mother

On the back of the card, also in gold-colored ink, she writes, in what looks like a poem she copied from somewhere:

This, too, Shall Pass Away
When skies are clear,
expect the cloud,
In darkness, wait
the coming light,
Whatever be thy
Fate today,
Remember, even this
shall pass away!

When she did die, there were suspicions that my father may have caused or encouraged her death by lacing an Ovaltine drink with an overdose of the barbiturates or antidepressants she was taking. The Oceanside authorities did not suspect foul play, and the police record shows that no forensic work was done at the house. Although no autopsy was performed either, her death certificate listed a drug-related "coronary thrombosis" as the cause. Nevertheless, Mama and Tuy were convinced my father somehow led her over the edge. There was the torn birthday card he received which my father mailed after she died. Mommy had written something to her brother, but it had been torn away. Had she been writing a plea for help? Tuy asks. Was she telling him in so many words that Armando was trying to kill her?

My uncle also feels his brother-in-law was hiding something in the master bedroom where she died. Otherwise, why did he ask my uncle to leave the room? Finally, my uncle and grandmother believed that he felt so guilty for what he had done that he tried to kill himself. When that failed, he went off to start a new life with another woman, severing all previous ties to his sons and the rest of the family. "I think his conscience was bothering him about something," Tuy says. "That's why he had to go confess to the Spanish priest in Colorado. He had to get religious to relieve his conscience. I remember he came back and told us he had visited the priest."

My brother Armand sees it differently. And aside from our father he was the only other person in the house the day Mommy died.

> *That morning I took you and Joan and little Michael to the airport in San Diego. Then I came home. Daddy was asleep on the sofa, and I went downstairs, because we had gotten up around five in the morning. I remember looking in on her and I saw her in bed, and I didn't think anything of it. I went downstairs to go to sleep. Well, shortly thereafter Daddy came down and woke me up. He was hysterical.*

"What do you mean?"

Well, he was crying, he was hysterical, because she had died, and he was totally incapable of doing anything. I had to do everything.

"This is incredible. This is a surprise. I mean he was such a guy in control."

I know, unless it was an act or something.

"You don't think—"

No.

"Was he shaking or—"

Just shaking and crying and saying things like, 'She's gone,' and then the rest—that is, the immediate rest—is a real blur as to who I called. I don't remember if I called the police or whether Tuy did. They took her away and the family was notified.

"Did you go in the bedroom?"

Yes.

"Was she under the covers?"

She had a way—not totally on her back but kind of halfway sitting up. That's the way she slept, and that's the way she looked when I came home, if I remember right. And that's the way she was when I looked in on her.

"Do you remember anything about the Ovaltine?"

He always used to make that for her, to help her sleep. So that's a possibility.

"But you don't remember any other details about the bedroom—open bottles, pills?"

No, no. If you're looking for that, no. There have been rumors that there was something underneath her when they picked her up, but I didn't see that. So I can't say. I have always thought, and it's my own feeling, that it was her illness, her rundown condition, that pushed her to her death. She was running on absolutely nothing. You know, on sheer will power.

"You mean foodwise?"

Minimum food. I mean, she was down to the low nineties in weight. She was running on sheer will power, which she had a lot of, just hanging on so she was able to see her grandson. Once she saw him, that was it—she gave up. She was fulfilled. Now she could let go—whether by her hand or by someone else's hand, I can't surmise because I was gone. I didn't see what happened. There is a possibility of the pills, because he did have access to them. He would hide them from her so she wouldn't take too many. He'd dole them out to her as she needed them. She'd beg him for more. So that's a possibility, that maybe he did doctor her Ovaltine. If he did, I don't know. It certainly could have been for humanistic motives.

"And then he tries to kill himself—not the act of a normal person."

Unless he felt guilty, or maybe it was delayed shock. But we never talked about it. It never happened.

"Do you think he killed her?"

No, I don't think he did it.

"Did he abuse her?"

I never remembered him abusing her physically. Maybe emotionally, psychologically, yes. The dislocated shoulder, she did it herself. She fell off the bed once, right on her shoulder. It was a high bed. That's how she injured herself. She was weak and drugged and refused to be taken to the hospital. He didn't push her down the stairs the way she told Mama. Remember, Mama could exaggerate. In the end, I think she just gave up. It wouldn't have taken much for her to die.

As for what our father told Father Jaime Prohens, the Denver parish priest said he would tell me as much as he could remember about my father's visit. More than twenty years had passed since that time, but since we first spoke he had been thinking about their long-ago meeting. I happened to be in Denver gathering information for a bank robbery and murder story, so I took a break from reporting to interview the man I hadn't seen since I was fourteen. He used to come for dinner when we lived in Colorado Springs, and I remember my mother would serve paella and wine, and they would play *Carmen* or Spanish *paso dobles* on the record player. The conversation would swing from serious to silly with lots of laughter in between. Whenever el padre Prohens came to the house, it was as if my parents were entertaining royalty—from the mother country, no less.

I located his church in a mostly Mexican and Chicano neighborhood on Denver's west side. When he opened the rectory door, I saw the same balding, bespectacled, kindly figure I had in my mind from four decades ago. We embraced, then went upstairs to his private office. After a few reminiscences about his visits to our home and the sporadic contacts he had with my parents since then, we began talking about my father's visit.

If Father Prohens had heard his confession a month after my mother's death, he wouldn't precisely say one way or another. As he went over the question in his mind, speaking to me with an earnest, lowered voice, there was an elliptical, word-relishing quality about the way he circled in on his answer. I listened to Don Quixote sermonize on the travails of ideal knighthood. We spoke in Spanish and I seemed to have opened a spigot for such fancy language as "in good time," "along these roads," "your letter brought to mind a marvelous memory of an excellent family," and "besides being a sign of filial gratitude and love, your project should be an homage to a meritorious and noble person." As I heard the words flow, I could see the pose and mission of knighthood described but made impossible in the modern world—or any world, for that matter.

From what I could gather, my father visited his old friend more for consolation and blessing than confession. The following is the plainest digest I could make of the patient padre's elegant answers to my many questions:

Actually, he visited me when I was still in Colorado Springs. He was staying in the Fort Carson officers' housing. As I remember, he was very disturbed. He was missing Emma. He was lonely and distraught. At one time they did love each other. Then at the end I believe he and Emma did not get along so well. He was tormented in those last years, but when she passed away, he was affected by her death. I also believe he was psychologically affected by his prison camp experience, and after fifteen or twenty years there was a delayed reaction. I think that was it. He was very Spanish in the old way—honor, chivalry, the values of his ancestors. And he and your mother found in me, a Spaniard from Spain, someone they could openly confide in. About his suicide attempt, let's leave it in a gray corner, or out—as they say—in the middle distance [tierra de por medio]. At the time he was unbalanced. I remember later he did go to Spain for rest and consolation. He was so proud to be an officer. And appearances aside, he was very sentimental. He was an officer of emotions.

Father Prohens was visibly affected as he spoke of my parents. From what he had seen, they were the ideal couple, my mother more Dulcinea than troubled wife, and my father more mounted knight than Casanova. Over the years, they had stayed in touch, and it saddened him that the marriage had fallen apart. Father Prohens admired them greatly and it grieved him to hear the news of my father's death in 1980.

Reluctantly I broached the subject of guilt regarding my mother's demise. In listening to his brief, head-shaking answer, I could not detect a whiff of indication that my father might have caused her death. If anything—and in this I agree with Father Prohens—we will never know if he actually killed her. What's important is that Daddy *believed* he somehow did cause her death, either by neglect or some unintentional slipup in doling out her pills—unless, as my younger brother suggests, her heart and body just gave out on their own. At any rate, having her die under his care was enough to convince my father that he was somehow responsible, that maybe he could have prevented her death.

Leaving the question of fault or guilt in the gray, ambiguous "middle distance," was, I believe, the proper and wisest answer to my question. The truth is that my distraught, lonely, guilt-ridden father was not "faking it" with his friend and likely confessor. He had no reason to make a trip to Denver just to act the part of a bereaved husband. He wasn't seeking forgiveness so much as seeking relief from the pain and guilt he was feeling.

Whether or not my father was beset by such ailments as post-traumatic stress disorder—as Father Prohens suggests—we can only guess. What we know is that his silent moods, screaming nightmares, and his sometimes strange, even cruel, behavior—as when he submitted Junior to a plague of insects—began after his Korean War experience. Certainly, in prison camp he was nothing like this. I wasn't able to locate his psychological profile from the Veterans Hospital where he was admitted after the suicide attempt, but I don't think I need it now. Some of his actions, which I or my relatives or his friends observed at close range, speak to the diagnosis.

In this regard, Max Medema, my father's erstwhile Arizona buddy Maximiliano, told me that when he saw him in 1962, it turned out to be the bleakest of visits.

> *We hadn't seen much of each other since he got back from Korea, what with your family moving around and all. But he called me one day out of the blue and we met in Glendale. We'd been real close before—I remember all the parties with him and your mom and just having a whale of a time. The thing I sensed at that last meeting with him was this alienation. He was alienated from everything, completely down in the dumps and just as gloomy as you could be. I could just sense it, and I thought, 'He feels distant from me and I can't get close to him.' Nothing I could say brought him out of it. Maybe it was the marriage going sour, as you say, but I know he was very upset that he couldn't get better jobs, that he was stuck working as a cook or still doing manual things. Whatever it was that brought him down, it was a huge weight. That was the last time I saw him.*

Medema, who spoke to me at his spacious, modern home next to the mountains bordering the north edge of Los Angeles, ended his recollection and excused himself. "He gave me something I want to show you," he said, then he left the room and returned moments later with something small and red which he carried in upturned, cupped hands. It was an empty, crinkled cigarette pack with Chinese writing and a flared-roof temple pictured on both sides. He held it out to me. "From his prison camp days," Medema said.

I looked at the wrinkled outer red-paper wrapping, the thin sheath of tin foil inside, and the minuscule bits of tobacco at the bottom.

"Keep it," he said.

"Thanks."

"Don't know why I kept it all these years, but it's yours."

Le Breuil
en Auge
MARTINI
AUBERGE
DU
DAUPHIN
UNICO
P
A 50 m

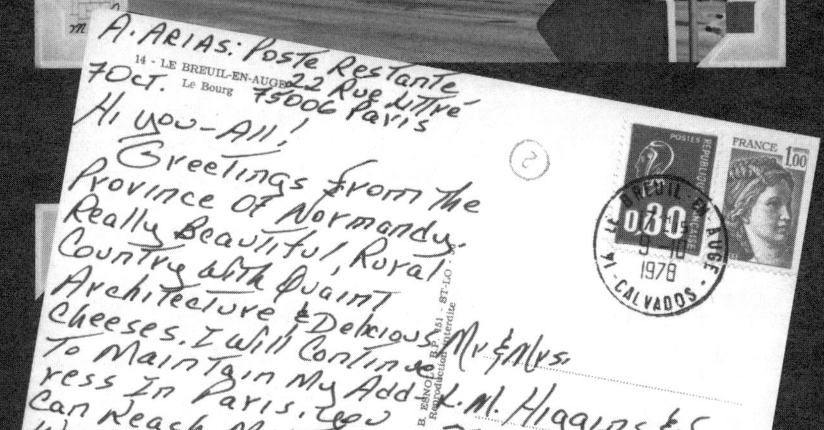
A. ARIAS: Poste Restante
22 Rue Littré
75006 Paris
7 Oct.
14 - LE BREUIL-EN-AUGE
Le Bourg
Hi You-All!
Greetings from the Province Of Normandy. Really Beautiful, Rural Country With Quaint Architecture & Delicious Cheeses. I Will Continue To Maintain My Address In Paris. You Can Reach Me There. Will Let You Know Well In Advance When I Plan to Move Out.
Au Revoir!
Armando
Éditions B. ESNOL B.P. 151 - ST-LO - Reproduction interdite
Couleurs Naturelles
POSTES REPUBLIQUE FRANÇAISE 0,30
FRANCE 1,00
14 BREUIL-EN-AUGE
9-10 1978
CALVADOS
Mr. & Mrs.
L. M. Higgins & Son
336 El Coneyo Dr.
Ojai, Calif. 93023
U.S.A.
PAR AVION

Rota, Spain - 13 Jul 79

GRENOBLE
Quais de l'Isère, téléphérique de la Bastille (Constructeur Pomagalski) et chaîne de Belledonne

NAVY FPO
JUL 14
PM
1979

PEOPLE'S RIGHT TO PETITION FOR REDRESS
USA 10c

Dear All -
Just Got Back from Greece - & Since I'm Beginning To Tire from Travel, & Also Feeling A Little Homesick, I Plan To Depart Spain for Ojai The End Of This Month. It's Been Fascinating & Loads Of Fun, But Now I Need Time To Sort Out & Evaluate All Those Sights & Impressions With Which I've Been Bombarding My Mind! Seeyas, Armando

Mr & Mrs
L. M. Higgins & Son
336 El Conejo Dr.
Ojai, Calif.
93023

Cliché et réalisation Editions GRENOBLE J. S. © SPADEM
Reproduction interdite

38 AB 196

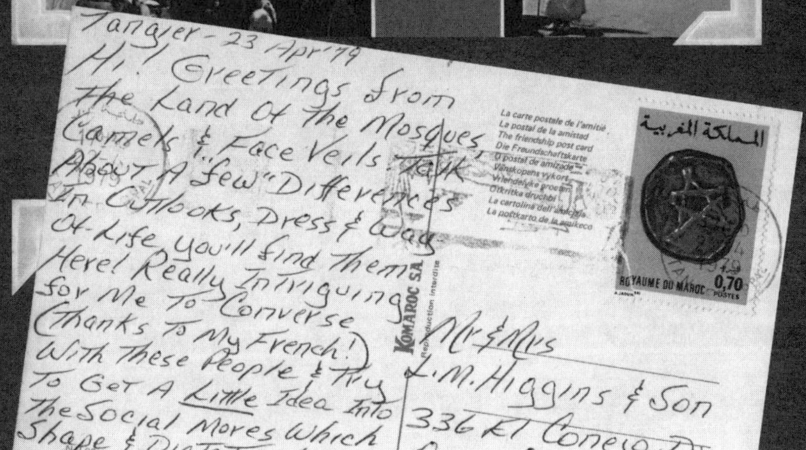

Tangier - 23 Apr '79

Hi! Greetings from
The Land Of the Mosques,
Camels & Face Veils. Talk
About A few "Differences"
In Outlooks, Dress & Way
Of Life you'll find them
Here! Really Intriguing
for Me To Converse
(Thanks To My French!)
With These People & Try
To Get A Little Idea Into
The Social Mores Which
Shape & Dictate Their
Every-Day Life Ac-
tivities. Tell you what I've
Learned Sometime. Au Revoir,
Armando

Mr & Mrs
L.M. Higgins & Son
336 El Conejo Dr.
Ojai, Calif. 93023
U.S.A.

Ojai

Yvette Veilleux was telling me that my father's family in Arizona had "cut him off." I listened for a silent moment while she left the phone to check something at her front door. On my desk the color picture of her and him standing side by side in the sunlight shows a handsome, buxom woman with long brown hair pulled back from her forehead by a pink-flowered scarf folded to headband width. She's smiling and holding a long-stemmed pink rose with both hands against her sleeveless pink dress. She looks at the camera, while my dad, left arm around her waist, looks at her with a grin. With a wisp of black hair combed back on top, trimmed mustache, white shirt, satiny-silver tie, and a pressed tan suit, he appears radiant and eager. The photograph was taken outside a courthouse either just before or after they were married.

"Ron?"

"Yeah, still here."

"Like I said, he'd been estranged from the family. I got him to renew his relations with them. It worked out fine. We went to Nogales and that was good. I met his brother Gene and everyone was very friendly to us."

"What about your relations with him?"

"We had six good years. We spent a lot of time together biking and going places. He enjoyed life. We traveled to Europe and Mexico. I liked Mexico a lot."

"What about Ojai?"

"We had a house and quite a social life, tennis, and lots of friends. Then we moved up to the mountain. He loved living on the mountain. The waterfall on the mesa was a very favorite spot for both of us. We'd hiked up there together or separately. It was lovely, so tranquil."

"Did he talk about us, his sons?"

"He spoke about you guys in the beginning. About Ronnie and Junior, I remember. That's what he called you."

"Did he ever—I mean, why didn't he want to see us? He kind of disappeared from our lives."

"He felt he'd been alienated from you. He thought you guys didn't approve of our marriage. I think he felt there was resentment. Maybe it was a misunderstanding, but he felt most of the resentment came from Bobby and his wife, Gloria. I remember him saying, 'Well, if they feel that way, we'll live in a world of our own.' We did a lot of talking about that."

"Did he ever talk about his war years?"

"Very little. You had to pry it out of him. He was very diplomatic about everything. He was unique, really—a kind, good man. I thought he was a great man, almost like a saint. He projected depth and you listened."

"You said you were married twice to him?"

"Well, after our first divorce, I moved back to Maine. We stayed friends, but he didn't like the separation. Then he visited me and asked to get back together. So we did marry again. Briefly, not even weeks."

"What happened?"

"We decided to separate. He didn't want this but agreed to it. So it was a mutual agreement. There's nothing bad I can say about him, but it just wasn't working. You know, he kept things inside. He was a listener. But it isn't good not to vent your feelings."

"Did you ever see him again?"

"We corresponded for two or three years. Then I went back to California for a visit to see my relatives and friends. I visited him for a few days. That's when he found out he was sick. He looked so old—I couldn't believe it. He was just skin and bones. Before, when we were married, he was so healthy and strong. He taught me to play tennis. It was a big part of our lives together. Then to see him like that. I just couldn't believe it. It was sad, almost pathetic."

"That was it?"

"That was the last time I saw him. About a year later, my mom called and told me about his death. I was shocked. My family, my mom, sister, they all loved him."

"Was there a funeral?"

"No, a cremation. That's what he wanted."

"Did he leave anything?"

"Nothing, really. He hadn't left a will. I don't even have pictures of him. My last husband had me destroy my photos of him and our past. If you want pictures, my sister might have some snapshots."

I didn't keep Yvette on the line much longer. She had nothing more to offer me, and though she was pleasant and generous enough on the phone, I felt she had closed that chapter of her life years ago and probably wasn't given much to reminiscing. Before we said our good-byes, she gave me the names of some of the people who knew him in Ventura and Ojai. Most of the names I already knew because he had listed them in his address book.

I made many calls before visiting the area one last time. I spoke with the oncologist who last treated him, I verified his death with the Ventura County Recorder's office, I got his death certificate, I contacted the Santa Barbara mortician who cremated his body, and I placed classified ads in the *Ojai Valley News*, asking anyone who knew Armando Arias, the horseman and tennis player, to call or write to me. A number of people did write, though it was Mrs. Lucien "Vesta" Higgins, a former next-door neighbor of the retired army major and his new bride, who gave the tidiest portrait of their time in Ojai.

Dear Sir or Madam:

I saw your ad and while I don't know the facts of his death or burial, I'll tell you what I can remember.

Armando and Yvette lived next door to us for a couple of years. They seemed to be so happy together. She raised a vegetable garden, played the piano like a professional—I mean really good—and they played tennis a lot.

Then they sold their furniture, even the pieces he brought from Europe, bought a mobile home and moved up on the mountain.

They took a trip up into Washington and Idaho, and I think they bought acreage around Coeur d'Alene. But apparently their plans didn't work out, for later that year Armando stopped by and in his quiet manner let us know he was alone. Yvette had gone back to Bangor, Maine.

We saw quite a bit of Armando—he had Christmas dinner with us, brought us fruit from his place. He and my husband fixed his motorcycle and one time his pickup truck. They really enjoyed talking together.

Then Armando took his tour of France, Italy, etc. He sent us postcards and letters, which I still have.

He once told us that he and Yvette had gotten together again, but it just didn't work out. And he never mentioned it again.

Then, around 1980, he told us that x-rays showed cancer in his lungs. He said he'd gone on a vegetarian diet. Then one day he came by and said he was on his way to see his mother.

That is the last time we ever saw or heard from our good friend. We often wondered but never saw anything in the paper and didn't know anyone to write and ask.

I hope this helps you in your quest for information.

The first person I visited in Ojai was Vesta Higgins, her husband, Lou, and their grown son Pinky, a former Vietnam War medic. As she was in her letter to me, Vesta was friendly and chatty. Even though my father had been gone from their lives for many years, they spoke excitedly and with affection about their ex-neighbors. Yvette was a "living doll," said Vesta. "She was always wearing cute summer dresses and had her hair in clever, long side-braids," while he was often "sitting in a hammock on the back porch listening to her play the piano." Yvette called him "maestro" and the two always seemed to be having a good time. Vesta said she would "scold" him for coming down the mountain on the motorcycle without a helmet and wearing only his tennis shirt and shorts against the morning chill. Lou said he was a "nomad," and Pinky added, "He loved to travel."

Vesta offered the most perceptive observation: "You know how you can meet some people for five minutes and feel you've known them all your lives? Well, your dad was just the opposite. He was the kind you could be friends with all your life and never really know. Not really and truly."

"Tell me about it," I said.

"It's a shame he couldn't share more of himself."

"I suppose he tried."

Lou: "He was very private."

The Higgins family couldn't recall my father discussing much about his past life as soldier and prisoner in two wars, or about having raised three sons. Most of his talk was about the here and now. "Sort of a tourist through life," Pinky interjected.

Before I left, Vesta handed me a rubber-banded bundle of the letters and postcards he had sent them during his travel spree in Europe before he died. When he departed Ojai in mid-1978, he was seemingly healthy, though the cancer most likely had already taken hold in his lungs.

Rose Boggs, who knew my father as a tennis player, said she spoke to him in the Ojai post office shortly after he returned from Europe. "He still stood tall," she recalls, "but he looked very depressed. He told me one lung was gone and it was too late to do anything. The last thing he said to me was, 'I'm terminal.' " From my brief chat with Rose, I went off in search of a place to read the letters and postcards.

Ojai, its boosters like to point out, was used as one Shangri-la filmsetting of the James Hilton novel *Lost Horizon*. As I drove through the town, which is still small enough to jog from one end to the other in about fifteen minutes, I did sense I was in a special place. Walking under oak trees with the a warm, citrus-scented breeze in my face, I felt Ojai was imbued with the kind of tranquility and tree-shaded beauty that would have drawn my father here in the first place. Of course, the valley's two main recreational obsessions, horses and tennis, also attracted him.

Around noon I sat down in a restaurant booth, ordered black coffee, and began to read through the small stack of picture postcards and letters. The earliest was a letter dated July 5, 1978, from Paris, and the last was a card postmarked July 14, 1979, from Rota, Spain. Thanks to his status as a retired army officer, my father flew practically free to and from Europe on military transport planes as a space-available passenger.

To tell from what he writes of his year-long sojourn in at least eight countries, I can safely conclude he left his California Shangri-la mainly for fun, adventure, and most likely, romance. While he was still able, he wanted to dance in the streets of Paris, run with the bulls in Spain, do whatever and go wherever his urges took him. He stayed for about five months in France, during which time he made forays to the beaches and back roads of Normandy, and to London and the countryside around Canterbury. In Paris, he writes, he is studying French at the Alliance Française, playing tennis at the Luxembourg Gardens courts, seeing all the usual tourist sites from the Eiffel Tower to the Louvre, riding a borrowed bicycle almost daily, and to save money, sharing room and board expenses with other students. As usual, his words are neatly printed, with most initial letters capitalized.

. . . I Dine OuT InfrequenTly Because of High CosT BuT Also Because I Live In An ApmT. WiTh 3 OTher STudenTs.

2 Of Them Are French & Very Good Cooks, & The OTher One Is U.S. & Also Good In The KiTchen. We All Share The KiTchen Of Course & You Should See The MasTer-Pieces ThaT Are frequenTly CreaTed There. (I Make No MenTion Of The CaTasTrophes Which Also EmanaTe from ThaT KiTchen!) We All Have A LoT Of fun EaTing Each OTher's ConcocTions, NoT To MenTion The STuff ThaT friends Of The 2 French Women Bring Over, from Time To Time.

On August 9, just back from a ten-day visit to England, he writes excitedly about the gardens and architecture, then recounts his July 14th Independence Day experience in Paris.

People Were All Dressed Up In Masquerade CosTumes WiTh The Make-Up ThaT Goes With IT. CosTumes Ran from A Couple Of Rags (AnyThing Colorful) To A few More SophisTicaTed Versions. I Was Made OuT Like An Apache Dancer from The LefT Bank & RighT In The Middle Of A Group of 25, Running Wild All Over Paris—STopping AT DifferenT OuTdoor LocaTions To Dance. Bands Were Playing AT 8-10 DifferenT LocaTions & Everybody Danced WiTh Everybody! AT MidnighT, We Had A BeauTiful Fireworks Display PuT On By The CiTy. Dancing ConTinued UnTil 4:00 A.M.! Everybody Was Everybody's friend & All, As far As I Could See, Had A Rip-Roaring Good Time! AfTer The Dance, We All

ReTurned To Our friend's ApartmenT Where We STarTed from & Had a Nice, HearTy BreakfasT.

In late fall, the weather turned cold, the Luxembourg courts closed for the winter, and my father writes that he will head south to "Greener Pastures & 'Sunny' Southern Spain." On the way, he stops for several weeks and wanders about the Ardeche River Valley, about a hundred miles south of Lyon. He describes the valley and its people admiringly and with an empathy for the common working man.

The Land Is Rocky & Poor, Making for RaTher Meager HarvesTs. Many Of The Small Farms Have EiTher Been Abandoned Or Sold As Summer Homes To CiTy Folk. IT Made Me Sad To See All These Apple Orchards, Berry Bushes & ChesTnuT Trees NeglecTed. The FruiTs Have Been Crying To Be HarvesTed, BuT There Aren'T Enough People LefT In The Valley To Take Care Of Other Land-Owners' ProperTy. I Also felT Sorry for The People Who Were finally forced To Leave Their farms & Go Seek Their Livelihood In The CiTies. There Is So Much Evidence Of Hard, Back-Breaking Work ThaT WenT InTo The Making Of Those farms Over A Period Of Several GeneraTions.

By early December he has moved his home base to Rota, Spain, which is near a U.S. air force base. At the base, he can shop cheaply, get medical attention if needed, and send and receive mail. He lives with a Spanish family and soon he's working in a warehouse moving casks of wine and sherry. Physical work, he reports to the

Higgins family, is helping to keep him healthy and in shape. Still, in a few picture postcards from Seville and Cordoba, he remarks that he's feeling unusually tired lately.

In March of 1979, his energy somewhat restored, he starts traveling again, sending back colorful, chatty descriptions of bullfights in Portugal, bull running in Spain, the Acropolis in Greece, dusty bus trips through Turkey, and a fragrant walk through the Casbah in Tangier. Some of his letters run to nine pages, and his postcards are full of exclamatory eagerness to share some new experience. As I read the chatter of details, most of it sounds superficial and traveloguish: "At the Syrian Border—Weather Here Is Hot & Terrain Is Semi-Arid." Then he ties this kind of thought to the personal: "This Country Also Reminds Me Of Latin America. Turks Look Upon Me As One Of Them. Am Really Pleased, As I Was In Tangier."

Perhaps he felt most at home among the more ancient cultures and peoples of Turkey and Morocco not only because of his Mediterranean, long-nosed appearance, but also because in this older world, male-held values were more to his liking. Some basis for this comes from observations made to me by a woman and poet my father lived with for about four months in Paris. Françoise is not mentioned in any of his postcards to the Higgins family. I discovered her name and what she meant to him in the box of his effects I found in the shed at Chorro Grande. The revelation was on the inside cover of a notebook he apparently gave to his Parisian lover and which somehow found its way back into his possession. In any case, all but the opening few pages are empty. The dedication, in his hand, reads:

July 14, 1978

Françoise –

May This Book Prove To Be The Key To A BeTTer, Fuller, Richer UndersTanding BeTween Two Individuals Wishing To Share Their Experiences, Inner-MosT ThoughTs

& Emotional Love & Affection, In The Most Profound & Intimate Way Imaginable. May It Serve To Bridge Any Gaps Of Cultural, Sexual Or Personality Traits & Thereby Afford Us The Opportunity To Be Mutually Supportive In Our Endeavors. To Achieve Self-Determination Within The All-Encompassing Embrace Of Our Being.

Armando Arias

The language is vintage Daddy as faithful lover and companion. I have cards, pictures, and notes he wrote to my mother with many of the same lofty phrases and sentiments. It was his way of being intimate on the page—his poetry, if you will. Curiously, there is one more sentence written in a different, more delicate script on the opposite page. Dated September 29, 1978, two-and-a-half months after he wrote the dedication, it is a question and appears to be Françoise's reaction to his kind of romancing. She writes in French,*"Alors, dites-moi, Armando, qu'est-ce que c'est: le machismo?"*—So tell me, Armando, what is this: machismo?

I found her address in his a battered black address book and wrote to her, enclosing some newsclips about him while he was a prisoner in Korea. Surprisingly—since their affair had ended more than ten years before—she answered me within a few weeks, writing in French, which I have translated.

> *I'm surprised to discover, through the photos and articles you sent, an entirely different Armando, a stranger, someone I never knew. It must have been the same with Yvette—he was a different man than he was with his family, as a husband and father. From the 1951 photo, which shows what looks like your mother's contented nature with her three children, I cannot retrieve Armando. Incredible!*
>
> *On the flipside, I found that he was a "playboy macho," a lot like in old retro films. And I think if I had seen that photo in 1978 when I was interested in the "Armando case," I wouldn't*

have reflected so casually on his education, his formation, everything that conditioned his mind and made him what he was.

He created internal barriers, blockages, for living a modern life. And this was probably the cause of his undoing, consciously or unconsciously.

Poor boy! He also had a sacred dose of "culpability" that he wanted to eliminate, without really being able to do so, which would explain his constant desire to break with the past in a universe where there is a sincere conviction about his bad conduct. What do you think?

He was running from himself.

In effect, in Ojai on his mountain ranch, in his trailer, he lived like a hermit, as the article says. He probably found it accessible and in harmony. It was a place where he could hear Krishna-Murti during his conferences in Ojai. For what reason? What was he looking for?

Why had he joined the Army so young? Was it simply a desire to leave his surroundings, which had become a bit stifling? Just a desire for action? Or to purge himself of some misdeed?

Your mother appears very beautiful in the group photo of all of you. She is exactly as I imagined her, without Armando ever having talked much about her.

I would think she should have been the feminine idea for this type of man, but as you see, it wasn't so. Then there was the big problem of Yvette and me. We were modern women, without feelings of guilt, and we were unable to join with him unless he made a great effort to adapt to our lifestyle.

But he was psychologically unable to. Perhaps this was the crux of the problem, and—who knows?—the origin of his cancer.

P.S. I find it very sad to see a life bungled because of unresolved problems. Armando was an illustration of this.

I believe Françoise perfectly captured one side, perhaps the unfulfilled intimate side, of his nature. Another side came from a man in Rota whose family opened itself to my father for six months in 1979. Enrique, as the epistolary spokesman for his extended clan, also answered my inquiry about whether or not he knew my father. Not only did Enrique know him, but also all his brothers, sisters, mother, father, cousins, and children treated him as part of their family. He lived in a downstairs room off a sunny courtyard with an arbor and many flowers. When he wasn't at the base or working at the winery warehouse or off on one of his touristy trips, my father would hang out with his hosts, eating with them, watching the kids play, joking with them, chatting with the adults.

One day he told my sister that he had three sons and that the youngest was 30 years old. And when he came and went from his favorite place in the patio, he would tell us that he missed "the united family." He said he was homesick for his sons.

Staring at these words, I couldn't help thinking a colossal misunderstanding had occurred sometime shortly after my mother died. He told Yvette that he believed Bobby and maybe by extension, Armand and I, disapproved of his marriage. I've asked my brothers and they, as I, really had no opinion one way or another about the marriage. We knew he was in a vulnerable state and just wanted him to stay afloat—and stay in touch, which he didn't. Enrique didn't know it, but he had given me one of the biggest missing pieces in the fractured story I had pursued for so many years. It seemed so simple: Daddy missed us and we missed him, but because we were all paralyzed by pride or perceived hurt, none of us ever forced a meeting that might have brought us together again.

Near the end of his letter, Enrique adds a final whimsical note. He writes that one day my father dressed up in a complete American cowboy outfit with a convincing hat, chaps, boots, and spurs. Then he and another American man went off to a fiesta in Arcos de la Frontera, a nearby picturesque town where a single fighting bull runs through the streets as a highlight of the fiesta. "Your father used to dress like that sometimes," Enrique explains, "but on that day he actually ran in front of a bull. He loved it. He was like a child again."

Enrique had learned of my father's death from one of his Ojai tennis pals, Grayson Rogers, a citrus grower who had notified some of the people listed in my father's address book. It was Rogers, as Enrique indicated, who offered my father a place to die. "Mr. Rogers told us that he cared for your father during his last twenty days," Enrique writes. "He mentioned that in his last days of life your father, when asked how he felt, would always say, 'Fine.' But of course he was obviously very sick."

Grayson Rogers opened the front door and invited me in with a handshake and a smile. A small man with short white hair and teary eyes, he was wearing old khaki trousers and a dirt-smudged sweatshirt with the sleeves rolled up to his elbows. His left arm ended in a stump at the wrist. Later, he explained he lost his hand in the early 1930s when he was doing stunt work for the movies. The gun he was using for a cowboy role somehow exploded and tore up his left hand so badly that it had to be amputated.

He showed me into a spacious living room with a large fireplace that was flanked by wide windows from which you could see thick rows of orange trees. Grayson was an octogenarian bachelor who had bought a small lot in the middle of a grove on the high ground east of Ojai. Then he had built his high-gabled dream home out of adobe-colored concrete blocks. "That's about when I got to know your dad," he said. "I was building a wall out front and he offered to pitch in and help me." Then he added, "You know, he knew he was going to die before he went to Europe. He'd already been spitting up blood before he left."

I said I figured my father knew something bad was going on.

"It was his choice," Grayson said. "He didn't want an operation or chemotherapy."

We sat at a large round table just off the kitchen, which was separated from the living room by a counter cluttered with carrots, oranges, celery, and several juice-squeezing machines. Grayson told me that one night he was asleep in bed and was awakened by a banging sound at the back door.

It sounded like wind banging the screen door. I got up to have a look, turned on the light, and there was Armando, lying on the ground, hitting the back door with one hand. He'd somehow gotten himself down the mountain on his motorcycle, and now was asking if he could stay with me because his condition was getting worse. I pulled him inside and helped him get to the spare bedroom. Later on, after he got worse, I moved him into the sofa bed in the living room. That way he might not feel so alone. I fed him a lot of juices and a doctor-friend from Nicaragua looked in on him pretty often. Not much you could do, though, because he was going downhill fast.

During his last ten days, he lay open-eyed on his back staring fixedly at the ceiling, headphones on, listening to classical music tapes. For a while he communicated with nods and headshakes, then there seemed to be no pain or reaction in his face. His expression remained fixed and blank. "He told me he'd rather live four months normally than four years as a cripple," Grayson said. "And that's what happened. He got weaker and weaker until there was no recognition. At the very end, his eyes were closed for a long time. Then he stopped breathing and died."

I looked at the sofa, imagining the fold-out bed in its place. He would have seen the orange trees directly in front of him out the big window. I glanced at the plain white ceiling. What did he see? Maybe at that point he could only hear. For hours and days the grand concertos and symphonies roused him higher and higher toward an overwhelming emotional finale. At least I would like to think so.

In those last days, was he thinking or just focusing on the pain, on getting past the pain? He knew he would not survive, that he would have to ride the wild horse bucking and kicking all the way to the end. He would hold on and never let go.

Did he see us or Mommy in his memory? Were there unspoken words, desires for what could have been, what should have been? If only I or my brothers had been with him during these days, we might have brought him some sweet consolation, some completeness, some sense that he still had us close to him. Knowing what we now know of his life, this would also bring us closer to a father we could understand and accept, a father that each of us in our separate, different ways, could love and remember.

Estero

Mommy: at the beginning of this story, I wrote that I would land on a single answer to all my questions. I wrote that it was something you probably knew all along. Well, I've told the tale as best as I could, going from place to place, island to island, until I've come back to the same kind of place where I started. I'm in the middle of an estuary, sitting on a small, barren island, watching a group of sea lions bask in the sun. I'm trying to stay as motionless as I can because I don't want to scare them off.

It's not the estuary where I used to live. It's not even on the same coast. And its name is simply Estuary, only in Spanish. It's a long finger of the Pacific Ocean with sand dunes and crusty tidal flats on one side and marshes leading to dry land on the other side. All along the estuary's edge the water is warm and limpid. A few sandbars break the surface in the distance, and across the way where the dunes are, only sparse patches of wild grass grow. There are no trees, and the only things moving are the pelicans and gulls gathered in clusters near the mouth where the ocean flows in.

Next to me in the water, I glimpse the slim shadow of a single fish pass by, and closer to me still, on the wet sand, I see tiny fiddler crabs scooting sideways, some backing into their holes. Suddenly, at the edge of the sunbathing pack of sea lions, a black flipper rises, followed by an eruption of snorting and harrumphing until the entire lumpish tangle of sluglike bodies ripples with movement to the sounds of much barking and grunting.

There's a rhythm here for everything. For some, it lasts only seconds, then it dies. For others, it lasts for years, maybe forever, like the motion of the waves or the rush of the wind. What's our rhythm? Do we have our moments for growth, for love, for turmoil, for loss, for triumph, for resolution, for peace? I am now ten years older than you were when you died. And yet here I am, with my boat pulled up on the sand, watching life around me and feeling as young as I've ever felt. I'm the lucky one. My rhythm, the beat of my heart, continues. But it continues for a reason, and that's part of my rhythm as a writer. Only now am I ready to write this story.

You nudged me into writing stories in notebooks. I studied, I worked, I had my mentors and guides, those who gave me what Daddy couldn't. I had my adventures. Finally, as I waded into middle age, I was compelled to uncover enough truth to tell our story, hoping to hit the target more often than not. I don't think you nor Daddy would like this story. For whatever reasons, you hid things, kept secrets, invented. I have invented nothing.

It's late and the sea lions have roused themselves and gone. The tide's coming in with a churning current, and my island is about gone too. I lift the boat, plunk it in the water, sit, and launch myself toward a crimson sky. In a while, following this day's rhythm, I should be eating dinner with Joan, talking, drinking something good, hearing voices at other tables, maybe laughter, maybe music.

But not to forget in case I haven't made this clear: the single answer I have for you is that Daddy loved us all, more than you might think, given his behavior in marriage. I don't defend him, I don't blame him for anything. If I had known him during his last years, I simply would have accepted him. I believe he was trying to do his best—as a soldier, a husband, a father, and a friend. But as we know, he had quirky, confounding limitations. That part of him is quite human. I think I even understand his spylike, secretive nature.

In Korea he became a hero by helping others survive conditions that went beyond the test of character. At least to some of those men and to me he's a hero. And he was a great one for telling me and my brothers that to survive in life you must first and always "take care of Number One." Obviously, that was not his focus when he was a prisoner of war or at home caring for you when you were ill.

I wish I could bring back our so-called happy days after the war in Europe, when both of you were younger and more passionate, more playful. Never mind your hurt and rage over his infidelities. I and others remember distinctly when you and he were intensely in love. What happened in later years seemed inevitable, given the circumstances. The man who came back to you from Korea was too serious, too controlled, too stoic, too damaged, too tightly wound in his own broodings and unfulfilled desires, professional as well as physical. And you, as your health declined, hung with the program of dutiful wife and mother, all the while living with—as you said—a stranger.

I'm sorry your last years were so lonely and loveless. I wish your life and your marriage to Daddy had not come apart. But you had no more control of that than Joan and I did in preventing the death of our son Jonathan Carlos.

We still visit his grave as often as we can. Joan sometimes pats the stone, or I trace my finger on the etched letters of his name. We never stay long and it seems we always walk away in silence, alone with our separate thoughts and thickened emotions. Our visits are devotional, sad, and sweet, which is how I've felt as I've written this book. In remembering, in gathering the evidence and voices of the past, I visited us, our family, in the same way I visit my son's grave.

I've just reached the beach. My afternoon sojourn is over. I pull the boat out of the water, shed my life vest, then stretch my legs and kick the sand. I think I've reflected long enough on this day and on the rhythms of wind and water, sun and sound, life and love.

Armando Arias' image may be in the center— the likenesses are all unnamed..

Korean War Veteran's Memorial Wall

Photo by Robert Arias